IMAGINING
THE WORST

Recent Titles in
Contributions to the Study of Popular Culture

IMAGINING THE WORST

CR

Stephen King and the Representation of Women

Edited by
Kathleen Margaret Lant
and Theresa Thompson

Contributions to the Study of Popular Culture,
Number 67

GREENWOOD PRESS
Westport, Connecticut • London

Library of Congress Cataloging-in-Publication Data

Imagining the worst : Stephen King and the representation of women /
    edited by Kathleen Margaret Lant and Theresa Thompson.
        p.   cm.—(Contributions to the study of popular culture,
    ISSN 0198–9871 ; no. 67)
      Includes bibliographical references (p.   ) and index.
      ISBN 0–313–30232–4 (alk. paper)
      1. King, Stephen, 1947- —Characters—Women. 2. Horror tales,
    American—History and criticism. 3. Women in literature. I. Lant,
    Kathleen Margaret. II. Thompson, Theresa. III. Series.
    PS3561.I483Z72   1998
    813′.54—dc21   97–48575

British Library Cataloguing in Publication Data is available.

Library of Congress Catalog Card Number: 97–48575
ISBN: 0–313–30232–4
ISSN: 0198–9871

First published in 1998

Greenwood Press, 88 Post Road West, Westport, CT 06881
An imprint of Greenwood Publishing Group, Inc.

Printed in the United States of America

The paper used in this book complies with the
Permanent Paper Standard issued by the National
Information Standards Organization (Z39.48–1984).

10 9 8 7 6 5 4 3 2

Copyright Acknowledgments

The editors and the publisher gratefully acknowledge permission for use of the following material:

From *Carrie, Christine, It, Dolores Claiborne, Gerald's Game, Misery,* "The Reach," and "The Raft"
by Stephen King. Reprinted with permission. © Stephen King. All rights reserved.

From *Carrie* by Stephen King. Copyright © 1974 by Stephen King. Used by permission of Doubleday,
a division of Bantam Doubleday Dell Publishing Group, Inc.

From "The Rape of the Constant Reader: Stephen King's Construction of the Female Reader and
Violation of the Female Body in *Misery*," by Kathleen Margaret Lant. *The Journal of Popular Culture,* 30 (Spring 1997), 89–114.

Contents

Preface

This collection of critical essays marks a significant passage into the electronic age of academic collaboration. The editors have "met" physically only once during the process of assembling these chapters. We first discovered our mutual interest in Stephen King when, over email, Peggy Lant put out a call for papers about King for a proposed MLA session. Lant, located at California Polytechnic State University in San Luis Obispo, California, is a professor of English while Theresa Thompson was, at that time, a graduate student at Washington State University preparing to write preliminary examinations for a Ph.D. What began as an on-going email discussion between two Stephen King enthusiasts eventually developed into an enduring friendship and this work.

Throughout the creation of this work, we, like many of King's characters, have been transformed. Lant has become a technology consultant as well as a professor. Thompson graduated with her Ph.D. and accepted a position at Valdosta State University in Georgia.

Our collaboration began during the winter of 1993 in recognition of the power King's works had exerted on our individual imaginations and on the imaginations of the many King readers around the world. As avid fans, we had read each of King's novels as it was published, and we had watched each movie as it hit the screen. We asked ourselves this question: what makes King's writing so powerful and why are women, in particular, so drawn to his works? Although a complete answer may never be possible, a partial answer, we hope, can be found in the following collection of essays.

This collection of essays about Stephen King's characterization of women, men, gender, and sexuality would not have been possible, however, without the cooperation and assistance of many diverse people and institutions over the course of the past several years. We would like to thank Stephen King for his prolific writing talent, which has permitted such critical studies as ours to exist. We also owe a large debt of gratitude to our publishers for their patience as we developed this collection.

Our gratitude is extended as well to the English Department at California Polytechnic State University in San Luis Obispo for funding Professor Lant's research and for their support and encouragement. We would also like to thank the student assistants at Cal Poly: Gerald Lamont Stokes and Kelly Claire Eick, for their work. A special thanks goes to Professor Lant's assistant, Diana Bernstein, who worked overtime many late nights, when she should have been dreaming about her garden. Cal Poly Kennedy librarians—particularly Paul Adalian, Ilene Rockman, and Lynne Gamble—demonstrated that most academic work depends on quality librarians. We are especially indebted to their tireless efforts. We also extend our gratitude to Washington State University, which provided Professor Thompson with an office and email services during the first years of this project, and to Valdosta State University, which now offers similar support.

Finally, we want our family and friends to know that their patience and assistance have not gone unnoticed. Many thanks to our spouses, Steve Thompson and Shann Chu, who tolerated many late nights and early mornings of writing and editing. We want to thank all our colleagues who listened patiently as we whined and grumbled about the difficulties involved in researching, composing, and editing. It has been a long process, but it is finished.

I

Introduction

Imagining the Worst:
Stephen King and the Representation of Women

Kathleen Margaret Lant
and
Theresa Thompson

[T]he horror writer always brings bad news: you're going to die, he says; he's telling you to never mind Oral Roberts and his "something *good* is going to happen to *you*," because something *bad* is also going to happen to *you*, and it may be cancer and it may be a stroke, and it may be a car accident, but it's going to happen. And he takes your hand and he enfolds it in his own, and he takes you into the room and he puts your hands on the shape under the sheet . . . and tells you to touch it here . . . here . . . and *here*.

Stephen King
Night Shift (xvii)

[O]nly the voice of the writer, low and rational, talking about the way the good fabric of things sometimes has a way of unraveling with shocking suddenness. He's telling you that you want to see the car accident, and yes, he's right—you do. There's a dead voice on the phone . . . something behind the walls of the old house that sounds bigger than a rat . . . movement at the foot of the cellar stairs. He wants you to see all of those things, and more; he wants you to put your hands on the shape under the sheet. And you want to put your hands there. Yes.

Stephen King
Night Shift (xx)

What is it about Stephen King? We complain harshly about his books—they need editing, they are overly long, they repeat themselves—but every time a new one appears, we rush to read it. If we have to wait for the paperback, we are impatient, cross. If we are fortunate enough to purchase the hardcover, we hoard it. We read about King on Internet news groups and visit the many websites eager fans construct for him (including sites in England, Germany, the

Netherlands, and Russia). We savor each mention of him in a newspaper or magazine and listen to interviews, hoping for some glimpse into his life, his mind, his *strangeness*.

Perhaps it is King's acumen about the world we live in that makes him so compelling to us, for King has focused his lens sharply on life in the late twentieth century. As Tony Magistrale observes, the "particular horrors of King's novels are aligned with, and often emerge from, culturally specific disturbances," disturbances that may be said to constitute the fabric of North American culture (26). But the persistent and obsessive interest we take in King seems to arise from so much more than the accuracy of his social commentary, and we often have the uneasy feeling, in fact, that some darker motivation lies at the core of our fascination with this enormously popular writer.

In an ironic demonstration of his power as a writer, Stephen King himself provides us with tools to elucidate our fascination with him: In our fixation on King, we resemble the violent, eerie fan he has fashioned in his novel *Misery*. The repulsive Annie provides an image of what we always already were—eager reflections of King's worst fears. King's art fulfills a need many of us share and none of us is ready, or perhaps able, to articulate without him. His ability to state so clearly our most basic, shared fears—the alien monster beneath the smiling clown, the lurking menace in the dark closet, the dark woods through which we must travel, the machines we cannot understand or control—compels us. We need his uncanny ability to give form to these inexpressible fears because we cannot speak them. Perhaps it is finally that in King's works we find not just our fears but ourselves. To many of us—his devouring, demanding fans—King's characters appear to be thoroughly the Everyman we see in the mirror—even as we tremble at the vision.

Although King must be praised for this accurate and potent rendition of Everyman in the late twentieth century, his representations of Everywoman often provoke hostility as well as admiration. When analyzing King's depiction of women, it is tempting to relegate him to the category of unregenerate misogynist or conversely to elevate him to the status of newly sensitive male. But it is probably more fruitful instead to examine closely the act of representation King practices in his works, to wonder how he constructs the female and the feminine and to consider what discursive communities inform his constructions. Such examinations reveal something about the psychology of this interesting man, Stephen King, but even more compelling and fascinating, they tell us something about our culture's own fears, anxieties, and obsessions with the female and the feminine.

King's audience has been moved and terrified by his fictional women for over twenty years now. Women, King's novels seem to show us, are often the perpetrators and the victims of a distinctly American domestic horror that hides its alien and terrifying face beneath a familiar grinning mask. There is something in his depiction of the female and the feminine that feels alien and familiar at once—perhaps because of King's insistent correlation of the writing of horror fiction with sexuality. His depiction of the horror writer as a man who "enfolds" your hand in his own and "puts your hands on the shape under the sheet," asserts an intimacy that, as he directs us to feel "here . . . here . . . and *here*," becomes increasingly erotic and provocative. And given that his perspective reflects, at least superficially, the heterosexism of our culture, this heteroerotic vision of author and reader becomes linked to the appalling and the inexplicable.

In King's vision, the macabre is often brutally and violently sexual because, male or female, the most unspeakable monsters do not always lurk uninvited in our closets; they might, indeed, share our beds. This vision of intimate horror is ineluctably tied in King's fiction to women and to the domestic realm. King's focus on women and the horror of the domestic links King to a gothic tradition that has for over two hundred years depicted the terrifying "other" face of the domestic sphere, where the angel in the house both dominates and is dominated, where that angel may suddenly become Charlotte Brontë's terrifying Bertha Mason or Louisa May Alcott's vicious and vindictive Jean Muir.

Many of the earliest novels written in England and America were domestic gothics of this sort, among them Mary Shelley's *Frankenstein* and Charles Brockden Brown's *Wieland*. King's gothic, though, often demonstrates a woman's abilities to assert domestic power and dominance that defy victimization—in part because, as we see in King's recent novel *Rose Madder*, his female protagonists successfully defeat not only the brutal men threatening them but also the foreign and terrifying territories within their own psyches. Within the female mind, King seems to imply in *Rose Madder*, resides something that both acquiesces to masculine dominance and violence and responds to that violence with an equally compelling power.

What King has done, then, with the gothic formula is to situate his gothic terror in our own minds, our own conflicts, and our own mundane reality. King's horrific domesticity, unlike the nineteenth-century precursors upon which King calls, has been neatly constructed within the confines of a post-Freudian world where the horror we must face, as women or as men, resides in the unfounded depths of our own repressed *id*. This personal landscape, then, is the horror that lies under the sheet—unseen, beckoning, compelling, yet repulsive. This hidden place provides a personal and internalized stage where monstrosity, fear, and alienation can be experienced in full force. Pre-psychoanalytic, nineteenth-century configurations of gothic alienation—that disjunctive feeling of otherness, which provides the basic fabric of horror in novels such as *Frankenstein*—are more squarely positioned within the extraordinary. Julia Kristeva defines this construction of the horrible as a "romantic leaning toward supernatural, parapsychology, madness, dreams, the obscure forces of the *fatum*, and even animal psychology [which] is related to the desire to grasp the strange, and by domesticating it, turn it into a component of the human" (180–81).

In Kristeva's terms, the otherness of horror is dealt with by our desire to domesticate it. In King's works, however, the alien who most frightens and horrifies is the alien who lives with and within us—who frequently *is* "us"—yet remains always Other to a male-centered culture: This creature is, of course, woman. This alien Other, this foreigner if you will, derives from the "Freudian notion of the unconscious" wherein the foreign is "neither a race nor a nation . . . [because] we are our own foreigners, we are divided" (Kristeva, 181). It comes as no surprise, then, that this divided and divisive female self—woman both as cultural Other and alienated subject—dominates so much of King's work.

Thus, many key aspects of King's representations of women appear firmly entrenched in a patriarchal economy of domesticity. An overwhelming sense of socially condoned masculinist violence and trespass haunts his women and men and their relations within these domestic spaces. King's use of the late-gothic tradition of the *doppelgänger*—that doubling and polarization of the self—reveals men and women trapped in a fatal struggle for power within King's construction of heterosexuality. His *femme/homme fatale* figures paradoxically provide both unknowing and conscious expressions of female sexual and social power as they battle within the constraints and liberties of an unbalanced discourse of pleasure and power. They, like King's eager readers, seem caught within what Michel Foucault identifies as an "ordered system of knowledge" about sex and sexuality that finds its strongest (and strangest) assertions in Freudian and neo-Freudian thought (69).

King's women—from Carrie to Rose Madder—suffer from both spatial isolation and social alienation, reminding King's readers that women have really not come a long way from the politically and discursively powerless times of their disenfranchised mothers and grandmothers. These women—and their female monster counterparts—remind us, eerily, of Betty Friedan's delineation of female consciousness, penned in her landmark work *The Feminine Mystique*; Friedan describes the "strange discrepancy between the reality of our lives as women and the image to which we are trying to conform" (9).

Within this context of sexual and social disorientation concerning the female and the feminine, we begin this volume with an examination of King's women. In "The American Context and Constructions of the Female," we offer three chapters, two about King's first novel, *Carrie* (1974), and one about recent works, *Gerald's Game* (1992) and *Dolores Claiborne* (1993), all of which foreground King's place in the American literary and cultural tradition. Ed Ingebretsen's chapter, "Cotton Mather and Stephen King: Writing/Righting the Body Politic," fixes King firmly in the American milieu—not simply with respect to the American gothic tradition but also with respect to American religion, politics, and identity. In these terms, Ingebretsen identifies in *Carrie* a struggle for female subjectivity and power that reflects many of the same conflicts, constructs, and dynamics as the struggle that arose during the Salem witch hysteria of the late seventeenth century.

Douglas Keesey shifts our focus in Chapter 3 to the twentieth century, placing King within the contemporary American context: Keesey traces the evolution of *Carrie* through its manifestations as book, as movie (directed by Brian De Palma), and finally as musical (produced, directed, and staffed by several members of the Royal Shakespeare Company). Keesey reflects on the fears of female sexuality or corporeality manifest in contemporary culture. Carrie is, Keesey argues, "patriarchal society's worst nightmare concerning women and their bodies."

In the chapter entitled "Rituals of Male Violence: Unlocking the (Fe)Male Self in *Gerald's Game* and *Dolores Claiborne*," Theresa Thompson examines the cultural context of King's metaphors of heterosexual containment and domestic violence. Thompson argues that King, especially in *Gerald's Game*, locates the site of American literary and cultural horror in the structure of the patriarchal household. She argues that the middle-class family structure of the 1950s and 1960s created a monster capable not only of haunting the female psyche but also of reconstructing that psyche in the image of the father/husband.

The three chapters in "Women and Genre" relate King's genre choices and narrative strategies to the power and danger of the female. Leonard Cassuto's "Repulsive Attractions: 'The Raft,' the *Vagina Dentata*, and the Slasher Formula" establishes a link between the slasher formula and images of castrating female power. King's genre, exemplified by such films as *Halloween* and *Friday the 13th* and characterized by the punishment of "adolescent sexuality with hideous, unconscious-driven aggression," is set in counterpoint to his central symbol of power—the consuming and emasculating *vagina dentata*.

André DeCuir also takes up King's appropriation and modification of the horror genre—specifically King's arrogation of Mary Shelley's gothic rendering of the horrors of birth and newborn life in *Frankenstein*. While DeCuir argues that King explores this path in *Pet Sematary*, he asserts that King brings together the themes of childbirth and horror more directly and more powerfully in his short story "The Reach," where he foregrounds a female consciousness and navigates the "cultural suppression of the female voice."

Carol Senf explores King's delineation of female power as it makes itself part of the creative process. In the chapter entitled "*Gerald's Game* and *Dolores Claiborne*: Stephen King and the Evolution of an Authentic Female Narrative Voice," Senf argues that King, despite charges from many serious critics that he is misogynist, is struggling in his narrative form to present a fully developed female character, to explore the contours of women's existence in our culture, and to speak with an "authentic" female voice.

The two chapters in the fourth part, "Evil and Female Essence," make clear King's association of what is frightening, what is horrible, and what is evil with what is essentially female. Linda Anderson and Karen Thoens address King's monumental *It* in these terms. The results make clear in differing ways that King has created in *It* his most horrifying and at the same time his most quintessentially female monster.

Anderson points out that the many monsters in the novel represent his attempt to portray "every monster you could think of" (in King's words), and she goes on to observe that all these monsters are male. Ultimately, however, when King unveils the essence of monstrosity—the monster to end all monsters—this monster is more horrible because it is not simply female, it is female and pregnant: the mother monster. Thoens, on the other hand, finds at the center of King's novels a power struggle in which beleaguered males seek to reassert an authority wrested from them by ascendant females. Thoens, examining *It*, locates this struggle in a masculine nostalgia for the past, a nostalgia translated into a longing for the master narrative of male superiority.

In the fifth part, "Masculine Power and the 'Problem' of the Female Body," Ed Madden and Kathleen Margaret Lant explore how King uses constructs of heterosexuality and metaphors of object-subject interactions to (re)assert male authority and authorship. Madden analyzes the American cliché concerning the bond that joins cars, femaleness, and evil in "Cars Are Girls: Sexual Power and Sexual Panic in Stephen King's *Christine*." As in Thoens's chapter, Madden finds masculine uncertainty and insecurity at the heart of the novel's representation of women. He contemplates the horrific proportions female power can assume in King's extended consideration of car as woman and as evil.

Lant's chapter, "The Rape of Constant Reader: Stephen King's Construction of the Female Reader and Violation of the Female Body in *Misery*," outlines how the fear of female power leads to a reinscription of male authority and authorship in King's depiction of a crazed yet devoted fan. According to Lant, King explores the tensions of creativity, popularity, and gender, delegating the privilege of speaking/writing to males and reserving the place of listener/fan for females. When fans become obstreperous, Lant argues, King's writer/protagonist resorts to the last refuge of the embattled man—rape.

WORKS CITED

Foucault, Michel. *The History of Sexuality*. Translated by Robert Hurley. New York: Pantheon, 1978.

Friedan, Betty. *The Feminine Mystique*. New York: Norton, 1963.

King, Stephen. *Night Shift*. Garden City: Doubleday, 1978.

Kristeva, Julia. *Strangers to Ourselves*. Translated by Leon S. Roudiez. New York: Columbia University Press, 1991.

Magistrale, Tony. *Landscape of Fear: Stephen King's American Gothic*. Bowling Green: Bowling Green University Popular Press, 1988.

II

The American Context and Constructions of the Female

2

Cotton Mather and Stephen King: Writing/Righting the Body Politic

Edward J. Ingebretsen, S. J.

> Let us not be like a *Troubled House*, altho' we are so much haunted by the devils.
>
> Cotton Mather
> *Wonders of the Invisible World* (91)

> [W]ithin the framework [of a horror story] . . . we find a moral code so strong it would make a Puritan smile.
>
> Stephen King
> *Danse Macabre* (368)

I

In "A Model of Christian Charity" John Winthrop uses a rhetoric of benevolent religious terror to create political identity (and, incidentally, to enforce social conformity). His strategy in 1630 was not new, nor since was it an isolated instance. Let us consider, for example, a particular form of Christian charity, first as it played out in the construction of New England's social polity and communal identity, and then, in these latter days, as it traces itself through a market-driven genre, the American Gothic tradition of horror and fantasy texts. I am speaking, of course, about the rite of witch-hunting (in Salem and elsewhere) and its reconstruction as perennial American myth, cultic ideology, and commodified terror. In this chapter I argue that contemporary American industries of horror (Stephen King, for particular example) are hardly "diversions" at all—or, that indeed they *are* diversions, and as such, should be paid attention. The Freddy Krueger-style dismemberings and violent fantasies indulged in the name of entertainment can hardly be considered innocuous. Or, to put it another way, the horrors dismissed as trash and consigned to the "literary basement," or, as Leslie Fiedler observes, those that we usher around to the "backdoor of culture" (54) are, as it were, the "real thing" (with apologies to the Coke ad).

By way of background, I argue that religious discourse is a narrative of considerable cultural importance; although silenced by law, it still makes itself heard, surfacing in places presumed to be dismissable—particularly in the genres of the horrific sublime, or those texts we call dark fantasy. Thus, though not about religious experience directly, this chapter is about its indirect possibilities in the civic theater. I begin with the premise that American cultic life presumes a metaphysics—perhaps one could call this the condition of interiority—that gives form to approved cultural feelings and desires. This framework is Christian in deep and pervasive ways and is, therefore, explicitly about power and implicitly about fear. Further, I argue that echoes of this discredited system—in a democracy religious discourse is rendered politically unspeakable—can be loudly heard in the fertile markets of horror and fantasy.

Horror films and texts are not merely "entertainments"—they are, as the word itself suggests, sites of erotic dalliance: "diversions," significant cultural deflections. Indeed, they embody significant political remembering. So often taboo in subject matter, their presentation is organized around titillation. Consider, for example the eroticization of the serial killer in such films as *Silence of the Lambs*. Fear and dread, once associated with the religious sublime, are now deflected into new venues; religious anxiety, marketed as commercial horror, is placed in the service of civic definition and social constraint. Thus, consumer fear may be the last vestiges, if you will, of a bankrupt religious vision. That is, they constitute cultural acts of remembering; they are politically invested, civic gestures of identity and *religious* acts of allegiance.

As an example, consider Stephen King's *Carrie*, with its distant echoes of the canonical American memory of the Salem witch trials. As Cotton Mather would use the term in *Wonders of the Invisible World*, King's "entertainment" is also an *exemplum*, a model or example. As a fiction, it employs the trope of witchery to play out an anxiety of social dis-ease; as a metaphysics it points toward a spiritual order that transcends this temporal order, while nonetheless authorizing its political arrangements and exclusions.

The year 1997 marks the 300th anniversary of the final chapter in "one of the three dark moments in New England history" (Pribek, 95–100), the Salem witch hysteria of 1692–1693.[1] On January 14, 1667, Samuel Sewall stood before his church's congregation in Salem while his pastor read Sewall's public repudiation of the part he played in the witch-trials. Salem is in so many ways the point at which American popular culture—especially its revisionist nationalism—comes of age and claims its peculiar political and economic tensions. Indeed, American "public" or even "popular" culture can be said to begin where Salem repudiated *illegal* witchery (for, of course, there were legal practitioners of the white arts, notably the clergy who first decried the presence of witches in the town). The events of 1692–1693 were to be an initial instance, following Anne Hutchinson and the Antinomian affair, of what would over time become an essential civic mechanism in the construction of normalcy. Witchery could serve as one of many excuses for invoking a rite of social expiation—a communal self-flagellation that could be invoked whenever the Body Politic was felt to need moral exercise or a gesture of self-definition and muscle toning. Yet such gestures represent a civic impulse older than the Republic, and R. I. Moore traces them back through medieval Christianity's formation, as he calls it, of a "persecuting society."[2]

History books are filled with such moments of civic crisis. The emergence of the witch in medieval Christian polity, and her ubiquitous presence in subsequent uncivil/theological politics, is a case in point. Hugh Trevor-Roper argues that a Thomistic mapping of heaven and its powers and principalities prompted in turn an extensive, even obsessive, map of an inverted, although parallel, region below, complete with its attendant minions (*The European Witch-Craze of the Sixteenth and Seventeenth Centuries and Other Essays*). He charts the bizarre internal logic by which what had been initially a matter of arcane scholastic metaphysics—witch-hunting—became in time a socially necessary effect of bully politics and then, increasingly, a spectacular civic rite.[3]

As late as 1636 John Cotton and other first generation Puritan Divines, pursuing a provisional and largely ad hoc polity to strengthen what they perceived to be a generalized spiritual and civic decline, used the language of witchery—specifically gendered—to turn back Hutchinson's religious challenge to their civil authority.[4] The Old World theologies by which they ordered Congregational polity did not—could not—admit Hutchinson's claim of religious authority; and so, with no sense of irony, the divines employed a language and ritualized civic repudiation that had by and large been abandoned in Europe. In this way, the land that was to become New England, still fluid in concept—new, yet old, royal, yet recently not, whose external boundaries lay vulnerable to all manner of political and physical enemies—turned inward. In this way the society-in-formation began systematically to map itself according to a metaphysical topography of boundaries and hierarchies, of scrutinies and surveillances, organized according to biblical precept. As John Winthrop, then governor, said in court to Anne Hutchinson, "You must keep your conscience or it will be kept for you."[5] In such an order, as Stout explains, "there was no inherent contradiction between civic loyalty and godly sanctification" (21) and "a willful rebellion against the social order was indicative of an endangered soul" (24).[6]

The Hutchinson affair anticipates Salem's witch-hysteria forty-five years later. Salem can be seen as engaged in a similar effort at righting (writing) the Body Politic. In a chaotic period of fluctuating, even nonexistent boundaries, when the Royal authorization on which the colony depended seemed in question, Salem needed a way to establish and ground itself. When demographic and economic tensions are added to the ones already mentioned, it is easy to understand why Salem turned to policing its internal boundaries. Seeking witches was, at least, a diversion that most people could agree upon. Thus, the demons Salem sought furiously to extirpate were, indeed, more visible than invisible, more human rather than less. Hutchinson, then, learned early—as did the Quakers twenty years later and still later, the unfortunate victims at Salem—that in this brave New World neither the theory of freethinking nor its practice extended inward; mental witchery must be repudiated, conventionality must be protected against the enthusiasm of the particular. Maps of heaven did, after all, shape those of earth, as metaphysics and its imperatives came to ground in the cast-off bodies of those repudiated for the civic good. For this reason John Calvin's *Institutes* remain important documents in social theory as well as in theology.[7]

Stephen King's many novels provide examples of how disowned theologies return, ghostlike, as moralistic social memory. King's position on the social margins participates more deeply than is sometimes recognized in an imaginative social project profoundly shaped by religious imperatives and sensibilities. In *Carrie*, for instance, he revisits a primary cultural scene played out between Hutchinson and Cotton and then later between Cotton Mather and the various women accused of witchery in Salem. In both instances at issue is the gendered, and therefore imbalanced, relationship between the single separate self's private intimacies and the metaphysical allegiances, imperatives, and repudiations of a theofederal state order. From the earliest days in New England, the rhythm of private spirituality was thought intimately to reflect its public, conventional expression. That is, private religious moments carried political import in that public confession of same was a requirement for participation in the Lord's Supper, and thus, in the public life of the community. Though theoretically the self and the *Civitas* echoed each other as metaphor, symbol, often they seemed embattled discourses whose terms divided the more they were thought to be unified. In due time theological discourse itself—the language of the public spiritual self—was, by federal law, rendered legally unspeakable. But though silenced, the discourse was not erased. Traces of its formidable presence could still be found, submerged in a nostalgic, revisionist nationalism and in the various rhetorics of normalcy, issuing from pulpits both political and secular. King's *Carrie* (1973) exploits these religious and civic tensions in a way reminiscent of Cotton Mather's *Wonders of the Invisible World* (1693). Both authors—Mather's theological fictions more obviously than King's commercial fantasy, though no less insistently—describe what might be called a rite of deviancy. This is the mechanism by which a threatened order organizes and defends its boundaries by repudiating those who fail them. Both texts reflect the instability inherent in the construction of the witch, because witch-hunting points inward toward the civic center: "The worst work of the Devil they looked for—and found—among their own kind" (Demos, 71).

But before considering King's downward revision of theology, let me turn for a moment to Cotton Mather's 1693 Miltonesque rendering of "the

Fiend's descent on Salem Village" (Starkey, 242). Mather calls his account a "true History" (107), stating that he reports "matters not as an *Advocate*, but as an *Historian*" (110). At the same time, however, Mather ingenuously admits that he "was not present at any of [the trials]" (109). Mather's anxieties about how to read the whole Salem affair constantly intrude upon his narrative: "The whole business is become hereupon so *Snarled*, and the determination of the Question one way or another, so *dismal*, that . . . *We know not what to do!*" (84).[8] Mather's problem, however, was less metaphysical than practical because he makes it clear that the trials matter more as *exempla* of the moral life than as history or fiction. Or rather, they were both. That is, his theological interests—or perhaps justifications—were by necessity subsumed within the constraints of narrative, even formula, as Mather finds ready to hand the discourse of witchery derived from Old England. Staking the witch, then, was a complicated business, partly a matter of doctrine but also partly a matter of the right mix of entertainments and formulaic "spells." If staking the witch was a kind of spell by which to "right" the Body Politic, Mather concluded that "telling" the witch—"writing it"—was also a reforming action, a dis-spelling of unauthorized witchery by the authoritative "spelling" of social agents like himself. Indeed, the symbolic construction of the witch as subversive agent within a community, and her subsequent exemplary trial and condemnation, encompassed a variety of often divergent ends. For one thing, such an act of communal finger-pointing defined the abstract, ideological boundaries of a community; the violence of this scapegoating melodrama underscores, but does not discredit, routine acts of violence throughout the Body Politic. In addition, witch-hunting constituted an approved social gesture, in a climate generally suspicious of ritual, for maintaining religious control precisely through ritualistic means; for shaping the civic imagination; and paradoxically, for transgressing that imagination as well.[9] The rite was both expiatory and explanatory, socially clarifying as well as purgative. A habitual cry of guilt and repudiation, the Calvinistic civic cosmology of expiation was, in addition, a primary means of self-definition. But the larger point I wish to address is that, as Foucault reminds us, deviancy needs to be cultivated in order that its suppression—and its exposition—might provide an occasion for a ceremonial display of civic power.[10] Some laws, then, are meant to be broken.

In Gothic lore, monsters generally haunt the margins of society, whereas in political realities, witches emerge from within communities. Observers of the dynamics of witchcraft conclude that the "bizarre mythology" leading to various resurgences of witch craze in Europe resulted from "social struggle" (Trevor-Roper, 165). Trevor-Roper notes, too, that it was a "social movement" but one that could be extended "deliberately, in times of political crisis, as a political device, to destroy powerful enemies or dangerous persons" (189): "At best, the myth might be contained as in the early sixteenth century. But it did not evaporate: It remained at the bottom of society, like a stagnant pool, easily flooded, easily stirred" (191). In *Entertaining Satan* John Demos argues that the witch hysteria served Salem in a traditional manner, acting as a "social strain gauge" (276) by which one could judge not only the intersection of demographic and economic forces local to Salem's geographically divided community, but also visible fissures, where an often overlapping series of discourses and rhetorics of normalcy (religious, civil, personal, ecclesiastical, institutional) failed to hold. Witchcraft was a necessary part of communal life because it served the group by "sharpening its boundaries, reinforcing its values, and deepening the loyalty of its membership" (14).[11] Indeed, witchcraft "most often occurs where there is *both* unusual tension *and* a lack of appropriate outlets (and/or means of resolution)" (Demos, 276). But these rather dry abstractions have particular and embodied consequences; social anxiety will manifest itself in behaviors of all kinds. Symbols can kill. That is, social constructions embody metaphysical assumptions, and symbolic repudiations often shed real blood. Thus it was that metaphysics came to ground. A constellation of historical pressures native to the New England colonies came to sharp focus in the township of Salem and its local neighbors.

Sociologists and historians suggest that the civic turbulence at Salem—which emerged, in concentrated form, in the witch trials—was a way of deflecting often unrelated anxieties. In particular they note anxieties arising from the revocation of the original Bay Colonies charter in 1688. In such an unsettled social context, then, the witch hysteria at Salem and the surrounding townships can be viewed as a work of political reformation, as well as—or instead of—a theological reformation. The action was an attempt to draw lines and reform personal as well as communal boundaries in a young community whose legal definition had been, quite literally, erased by the political upheaval in Old England. In addition, however, and moving from a political map to a metaphysical one, the charge of witchcraft is rhetorically dense, a metaphor drenched with moral imperative. In the first place, although framed in conventional religious terms as *maleficium*, witchcraft in fact constituted a civil, rather than a religious, offense. Witchcraft focused social unrest within a divided community, and it was a charge tantamount to disturbing the social peace.

David Hall writes that "From the preachers' point of view, then, the lesson of the Quakers . . . and Anne Hutchinson was exactly this: they allowed Satan entrance to the self" (*Worlds of Wonder*, 146–47).[12] For residents of Salem in 1692, beleaguered by internal conflict and international confusion, the witch's body provided the same *exemplum*, and the public rending of that body ceremonially displayed the same power as did the exile (and later death) of Anne Hutchinson and the later execution of the Quakers (Boston Commons, 1656). Metaphorically, witches, Quakers, and other "freethinkers" established a wilderness site ready for settlement and domestication. The witch's body was a site of public strife—a platform on which to inscribe the authorizations of Genesis, and from which to promulgate its repudiations: Enter the land and possess it; divide, subdue, and occupy it. Confess it. Textify it. Read it in terror.[13] Clearly more was at stake at Salem than just the witch's physical person; although for that matter, even the stake was an ambiguous tool, useful for burning as well as for demarcating possession of the land.

In the witch's person—or on it in crimson letters, as in the case of Hawthorne's Hester Prynne—was written a complex grammar, a kind of palimpsest, writing over previous erasures and delineations society's exclusions and its fears.[14] For people governed by the Word, the witch embodied—and expiated—the contradiction between a law-obsessed, literal-minded people and its strongly Antinomian tendencies. Yet the witch was more than a legal marker; the stories of Susanna Martin and Bridget Bishop and other witches cobbled together by Cotton Mather also provided a sanctioned way of surreptitiously enjoying the "delights" of the immoral life while obediently repudiating them.[15] If some laws are meant to be broken for the social good, then some perverseness and demonstrations of wickedness could likewise find good social use for edification and example. And even more. For example, Increase Mather's account of Elizabeth Knapp's possession (in Groton, 1761) was described by the book-seller as "entertainment" for the "curious" (Hall, *Worlds of Wonder*, 282). Cotton Mather, likewise, recognized that witchcraft was a source of unflagging social interest. So had *news* become entertainment? Or was it the other way around? And whatever happened to theology? Mather's breathless accounts of the "Witches *Extasies*" [*sic*] (35), served as a diversion and distraction—a "scarlet thread" (Starkey, 239) in an otherwise mundane daily world. Whatever their theological implications, witch trials provided life and color, however perversely and voyeuristically, to an otherwise monochromatic life. As Marion Starkey notes, the "hangings were made a spectacle by intention" (208). To anticipate a later genre of tabloid political gothic, witchcraft was news. It made celebrities (not always fortunately) of those accused of witchery, while bringing fame and (or) notoriety to those sharing the spotlight. Indeed, says Demos the "metaphor of theatre suggests itself quite naturally; every witchcraft case was, in part a public drama" (117).[16] Reconstructing such an event Demos observes:

Meanwhile a triumphant Cotton Mather is working long and late in his study to complete a book that will soon be published under the title *Memorable Providences Relating to Witchcrafts and Possessions*. A central chapter presents some carefully selected "examples," and includes the events in which Mather himself has so recently participated. The Goodwin children will be leading characters in a local-bestseller. (9)

The charge of witchcraft offered power and individuality to witch and victim alike—who found themselves, accused and accuser, for the first time in the center of public attention and control. As Keith Thomas explains in *Religion and the Decline of Magic*, witches were "the persons whose position in society was ambiguous or insecure" (168–69). Of course, by self-definition, this could characterize an entire New England society: strangers in a strange land; outcasts, deviants by public outcry—at least to the folks left behind in Old England. Salem's example would be only one of many in which theological discourse would intersect with a normalizing rhetoric of the polite (*polis*) during periods of social unrest. Reminders of Salem echo from time to time; indeed, in contemporary formulations of the rite of deviancy, the "witch-hunt" demonstrates how ready to hand is this social corrective in times of civic distress. The language of religious terror and an appeal to the safety of the Body Politic conjoin most "naturally" in times when the *polis* is threatened, whether by actual external, historical event or by some perceived ideological threat. But thus it is that memory, in the name of nostalgia, invents the tradition it needs in order to justify its present needs, and this is as true for established cultural orders as well as individuals. Salem, then, is an early preparation for the later political melodramas and civic theater in which a socializing theology becomes normative cultic narrative of exclusion.[17]

I have briefly discussed how under pressure of a variety of social and political forces the accused witch was erased as an individual and rewritten as symbol. Like Hutchinson, the Quakers—even Hawthorne's fictional version of Hutchinson, Hester Prynne—the accused woman focused community energy for correction and vigilance, becoming at the same time a (tacitly pleasurable) religious memorial. Ironically, however, it is in her hapless role as religious memorial that the witch bears out a community's symbolic rejection of itself in the very terms by which that community defined itself. That is, the witch was feared precisely because she made explicit her unmediated relationship to the powers and principalities; she denied the efficacious mediation of the priest or minister and presumed to invoke interdicted power by virtue of her own authority. In so doing she both confirmed the Protestant principle of immediate access to the Divine while, as a woman, she challenged the male-organized civic order set in place to enforce that principle. Thus an ideology of Christian obedience—since St. Paul, a complex matter of submission to the law and an ironic freedom from it—continues to trouble American civic history. There is no place in American theological or civic history for the strong woman, of course, because that contradicts a favorite cultural narrative. As such, the witch cannot live.

We have seen how, despite Mather's attempt to moralize his accounts of Salem's witch-trials, these accounts became, however covertly, an accepted form of "entertainment." Indeed, a vestige of that function still lingers in the language of the ancient charge: a witch was brought to trial charged with "giving entertainment to Satan" (Demos, 10).[18] Let me turn next to Stephen King's *Carrie*, and see what happens when an originally theological discourse of witchcraft becomes a paradigm of civic imagination in which witches not only live for the civic good, but must, of course, die in order to be repudiated. Ideology connives in the writing of fantasy, whether deployed as civic ritual or marketed as diverting entertainment—with all that word's lethal history.[19]

II

Stephen King was not long out of college, teaching part-time and working in a laundry when he sold *Carrie* to Doubleday. Although he had written (though not yet published) other novels, *Carrie* was his first experiment in the genre of horror. Thus, King's publishing career begins with his serendipitous discovery that Cotton Mather was right: the devil—or at least deviltry—did sell. At that point, as King puts it, "Life began to move at Concorde speed" *(Danse Macabre,* 372).[20] In conversation King discounts this early novel as being the hesitant work of a "young writer," and he may not realize all the reasons for the tale's success. Carrie White is the daughter of a religious fanatic, a girl troubled by (or gifted with) telekinetic power, and King's decentered narrative is in some ways a most traditional American tale. In *Carrie* King adapts the formulas of the Captivity Narrative and Spiritual Autobiography to the ends of "horror." Captivity and possession have been metaphors with deep cultural resonance since Winthrop and the Great Migration. Jonathan Edwards probably never realized how much his terrifying sermon, "Sinners in the Hands of an Angry God" depended for *its* success upon a tradition of such images of captivity.

Even as early as 1742 Edwards's terrifying vision of the sinner captive in the hands of a relentlessly loving God offered a formulaic representation of a basic religious, and civil, fear. The possession/captivity motif has been played out since Anne Hutchinson in a variety of narratives, ranging from sermon to Indian narratives, from slave narratives to tales of domestic entrapment. King, too, reworks the formulas. Particularly, in *Carrie* King charts the dynamic, transgressive oppositions of a derivatively Calvinist cosmology, where, in Mary Douglas's terms, an insistence upon boundary, purity, and law organize and actually create the conflict they enact; and where transgression and scrutiny, rather than love, organize the community. In this social order orthodoxy and heresy create, and depend upon, each other for definition. In this respect, then, *Carrie* emerges from the same social world in which Cotton Mather struggled to define a visible world of order against an invisible world of providence and disorder. Further, King's novel can be helpfully read against the tradition of spiritual autobiography as a darkly parodic captivity narrative reminiscent of Rowlandson.

Carrie is the tale of a 16-year-old, socially-inept girl in the small New England town of Chamberlain. Her powerful and uncontrollable telekinetic powers are triggered by an abrupt and chaotic passage into menstruation, a public event that is both chaotic and humiliating for Carrie. Her subsequent destructive use of her telekinetic powers, partly in response to the visceral repudiations she experiences at the hands of various individuals, drive the plot of this fairly short (for King) novel. King's tale permits a glimpse into a moralistically Calvinistic, Lovecraftian cosmology of distance and power, where the Inscrutable Deity of Margaret White is also the Inescapable Wrath—the Great Transgressor God who is, Carrie insists, at least partly to blame for her captivity and trials. King could hardly have chosen the girl's name by accident, and he is perhaps too clever here by half. For one thing, "white" evokes a tradition in American letters in which whiteness and inscrutability are two points of a triangle, and whose third point is the futility of interpretation—a theme central to the metaphysical puzzlings of Poe, Melville, even Frost.[21] In addition, the name "Carrie" echoes in America's checkered history of social violence doled out in the name of the public good. Martha Corey was the first Salem woman cried out as a witch by Ann Putnam. The name also recalls Martha Carrier, likewise executed at Salem for witchcraft in 1692. Cotton Mather, who witnessed Carrier's execution, called her the "Queen of hell" (*Wonders*, 159). Further, White etymologically suggests witch, and both words are cognates of the word "knowledge." Like Hawthorne's revisionist Hester, Carrie's fatal difference from others is that she knows too much and disowns too little. She can not, like Sue Snell, "conform" to the socializing dictates of her community, partly because she has never been educated in the social literacy that could now help her read that text herself. Less possessed by demons than by her own dark self, her social sin is the power she refuses to cede to the girls who taunt her and the adults who ignore or misread her. Her tragedy, like the earlier social traumas in New England history, centers on the hidden, or at least disguised, center of Calvinist metaphysics—power and authority. The irony of course, is that while Carrie has power, one asks, with Yeats, has she put on the god's knowledge along with his powerful gift?

The novel's opening scene graphically portrays the social exclusionary tactics at work, although King's clumsiness in this spectacle of gender-horror reflects a larger inability to escape the trap of representing women as erotic spectacles, however debased. In this, of course, he is only following patterns set in place by, among others, Mather himself. Carrie's dark menstrual blood flowing into the school shower is meant to signal that she has come of biological child-bearing age. Carrie's body is itself the prime source of her power and mystery, and her blood flow symbolizes the various metaphysical uncertainties against which the community must arm itself. Almost in spite of King's efforts, the scene is luminous with a variety of cultural anxieties: blood, women, witchery, fear of difference. The other girls surround Carrie and respond quickly—and negatively—to her shock and embarrassment. By distancing themselves from her, they hope to secure their own "girlish" purity, although they are clearly more sexually experienced than Carrie. Their repudiation, however, also re-enacts a wider community's fear and rejection of the woman—who, biologically powerful and "ungovernable," must be rendered ideologically powerless, either by being ennobled and feminized, or debased and spectacularized. Carrie, therefore, is a convenient token for the community's intense strategies of repudiation; she embodies social self-hate. She is the foreign witch woman among the innocents, and her unchallenged presence is a powerful threat to their purity (a traditional charge against witches, of course: They prey on the children).

Carrie is a "fractured fairy tale" (Winter, 29), an Ovidian tale of implacable fate and metamorphosis. It is an apocalyptic text in which cosmic psychomachia, a war between invisible and visible worlds, is rewritten as private obsession and narcissism. In a moment of sudden stress, Carrie transforms from victim innocent of knowledge (in her ignorance Carrie thinks that tampons are for applying lipstick), into the powerful Other whose ungovernable secret threatens community stability just as literally as she threatens to deconstruct the town's sense of itself. Carrie's passage to biological maturity means, most simply, that her powers do not easily lend themselves to management, either personally or socially. Neither tampon nor the coercions of ideology effectively constrain her for very long. The speed and the thoroughness of the change from virgin to Cinderella to dark destroying Mother, and the speed with which townspeople—teachers, neighbors, fellow students—rapidly align themselves against her, indicates that here, as at Salem, witchcraft is functional rather than personal.

Throughout the novel King intersperses a variety of texts—newspapers, biographies, sensationalist accounts, scientific "explanations." The effect of these is to erase the personal, to subsume Carrie's individuality in the deceptively bland and universal rhetoric of a socially (or in some cases, biologically) determined fate. The cruelty of this fate is disguised beneath theological, communitarian sanction, as happens to the hapless women in Salem, who find themselves written *in* to Mather's text as theological justification. In *Carrie*, the reader loses sight of Carrie as she is dispersed throughout a range of rhetorics and genres. Various discourses of social defense, rituals of transgressions and victimization, merge to defend the social order of convention. In effect conformity becomes the new interiority. Carrie White, always different, writes in her school notebook a short couplet: "Everybody's guessed/that baby can't be blessed/'til she finally sees that she's like all the rest" (37).

In *Natural Symbols: Explorations in Cosmology*, Mary Douglas argues that witch beliefs flourish under certain conditions, whose structure she metaphorically calls cosmologies. Her comments are applicable to Salem and Chamberlain; to the fictionalized history of Mather and to the historicized fiction of King. In such societies,

the body politic tends to have a clear external boundary, and a confused internal state in which envy and favouritism flourish and continually confound the proper expectations of members. So the body of the witch, normal-seeming and apparently carrying the normal human limitations, is equipped with hidden and extraordinarily malevolent powers. The loyalty of the witch, instead of being committed firmly to his group, flies out loose. He goes alone to contend with alien personifications of lust and power. The witch himself has no firm anchorage in the social structure. In appearance he is present, but only bodily; his real inner self has escaped from social restraint. (113)

As witch, in a society governed by metaphysical mappings of proscriptions and imperatives, Carrie White is a commonplace. That is, Carrie embodies a formula of repudiation that was ossified long before Mather reworked its conventions. As a common ground of social contention and conflict, in her, visible and invisible worlds intersect; in other words, Carrie forms the boundary between the human and its (ill-human) sense of itself. Like the clergy in this respect, who are witches of a more legal sort, Carrie assumes a role prepared for her—one that is sacrosanct, taboo, and a matter of communal ritual. Carrie, like the witch, must exist, if only as type and scapegoat of what the society fears and must repudiate. Obligingly, her community reads her— interprets and confirms her—in the role, if only to prevent themselves from occupying it. She embodies, in quite literal fashion, a social order's habitual need to establish, above all else, and authorizing all else, a sacred hierarchy of pain and victims, one made holy—and horrible—in the name and suffering authority of Jesus.

Carrie is not only the story of an isolated case of repressed telekinesis. It is also the story of a culture's ghosts, chief of which is its Calvinistic idealizations, a suppression of the body in favor of the spirit. Carrie is apocalypse rendered as personal metaphor, shattering not only the ill-fated individual life but also the larger town and the discourses designed to contain its extravagances. What is socially discredited is often symbolically central; thus, a culture that privileges the spirit, by inverse necessity, repudiates the body— displaces it into a rhetoric of moralizing concern over its place and functions. In Carrie this is reflected in the pattern of anxieties about the body, and, obliquely, about the place of women in the larger Body Politic.[22] As metaphor, the body provides a convenient site on which a culture can imagine and protect its vulnerabilities; as such the body is the object of managerial control. Women's bodies, especially, are considered both extraordinary in their dangerous appeal and remarkable in their weakness; traditionally they are the objects of social regulation, and the occasion, too, for much noble-sounding rhetoric. But this, of course, is simply discourse reworked as a kind of policing. Theologies are not dissimilar from political myth in this respect, and, as the Inquisition knew well, the body is the soul's guarantor, and control of the body is tantamount to domesticating the soul.[23]

Carrie, then, is a social cipher. Her presence highlights, and energizes, a socially authorized politics of interpretation and its powers of coercion. In the semiotic exercises of gossipy Chamberlain, she occupies the center of an interpretive storm, a "gaping, whistling hole" (41). She is an emptiness, vulnerable to the powers of society in whose interests she will be "read" and violently interpreted—first as the "frog among swans," then as society's "butt," and then, as a Dark Cinderella. Finally, as "Typhoid Mary," empowered by her telekinetic strength, she is "capable of destroying almost at will" (102). Carrie, however, is not the problem; rather, she is the victim, structured to articulate an otherwise unspeakable town dynamic of exclusion. She enables the classist and mysogynist community to function—its demonstrable acts of violence expended on her deflect away from the casual and daily violences by which it defines itself. More broadly speaking, Carrie functions as a buttress and demonstration; she calls into play the metaphysics of repudiation by which certain exclusions are authorized as socially necessary, approved as they are by a presumptive "right" reading of Revelation. As a witch, then, like Martha Carrier (Starkey, 146*ff.*) Carrie White is both victim and expiation; transgressor and exemplary subject of the law; witch and messenger of a dark god. As a witch, Carrie inscribes a society's long memories in her own blood. She symbolizes the social order's need to repudiate at all costs that which it can neither understand nor manage, its fears of radical instability and boundarylessness—anxieties as old as Winthrop and Mather.

In her final conflict with the religiously paranoid Margaret White, Carrie offers her a present: "What you always wanted. Darkness. And whatever God lives there" (211). For theologies, no less than fantasies, are constrained by the urgent need of the human imagination, to which no scrap of usable memory, pain, or pleasure, goes wasted. Yet Carrie's unsophisticated although nonetheless astute reflections emphasize the real experience behind theological abstraction. However heretical it might be as doctrine, the thought is comforting that somewhere the All-powerful God of love has his All-horrorful equal—or as Whitman suggested, is Himself such an equal, the Square Deific. Carrie "did not know if her gift had come from the lord of light or of darkness" (98). For the community, for her mother, it didn't matter. There had long ceased to be any difference between either of the two inscrutable lords, and a community order that posed terror as the proof of the Divine could no longer understand love or the Divine except as a variety of fear. For this reason Margaret White can find no distinction to be made between Carrie's "devilspawn, demon-power" and the "kind, vengeful hand" (55) of the deity whose portrait she keeps locked in the closet. If Carrie on occasions needs to be locked away, her power suppressed by fear and silence, so, too, does the God she fears. Ironically, then, she locks "Derrault's conception of Jonathan Edwards's famous sermon, *Sinners in the Hands of an Angry God*" in the closet with Carrie, and both languish "below a hideous blue bulb that was always lit" (54). Both need vigilance; both need to be watched. Alone and locked in the closet with the shadow of Jonathan Edwards, Carrie bears the repudiations of "Momma's angry God" (57), which are played out in the secrets and in the silences of a closet-happy society. If the apocalyptic mind gets what it imagines, Carrie becomes for her society the apocalypse uncovered, the closeted God of terror uncloseted, its love revealed as something quite awful to behold. She is one point of an unholy trinity, whose other "twin shadows" are the "crucified Jesus and Momma" (52). Carrie is the pig-bloody sacrifice, the "angel with a sword" countering the sentimentality of the "savior jesus meek and mild" (22).

"To deny King's worth . . . is to deny the society in which we live" (Magistrale, xiv). Indeed, in Carrie's possession by inscrutable forces, in her subsequent isolation and expiatory death, King's tale "enact[s] the recurrent American nightmare" (Winter, 2). She embodies, in the most literally unspeakable way, the Jeremiad—a communal self-narrative drenched with an obsessive sense of responsibility and denial. Though doctrine might be debased over time, religious metaphors remain constant, though shifting, centers of symbolic energy. There will always be a victim, sentimentally divinized even as repudiated. No wonder the cross in their home had "given Carrie endless nightmares in which the mutilated Christ chased her through dream corridors, holding a mallet and nails, begging her to take up her cross and follow Him" (39). Carrie is the new Jesus, as there will be, in time, others after her. In her final moments of agony, praying in the Congregational Church before her final destructive walk home, Carrie understands the emptiness at the center of religious practice. In her misery she becomes Jesus in the Garden, praying to the dark: "No one was there—or if there was, He/It was cowering from her" (200). And, she wonders, why not? This "horror was as much His doing as hers" (200). Mather harbored similar suspicions, and in classic dysfunctional fashion, turned his doubts not upon God, who deserved them, but onto his fellow citizens in Salem, who did not.

Mary Douglas writes, "The reasons for any particular way of defining the sacred are embedded in the social consensus which it protects" (*Implicit Meanings*, viii–ix).[24] Carrie is important for what she suggests about the role of the demonic in a social order; that is, what sort of "social consensus" is created by means of the ritual communal gestures of cleansing and purging that gather around her? To her mother, Carrie signifies that "the devil has come home" (210). To Mr. Quillan, her presence likewise signals that "the Devil came to Chamberlain" (181). For the demonic is less object or agent than a necessary and tacitly agreed-upon civic mechanism in which Carrie exists in order to facilitate, even justify, a process of exclusion. She is the prohibition, the taboo, the ritualized effacement by which the community, however haltingly and imperfectly, comes to self-knowledge. As happened in Salem, community needs—social cleansing, role clarification, boundary vigilance—connive to isolate Carrie, first as agent of the demonic, and then, as the Demonic itself. When she attends the Prom in her deep red dress, and stands before the assembled community, she is similarly attired as Hester Prynne, who similarly is the meaning behind a communal convocation. Carrie's humiliation in and exclusion from the social fabric is a social event; the carnivalesque moment in the shower is repeated at the Prom, where the threat of change, social upheaval, is made visible and its agent effaced. Carrie intends the meaning her community needs for itself, but which it cannot read or interpret clearly. She is the ritual speech by which the society says what it cannot understand. By erasing Carrie, by placing her as the central icon at the center of a community ritual, the townspeople draw a line between her and themselves, and thus, at least temporarily, they escape the same fate.

It is in this respect, then, that the novel *Carrie* is deeply respectful, if also unaware, of its own religious roots. In the inscrutable universe of spiritual determinism, a hunger for victims seems a divine logic, and anxieties of communal annihilation and personal expiation go hand in hand. *Carrie*, then, as the tale of one chosen for this role, is a narrative of vocation and exceptionality. She is the one chosen of the gods as *Monstrum*, the ambiguous and unspeakable sign of human complicity in the responsibility for evil. Thus, the final irony: Carrie is not only witch, not only a feminized Jesus, but silenced woman and hero—etymologically, the powerful one offered to the goddess Hera. She is, then, the saving sacrifice of the people.

III

Salem's abjection of its witches establishes the crucial beginnings of an Anglo-American religious community, a "People of the Word" governed almost obsessively, however obliquely, by rituals and by texts.[25] In such a civic order, allegory is privileged meaning, and revelations are the chief currency of exchange. Accordingly, Carrie dies as expiation only to be resurrected in the symbolic order. She signifies the meaning of transcendence that gives her society its shape. She is what transcendence means, an inevitable distortion, even denial of the self, in favor of its "unselfing" and effacement. Carrie is *Monstrous* in the word's original meaning: revelatory of Divine intent, a sign revealing the order and purpose of the cosmos—at least as that order is humanly construed for social and political purposes. Stephen King, then, like Cotton Mather, could agree that the history of human pain can be read as a trace of religious iconographies. Even debased religion can be peculiarly, sometimes brilliantly revelatory, as it is here. Despite the rhetorical, even nostalgic commitment to love in the sentimental American practice of religion, transgression is religious clarification; pain is privilege and grace; expiation is justification and final triumph.

So, despite the contrivance of so much contemporary horror, the real horror of King's fiction, or of Blatty's *The Exorcist*, or, further back, of Mather's witch narrative, is the evidence these pose of how a religious society "reads" and interprets itself in terms of its metaphysics. Carrie's dark powers— arbitrary, vengeful, inscrutable—terrify the people of Chamberlain (and, vicariously, the reader?) because in them can be seen inscribed the metaphysics of contradiction and opposition against which, historically, the American private and most intimate self has been defined. The social order that makes Stephen King possible is one in which the marginal monsters speak directly to the gods in the center. Those gods continue to be supported, as Douglas notes, because they permit, even secure, a way of life and means of power. We are invested in our religious practices for the same reason Mather is; in our vigilance (hear the religious echo in the word) keeps ever secure the fluctuating boundaries between the human and ill-human, between human and the unhuman. And, as tradition teaches, the Deity, whether Blake's "Nobadaddy" or Margaret White's "Three-lobbed Eye," is the most unhuman of all—and especially so, thank you, Mr. Jonathan Edwards—when dreadfully provoked and holding us over the fire, he manifests his unconditional love. Thus, no wonder that this derivatively Calvinistic social order, badly parodied as it is in Mrs. White, keeps the threatening deity in the closets of fantasy. A society of transgression learns its way from the gods it chooses to worship; whereas that same society defines the "real" of its social order by the fantasies and horrors it feels it must repudiate.

To end where we began. Lastly, the charge of witchcraft in the Massachusetts Code represents a specific civil violation, a rending of the social fabric. Nonetheless, in important ways, "entertaining Satan" was a weaving together of the fabric, a construction of the Body Politic on the dismembered bodies of its victims. Whereas Weisman argues that "secular and ecclesiastical concerns were synthesized in the social regulation of witchcraft" (10), so, too, were less tangible concerns of the imagination. Dismembering is a remembering, after all. The social fabric continues this somewhat schizoid process of rending/mending itself through its well-oiled machineries of terror. The great Silenced Text of religious discourse continues to be written, evident most clearly in the ephemera and entertainments that are, after all, "diversions." Indeed, and diversions from what, one wonders? After all, the writer of horror fiction is, says Stephen King, an "agent of the norm" (*Danse Macabre*, 58), someone who, in King's pithy expression, "watches for the mutant."

So our horrific entertainments are the formulaic diversions by which we divert ourselves from other lies. They are, in effect, religious rituals, by which we encounter the sacred and the cultically taboo.[26] Back to a question hinted at earlier: Why *did* William Blatty find it necessary, in *The Exorcist*, to exchange the real-life young boy with a fictionalized adolescent girl? Many reasons come to mind, not all of them salutary. This is a question we may not be able to answer at the moment, except to draw a backward line to Salem. The dispossessed Regan is the Body Politic, sanitized—the little house on Prospect Street, domesticated, swept, and cleaned. Regan, demonless, domesticated as well, sounds rather like a character from a different kind of text, *Little Women*. Securely domesticated by a society's repressions, she is, of course, safe—as indeed, was Ann Putnam years later, as she confessed to the crowded church the error of her earlier witchlike ways. Conversion—of the body, of the soul—is an important civic motif, and it is, finally, about control. That is why possessed boys, in real life, become girls in fiction. It is also why King, ignorant finally of all irony, can say that *Carrie* is "largely about how women find their own channels of power, and what men fear about women and women's sexuality" (*Danse Macabre*, 170). Indeed. If Carrie is the powerfully sexual woman men fear, she has still not escaped the narrow confines of the patriarchal imagination.

NOTES

1. The other two "shames" were the 1656 persecution of the Quakers and the 1721 campaign for smallpox inoculation.

2. See R. I. Moore, *The Formation of a Persecuting Society*. The connection between the articulation of the soul (theology) and the description of the *polis* (politics)

thus makes itself still heard. See, for example, Sacvan Bercovitch, *The Puritan Origins of the American Self*, and Garry Wills, *Under God: Religion and American Politics*.

3. Norman Cohn traces remnants of this process in a recent review of Elaine Pagels's *Satan*; speaking of the expiatory quality of the Judeo-Christian metaphysical tradition, Cohn writes, "for all the differences between [the gospel accounts], they embody a characteristic world view, and one which has remained potent down to the present day" (18). Further, "[Pagels] has demonstrated, more fully and convincingly than has been done before, how ancient the demonizing tradition in Christianity is" (20).

4. The text of Excommunication reads as follows:

Forasmuch as you, Mrs. Huchison [*sic*], have highly transgressed and offended and forasmuch as you have soe many ways troubled the Church with your erors and have drawen away many a poor soule and have upheld your Revelations: and forasmuch as you have made a Lye, etc. Therefore in the name of our Lord Jesus Christ and in the name of the Church I doe not only pronounce you worthy to be cast out, but I doe cast you out and in the name of Christ I doe deliver you up to Sathan that you may learne no more to blaspheme to seduce and to lye. And I doe account you from this time forth to be a Hethen and a Publican and soe to be held of all the Bretheren and Sisters of this Congregation, and of others. Therefor I command you in the name of Christ Jesus and of this Church as a Leper to withdraw your self out of the Congregation; that as formerly you have dispised and contemned the Holy Ordinances of God and turned your Backe on them, soe you may now have no part in them nor benefit by them. (Hall, *The Antinomian Controversy*, 388)

5. Winthrop to Hutchinson.

6. Richard Bushman draws a portrait of this society some years later:

The whole society suffered from a painful confusion of identity. People were taught to work at their earthly callings and to seek wealth; but one's business had to remain subservient to religion and to function within the bounds of seventeenth-century institutions. The opportunities constantly prompted people to overstep both boundaries, thereby evoking the wrath of the powerful men who ruled society. Even relations with neighbors deteriorated as expansion multiplied the occasions for hard feelings. (15–46)

7. See *Puritanism in America: New Culture in a New World* by Larzer Ziff; *Puritan Influences in American Literature* edited by Emory Elliott; and *Saints and Revolutionaries: Essays on Early American History*, edited by David D. Hall, John M. Murrin, and Thad W. White.

8. Mather comments on the ambiguities that had prompted his essayistic justification of the trials: "If the Evil One have obtained a permission to Appear, in the Figure of such as we have cause to think, have hitherto Abstained, even from the Appearance of Evil: It is in Truth, such an Invasion upon Mankind, as may wee Raise an Horror in us all" (101).

9. Mather shows the degree to which boundaries and borders possess him, if I may use the word: "but indeed, all the Unreformed among us, may justly be cry'd out upon, as having too much of an hand in letting of the Devils into our Borders" (95). Throughout my argument I am indebted to Peter Stallybrass and Allon White's discussion of boundaries in *The Politics and Poetics of Transgression*.

10. See Weisman, especially his introductory chapter.

11. Kai Erickson and Weisman extend Demos's observation by arguing that witchcraft fulfills a crucial social function. It is, says Weisman, a ritual by which a society oversees the "creation of social meanings" (10)—specifically the exclusionary politics encoded around social deviancy. In addition, other functions can be discerned. As D. H. Lawrence observes, America has been "the land of Thou shalt not" (5). So from the

very first days of the Republic the trials served as a socialized rhythm by which a community defined the parameters of the acceptable by repudiating the unacceptable.

12. See Carol F. Karlsen, *The Devil in the Shape of a Woman: Witchcraft in Colonial New England*.

13. See Michael Clark, "Witches and Wall Street: Possession Is Nine-Tenths of the Law." Clark argues that in the witchcraft trials "authority performs the same hermeneutic function that interpretation performs for Mather. In the trials that knowledge ['right interpretation' of often contradictory evidence] was constituted not by providence, but by power, the very channels of social hierarchy through which evidence emerged" (133). In *Witch-Hunting in Seventeenth Century New England: A Documentary History, 1638–1692*, David D. Hall similarly observes that "Witch-hunting was thus a process of interpretation that began at the village level before moving to the courts" (10).

14. For a provocative discussion of the Body-as-Text see Robert Detweiler's *Breaking the Fall: Religious Readings of Contemporary Fiction*, especially "Sacred Texts/Sacred Space."

15. Demos writes, "the qualities of witchcraft are at the heart of the story. In one broad aspect they are everywhere similar: they express a tendency to 'project,' to 'scapegoat,' to extrude and expel that which individuals (or groups) define as bad. . . . Diversity is the rule in the fantasies, the generative circumstances, the contingent values, the interpersonal structures—which support and reflect any given 'system' of witchcraft belief" (13).

16. Marion Starkey likewise comments that the "possession" of Margaret Rule, in which Mather had a hand, was the "major theatrical attraction in Boston" that season (243).

17. Indeed, the popular reclamation, as national memory, of Salem's disowned and repudiated politics, provides us still a ready-made vocabulary and model for policing the Body Politic—a point made pellucidly clear when Clarence Thomas, in Senate hearings, deftly recontextualized a charge of sexual harassment into a racially tinged "witchhunt"—it will be recalled that the diversion had its desired effect.

18. Further, the word itself speaks more than a little history, in its evident erasures and the slippage of discourse: Is Satan entertaining? Are we entertaining Satan? Who is at dalliance with whom? In the language of Rosemary Jackson and Terry Heller, societies strengthen themselves by "reenacting repression." That is, they channel threatening energy into sanctioned forms of deviancy that can then be safely abjected, [dis]spoken, silenced. See Rosemary Jackson, *Fantasy: The Literature of Subversion* and Terry Heller, *The Delights of Horror: An Aesthetics of the Tale of Terror*.

19. To cite one example, important thematic, social, and even literary links can be made between Elizabeth Knapp, the "'demoniac'-girl" of Groton (Demos, 111) and Regan, William Blatty's demon-girl of *The Exorcist*.

20. It was on the heels of the rejection of one novel that Doubleday published *Carrie*. Four of King's previously unpublished novels were subsequently published under the pseudonym of Richard Bachman. See Bill Thompson, "A Girl Named Carrie" (especially pages 29–34) as well as King's, *Danse Macabre* (372).

21. See Harry Levin, *The Power of Blackness: Hawthorne, Poe, Melville*.

22. King is accurate in his assessment that horror American-style is constructed around cultural anxieties about the power and place of women—especially power as it is wrested back from an inscrutable God and, often, less scrutable social systems in service

of that God. Nonetheless, despite Tabitha King's introduction to the text, "explaining" it, King's *Carrie* is not the book "of woman's power" that King would like it to be.

23. In *The European Witch-Craze* Hugh Trevor-Roper suggests that a debased language of religion and prescribed (unmanaged) sexuality are commonly found linked in the ritual symbologies of the witch-hunt.

24. This is even more clear in a culture that still is, in many respects, a sectarian culture, organized around the specific revelation of an Unspeakable [Unspeaking] metaphysic. Bryan Wilson makes the point that in a sectarian society "worship of God is worship of the community" (cited in Douglas, *Natural Symbols*, 115).

25. See Julia Kristeva, *Powers of Horror: An Essay on Abjection.*

26. For a discussion of New England and ritualism, see *Worlds of Wonder, Days of Judgment: Popular Religious Belief in Early New England* by David D. Hall (especially Chapter 4, pages 166–212); *Puritan Influences in American Literature*, edited by Emory Elliott; *Saints and Revolutionaries: Essays on Early American History*, edited by David D. Hall, John M. Murrin, and Thad W. White.

WORKS CITED

Bercovitch, Sacvan. *The Puritan Origins of the American Self.* New Haven: Yale University Press, 1975.

Bushman, Richard. "Jonathan Edwards as Great Man: Identity, Conversion, and Leadership in the Great Awakening." *Soundings* 52 (1969): 15–46.

Clark, Michael. "Witches and Wall Street: Possession Is Nine-Tenths of the Law." *Herman Melville's Billy Budd, Benito Cereno, Bartleby the Scrivener, and Other Tales.* Edited by Harold Bloom. New York: Chelsea, 1987, 127–47.

Cohn, Norman. "Le Diable au Coeur." Review of *The Origin of Satan*, by Elaine Pagels. *The New York Review of Books*, 21 September 1995, 18–20.

Demos, John. *Entertaining Satan: Witchcraft and the Culture of Early New England.* Oxford: Oxford University Press, 1982.

Detweiler, Robert. *Breaking the Fall: Religious Readings of Contemporary Fiction.* San Francisco: Harper and Row, 1987.

Douglas, Mary. *Implicit Meanings: Essays in Anthropology.* Boston: Routledge & Paul, 1975.

———. *Natural Symbols: Explorations in Cosmology.* New York: Random, 1970.

Elliott, Emory, ed. *Puritan Influences in American Literature.* Urbana: University of Illinois Press, 1979.

Erickson, Kai T. *Wayward Puritans: A Study in the Sociology of Deviance.* New York: Wiley, 1966.

Fiedler, Leslie. "Fantasy as Commodity and Myth." *Kingdom of Fear: The World of Stephen King.* Edited by Tim Underwood and Chuck Miller. New York: Signet, 1986, 47–52.

Hall, David D., ed. *The Antinomian Controversy, 1636–1638: A Documentary History.* Boston: Northeastern University Press, 1991.

———. *Witch-Hunting in Seventeenth Century New England: A Documentary History, 1638–1692.* Boston: Northeastern University Press, 1991.

———. *Worlds of Wonder, Days of Judgment: Popular Religious Belief in Early New England.* New York: Knopf, 1989.

Hall, David, John M. Murrin, and Thad W. White, eds. *Saints and Revolutionaries: Essays on Early American History*. New York: Norton, 1984.

Heller, Terry. *The Delights of Horror: An Aesthetics of the Tale of Terror*. Urbana: University of Illinois Press, 1987.

Jackson, Rosemary. *Fantasy: The Literature of Subversion*. New York: Methuen, 1981.

Karlsen, Carol F. *The Devil in the Shape of a Woman: Witchcraft in Colonial New England*. New York: Random House, 1987.

King, Stephen. *Carrie*. New York: Signet, 1974.

———. *Danse Macabre*. New York: Everest, 1981.

Kristeva, Julia. *Powers of Horror: An Essay on Abjection*. Translated by Leon S. Roudiez. New York: Columbia University Press, 1982.

Lawrence, D. H. *Studies in Classic American Literature*. New York: Viking, 1964.

Levin, Harry. *The Power of Blackness: Hawthorne, Poe, Melville*. New York: Knopf, 1964.

Magistrale, Tony, ed. *The Dark Descent: Essays Defining Stephen King's Horrorscape*. Westport, CT: Greenwood, 1992.

Mather, Cotton. *Wonders of the Invisible World*. Boston, 1693; reprint, John Russell Smith, 1862.

Moore, R. I. *The Formation of a Persecuting Society: Power and Deviance in Western Europe, 950–1250*. New York: Basil Blackwell, 1987.

Pribek, Thomas. "Witchcraft in 'Lady Eleanor's Mantle.'" *Studies in American Fiction* 15 (1987): 95–100.

Stallybrass, Peter, and Allon White. *The Politics and Poetics of Transgression*. London: Methuen, 1986.

Starkey, Marion. *The Devil in Massachusetts: A Modern Enquiry into the Salem Witch Trials*. New York: Knopf, 1949.

Stout, Harry S. *The New England Soul: Preaching and Religious Culture in Colonial New England*. New York: Oxford University Press, 1986.

Thomas, Keith. *Religion and the Decline of Magic*. New York: Scribner's, 1976.

Thompson, Bill. "A Girl Named Carrie." *Kingdom of Fear: The World of Stephen King*. Edited by Tim Underwood and Chuck Miller. New York: New American, 1986, 29–34.

Trevor-Roper, Hugh. *The European Witch-Craze of the Sixteenth and Seventeenth Centuries and Other Essays*. New York: Harper, 1969.

Weisman, Richard. *Witchcraft, Magic, and Religion in Seventeenth-Century Massachusetts*. Amherst: University of Massachusetts Press, 1984.

Wills, Garry. *Under God: Religion and American Politics*. New York: Simon and Schuster, 1990.

Winter, Douglas E. *Stephen King: The Art of Darkness*. New York: New American, 1986.

Ziff, Larzer. *Puritanism in America: New Culture in a New World*. New York: Viking, 1973.

3

Patriarchal Mediations of *Carrie*: The Book, the Movie, and the Musical

Douglas Keesey

The Curse: Telekinesis and Menstruation in Stephen King's *Carrie*

The novel's birth was almost as difficult as its title character's. Conceived at the suggestion of a friend who challenged King to create a credible female character ("Why are you writing all of this macho crap? . . . You don't have any feminine sensibility at all"), the work was soon aborted when King realized just how difficult the task of writing a woman's story could be (King, quoted in Underwood and Miller, 85–86). King's wife Tabitha then retrieved the manuscript from the wastebasket, launching him again into the unfathomable depths of a woman's world but also, by answering his questions, helping him to survive in that world; hence, the dedication: "This is for Tabby, who got me into it—and then bailed me out of it" (*Carrie*).[1] Despite his wife's collaboration and the novel's successful coming to term, King remains ambivalent about his ability to create a believable woman, fearing that he may have fallen into the stereotypes identified by Leslie Fiedler in *Love and Death in the American Novel*: "When I think I'm free of the charge that most male American writers depict women as either nebbishes or bitch-goddess destroyers, I create someone like Carrie—who starts out as a nebbish victim and then becomes a bitch goddess, destroying an entire town in an explosion of hormonal rage" (quoted in Beahm, 38).

"Hormonal rage" suggests the connection between menstruation and telekinesis that is the book's main focus; as King readily admits, *Carrie* is in many ways the sexist nightmare of an immature male who, like Billy Nolan, fears female equality as a threat to his masculinity: "*Carrie* is largely about how women find their own channels of power, and what men fear about women and women's sexuality . . . which is only to say that, writing the book in 1973 and only out of college three years, I was fully aware of what Women's Liberation implied for me and others of my sex. The book is . . . an uneasy masculine shrinking from a future of female equality" (*Danse Macabre*, 170). But King has tried to get beyond a masculinist perspective and to bridge the gender gap: Not only has he given *Carrie* aspects of his own life as a child—King too was "fat," "estranged from other kids my age," "deserted" by his "father," and prone to "violent" feelings, "particularly in my teens" (King, quoted in Beahm, 27)—but King has also attempted to tell the story from a feminist perspective, interpreting his own "male fears—about menstruation and about dealing with women who eat you up" as misunderstandings of nature, fears so strong that they become self-fulfilling prophecies (King, quoted in Underwood and Miller, 95).

Though never explained, it is clearly no mere coincidence that the awakening of Carrie's psychic abilities is tied to the onset of her first period: Menstruation and telekinesis are both referred to by an uncomprehending society as "the curse," and it is patriarchal society's very attempt to repress the power of female sexuality, to keep the blood hidden, that causes the defiant eruption of Carrie's paranormal powers. In Carrie, the supernatural rises to assert the inevitability of natural female forces that society has tried to deny; if Carrie's power is a "curse," it is one society has brought upon itself. The fantastic elements in the book are thus an integral part of its social commentary: The metaphysical power of mind over matter is the only channel of force open to Carrie in a society in which men have monopolized all the physically active roles. As King explains, Carrie is "Woman, feeling her powers for the first time and, like Samson, pulling down the temple on everyone in sight at the end of the book" (*Danse Macabre*, 170). At crucial moments in the novel (3–4, 7, 37), King compares Carrie's psychic powers to the force of a nuclear bomb, suggesting that natural energy (female or atomic) will inevitably backfire on society if that energy is directed toward misogyny or war. King likens society's oppression of Carrie to a "chain reaction approaching critical mass": the explosion of Carrie's feminist rage. Nature has her laws and will not be denied.

The young women who bombard Carrie with tampons in the opening shower scene display the "revulsion" and "disgust" (6) they have been taught to feel at the sight of their female natures. Even the gym teacher, Miss Desjardin, whose "nonbreasted," "muscular" physique and skill at "archery" suggest a feminist identification[2] and whose close mother-daughter relationship helped her feel pride in her first period (5, 9–10), is overwhelmed with "self-shame" when she sees Carrie's bleeding and confesses that "Maybe there's some kind of instinct about menstruation that makes women want to snarl" (10, 16). As on the day when she used a tampon to apply lipstick (8), Carrie in the shower scene has once again exposed an aspect of female nature that is considered unnatural and unfeminine. Like her menstrual blood, the fat, sweat, mucus, and shit Carrie exudes are all mocked by a society that considers the body a threat and that associates women with the body (7, 8, 13).

Thinking about it later, Sue Snell realizes that she and the other young women in the shower scene were unconscious participants in a social ritual:

women finding a place in patriarchal society by projecting their own unacceptable female traits onto Carrie and making her the scapegoat for them. To rise in society, Sue must see through men's eyes, oppressing undesirable females like Carrie and repressing the undesirable femaleness within: Wearing hair rollers and taking birth-control pills, Sue ensures that her body will be presentable to the male gaze (34). Sue comes to realize that her social popularity is bought at a high price; in ostracizing Carrie, she is not only denying sisterhood, she is also repudiating her own female independence: "And having something she had always longed for—a sense of place, of security, of status— she found that it carried uneasiness with it like a darker sister" (33).

For her own sake as well as Carrie's, Sue attempts to reintegrate femaleness back into the social body before it surfaces vengefully as a "dark thing" to destroy the society that denied it light. First she reintroduces a female awareness of the body into her relationship with Tommy. Whereas earlier she had viewed their relationship through society's eyes ("they fit together walking . . . she could look at their reflection in a store window and think, There goes a handsome couple"), now she begins to see things from her own perspective: Having sex to gain social advancement is not true love but a brutal, unfeeling act: "[S]he had let him fuck her (do you have to say it that way yes this time I do) simply because he was Popular" (33–34). Only when Tommy stops trying to score and admits to her that he got the rubber on wrong, only when she stops trying to be the perfect model she thinks he wants her to be and confesses that the first time was painful, do they really make love. Sharing with each other their doubts about the future, Sue and Tommy find that an admission of bodily weakness brings not repudiation but a mutual recognition of their common humanity. It is no accident that Sue finds the sight of Tommy "looking pensively out the back window with his pants still down around his ankles" both "comic and oddly endearing" (32): The male mind that admits to physical vulnerability is more attractive than a sham of invincible intellect.

Sue's second step toward reintroducing a female acknowledgment of the physical is to undo her earlier scapegoating of Carrie and ask Tommy to take Carrie to the prom in her place, thus claiming her own ability to do without social affirmation and giving Carrie a chance at the acceptance she herself has had. Tommy's acquiescence to Sue's request shows his unchauvinistic regard for Sue and her need to atone for her cruelty toward Carrie; it also shows Tommy's truly masculine willingness to face society's censure at his association with Carrie in a romantic setting.

Like dark doubles of Sue and Tommy, Chris Hargensen and Billy Nolan also chafe at social conformity, but only work their way in deeper in an effort to get out. Chris's conformist assault on Carrie (and refusal to atone for it by doing the gym exercises set as penance) has gotten her barred from the very prom to which Carrie has now been invited. The ferocious zeal of Chris's conformist assault has backfired, excluding her from her place as leader of an adolescent rite of passage (Queen of the Prom) and alienating her from her former entourage, who agreed to submit to the punishment prescribed by authority. Chris's overzealous attempt to conform is both a sign of her deep insecurity about fitting in and an indication of a female independence trying to get out: Chris has channeled all her nonconformist rage into being an exceptional conformist, a standard of standardized womanhood; in Chris, the goody-goody and the bad girl are one and the same.

Like Sue, Chris finds that packaging herself for male consumption makes her attractive to society men, but the sex that ensues is also prepackaged, already programmed, a simulacrum of feeling between a commercial-perfect couple, a consummate joining of gender stereotypes. Having stereotyped herself to be attractive, Chris finds that she can attract only stereotypes: These men love her only for her image, an image they had her create only to reinforce their image of themselves. Chris's "passivity" during intercourse makes them feel more actively virile; they don't want an individually responsive woman. The fact that Chris later "achieved her own solitary climax while viewing the incident as a single closed loop of memory" (94) shows both her isolation in a world of conformity and her desire for personal fulfillment, even if this must be merely masturbatory or through a voyeuristic fantasy.

Seeking the real in a world of simulacra, Chris is understandably attracted to Billy Nolan, whose "old, dark" 1950s car promises delivery from the false light of the new, the "machine-stamped, anonymous vehicles" of her 1970s boyfriends (95). Chris's nostalgia is for a genuineness she has never known, a passionate individuality that will bring out her own; as the "first [lover] she could not dance and dandle at her whim" (94), Billy seems more than just a stereotype responding to her stereotypical beauty. Unlike her white-collar yuppie boyfriends, sweaty, grease-monkey Billy seems at home with physical labor, with fluids, and with the body. Not having cordoned himself off from the facts of life within a "ventless" car smelling of "plastic seat covers and windshield solvent" (95), windows-open, fast-driving Billy gleefully faces death and loves to get his hands dirty. As Chris exhorts him to "Feel me all over. Get me dirty," Billy's unrepressed physical desire and the memory of their "sudden brush with death" in the car thrill Chris with the feeling that at last she has broken out of her society's mandate to conform, its repression of natural instinct (96).

But Billy's dirty machismo is as much a stereotype as the yuppie lordliness for which it is designed to compensate. Billy's craftsmanlike pride in making things with his own hands is tainted by vengefulness: His father failed in the gas station business, and Billy's independent workmanship is used to make a special tool to break into the school building and set up the blood bath for Carrie (100, 102). After running away in disgrace, Billy's father was replaced in his mother's affections by a man named Brucie; Billy runs over stray dogs with his car and plans to dump blood on Carrie, imagining that the dogs and Carrie are Brucie (161). His rough sex with Chris is a way of getting back at her moneyed father and all the men with their "plump, glistening daddies' cars" whom he blames for doing in his own father (101). Finally, his association with Chris is both a wish-fulfillment fantasy of being accepted into a society that had rejected his father and also his way of taking revenge on that society, and on his mother, for his father's rejection (82). His interest in Chris is no more personally affectionate than his masculinity is individual or affirmative: From his "stuffed crotch" to his massaging of Chris's shoulder as if he were "testing a cut of beef" (54), Billy is a walking stereotype of a man puffing himself up and scapegoating women for what goes wrong in a man's world.

Even if Billy were what she was looking for, indications are that Chris is too insecure about losing her position in society to date him for long. In the end, she finds her inability to control him more of a threat than a thrill, and plans to withhold her sexual favors as punishment for his independence: "[W]hen this is over you're going to get it buddy maybe you'll go to bed with lover's nuts tonight" (117). He, in turn, plans to rape her, as his own insecurities about his masculinity get the better of him and his nightmare of rejection becomes a self-confirming prophecy: "When this was over he was going to have her until every other time she'd been had was like two pumps with a fag's little finger" (121). "When this was over"—in each case Billy and Chris temporarily channel their hatred of society, each other, and themselves onto Carrie: The blood bath at the senior prom is thus the (un)natural extension of the scapegoating that occurred in the bloody shower scene.

Just as the actions of Billy and Chris and of Sue and Tommy can best be understood within a larger familial and social context, so Carrie's unnatural acts can be seen as the consequence of her parents' and grandparents' failure to reconcile natural desires and social strictures. Turning to religion for consolation at the loss of her father, Margaret White also uses religion as a weapon to get back at her mother for seeing another man in her father's place, accusing her of "living in sin" with a boyfriend (44). In reaction to what she sees as her mother's infidelity and in line with certain fundamentalist attitudes toward the body, Margaret comes to view all sex as sinful and any female desire as a temptation that must be resisted, as her mother did not. When Margaret and her husband Ralph find themselves giving in to their sexual urges, Ralph runs off and is subsequently killed in an accident that strongly suggests that he simply could not live with his own body's tendency to break out of its religious confines: Ralph dies "when a steel girder fell out of a carrying sling on a housing-project job" (10). So that she can still believe in Ralph's purity and in her own worthiness as his sinless wife, Margaret attempts to forget the fact that they ever had intercourse and to deny responsibility for the child growing within her: "Mrs. White believed, from her fifth month on, that she had a 'cancer of the womanly parts' and would soon join her husband in heaven" (11). Despite her self-mortifying need to live up to Ralph's and God's expectations, Margaret stops herself from aborting the child and allows her maternal nature a momentary triumph over paternal law.

But the fear that her daughter Carrie may one day give way to sexual desire causes Margaret to conceal from her all knowledge of female nature. Although Carrie insists that the real sin was her mother's keeping her ignorant of the facts of life, Margaret views Carrie's menstrual flow as itself a sin, a sign of female desire that Carrie could have willed not to express. As Carrie begins to show a natural interest in boys and to assert her supernatural powers against her mother's social strictures, Margaret's maternal instincts intensify in an ironically patriarchal and conformist direction. Like the goody-goody bad girl Chris, Margaret asserts her female independence by her overenthusiastic adoption of a social role: She becomes a fanatical fundamentalist, an extreme version of patriarchal religion's ideal—the piously protective mother. In attempting to save her daughter from men with lust-inciting "Roadhouse Whiskey" on their breath, men like Ralph who "took" Margaret in a moment of weakness (70), Carrie's mother associates men, sex, and death in her daughter's mind. It's true that Margaret's father died in a "Roadhouse" shootout, but Margaret represses the fact that this very roadhouse owned by her parents was also probably the site of her own conception, just as Carrie was conceived the night Ralph came home with "roadhouse whiskey" on his breath (43, 154). Carrie's attempt to shock her mother into a recognition of her female nature—"'You FUCK!' Carrie screamed. (there there o there it's out how else do you think she got you o god o good)" (42)—can only be heard as a curse, a blasphemy from her mother's body-fearing, fundamentalist perspective.

Carrie's natural interest in sex threatens Margaret's sense of her own purity: If she cannot protect her daughter from female desires, then she must defend herself to ensure her own salvation and marriage in a male heaven: "'It says in the Lord's Book: "Thou shalt not suffer a witch to live." Your father did the Lord's work'" (71). The sight of "Momma holding Daddy Ralph's long butcher knife" (67), the nightmare vision of her mother as the insane embodiment of patriarchal religion's ideal of motherhood, greets Carrie when she returns from the prom, and the knife descends as Margaret carries out the religious imperative she feels is her duty: Thus the mother commits the very rape and murder from which she had hoped to save her daughter. The mother's fear grew fantastic enough to become reality.

Margaret's murder of her daughter at the end is doubly ironic in that, by the time Carrie returns home, she is truly her mother's daughter: The blood bath at the prom has made her as fearfully destructive of society as her mother, seeming to confirm all her mother's worst nightmares about the outside world. From King's point of view, Carrie is no more responsible for the terrible direction her female power takes than is her mother for her murderous maternal instincts; in interview after interview, King insists on the social cause behind Carrie's actions, on society's responsibility for its own destruction: "I never viewed Carrie as evil. I saw her as good. When she pulls down the house at the end she is not responsible"; "when she perpetuates destruction on her hometown, it's because she's crazy. She doesn't want to make fires any more than she wants to wet her pants" (quoted in Underwood and Miller, 202). Like a madwoman who in the extremity of her fear loses control of her bodily functions, Carrie can no longer contain her female powers from drowning the world in the very blood it would disown. Mirroring her mother's own murderous assertion of a blood tie, Carrie brings Margaret's heart to a dead stop, taking revenge and at the same time fulfilling her mother's masochistic desire to cut out the evil body so that her purified spirit may ascend to heaven.

Playing to the hilt her assigned role as bloody female, Carrie vengefully becomes patriarchal society's worst nightmare concerning women and their bodies: Mother Nature as a force greater than man's or God's. If the supernatural is merely an extension of the natural, then what chance has society to win redemption from death through scapegoating? Despite its attempt to place the blame for Carrie's actions on another woman—Sue is the preferred scapegoat (58)—the White (male) Commission will eventually have to acknowledge its own responsibility in the creation of a Carrie, or the next girl-child to be born will grow up to be a "world-beeter" in the literal sense (181). Believing that "Momma wanted her to be the Angel's Fiery Sword, to destroy" (164), Carrie turns a male society's stereotypes against itself and wreaks a terrible revenge on behalf of her mother and other sisters in oppression.

The Transformation of Carrie: Novel into Film into Musical

Because of King's subsequent reputation for writing slangy, fast-paced horror, readers tend to forget that *Carrie*, King's first novel, is highly experimental in form. Whereas his later works display the predominantly linear plotting and linguistic transparency typical of much nineteenth-century realism, *Carrie*'s collagist juxtaposition of disparate print-forms is closer to modernism or postmodernism in style. King's verbally conspicuous conjoining of newspaper clippings, book and letter excerpts, investigative hearing transcripts, Associated Press wire reports, classroom desk graffiti, slang definitions, and a death certificate function like a Brechtian alienation effect to make readers question customary modes of representation. By emphasizing the literariness of his literature, King demystifies print, making readers read the words on the page not as some natural, transparent reflection of the truth, but as a personally and politically motivated refraction of reality. As Sue Snell muses on the newspapers' transformation of Carrie into a story, "They've made her into some kind of a symbol and forgotten that she was a human being, as real as you reading this, with hopes and dreams and blah, blah, blah. Useless to tell you that, I suppose. Nothing can change her back now from something made out of newsprint into a person" (97–98). "Hopes and dreams and blah, blah, blah" suggests the rapidity with which real human emotions become sentimental clichés when they are put into words, and "she was a human being, as real as you reading this" describes Sue's and King's effort to counter this tendency, to make the reader conscious of the reading process and of how most print derealizes people even as it seems to convey the truth about them.

If "The White Commission Report" is published by "Signet Books," then so is the paperback version of King's novel (130). The Commission attempts to whitewash Carrie's story, circumscribing her terrible power within scientific jargon ("A View Toward Isolation of the TK Gene with Specific Recommendations for Control Parameters") and writing it off as a "once-in-a-lifetime phenomenon" or the more colloquially reassuring "fluke" (165, 179, 165). Against the bureaucratese of the "State Investigatory Board," which concludes that "we find no reason to believe that a recurrence is likely or even possible," King juxtaposes the letter of a near-illiterate whose report of a frightfully telekinetic young "Annie" rises like a return of the repressed to disturb the smooth surface of official narrative's secondary revision (180). King's self-reflexive fiction warns against the normalization of horror, society's tendency to translate what it cannot bear to look at into more acceptable terms, as in "Slang Terms Explained: A Parents' Guide," with its neat definition of "to rip off a Carrie" as "To cause either violence destruction; mayhem, confusion; (2) to commit arson" (179). As Douglas E. Winter puts it, "Carrie has been defined away as a comfortable colloquialism, memorialized for her act rather than herself" (33).[3] In the war of the words King dramatizes between an oppressive/repressive official discourse and an uncannily resurgent speech, we can see the beginnings of a literary mode that will become a King trademark: stream of consciousness, that form closest to the unvarnished truth of primary process mentation. In parenthetical run-on sentences with lower-case I's—"(i killed my momma i want her o it hurts)" (170)—King sets a fluid, feelingful language of the unconscious, both Carrie's and the town's, against the officialese that insists on distinguishing high from low, victors from victims, and the innocent from those (scapegoated as) responsible.

Both this communal stream of consciousness of primary and primal truths similar to Jung's universal archetypes of the collective unconscious (as Carrie may be likened to the anima or vengeful dark side of an unaccepting patriarchy) and King's use of collagist technique or dialogic form serve to challenge society's pretended monopoly on truth. And yet the novel's multiplicity of perspectives may also be read as a sign of psychic splitting: Whereas a part of King clearly identifies with Carrie and understands her power as the vengeful return of natural female energy that patriarchy is responsible for having repressed, another part of King shares patriarchy's horror at women, amply embodied in the novel's misogynistic officialese. Asked by a Penthouse interviewer about his "greatest sexual fear," King responded, "The vagina dentata, the vagina with teeth"; his second greatest, King said, was represented in a "horror story . . . about a pregnancy" (quoted in Underwood and Miller, 189). That King's first novel is evidence of a horror at what terrible powers castrating women may give birth to is something King readily admits: "*Carrie* expresses a lot of male fears—about menstruation and about dealing with women who eat you up" (quoted in Underwood and Miller, 95). As openly confessional in his first novel as he is in later interviews, King's split form displays both his patriarchal gynephobia—his fear of the "bitch goddess['s] . . . hormonal rage" (quoted in Beahm, 38)—and his feminist social satire, his sincere desire to depict women in sympathetic and nonstereotypical ways. The formal experimentation of *Carrie* represents the ideological conflict in King's psyche and society.

Just as King's novel departs from the conventions of narrative realism, so Brian De Palma's film version of *Carrie* (1976) marks a spectacular divergence from the standard practices of classic Hollywood cinema. Whereas most Hollywood horror occludes its means of production by hiding its film technique so as to further identification between viewer and victim (or between voyeur and victor), De Palma's movie keeps flashily calling attention to its style. The opening shower sequence is shot in soft focus and slow motion, dollying lyrically by a scene of high-school girls cavorting like nymphs in various stages of undressed innocence; this is followed by a fluid dissolve to Carrie in the steamy gym shower, caressing her breasts and thighs. Though logically impossible, the entire scene seems to be presented as if from Carrie's point of view, a wish-fulfillment fantasy of laughing female community and innocent sensuousness. Abruptly, the tempo jolts from slow to regular motion as dream turns to nightmare: Carrie bleeds, fears she is dying, and encounters a shocked, ashamed, and contemptuous circle of sexually repressed young women who jeer at her and pelt her with tampons like stones.

But the unusual slow motion and the unusually public view of young women's private spaces have distracted most viewers from imagining this opening shower sequence as depicted from Carrie's point of view; instead, the scene is more often criticized as voyeuristic, as the typical male director's and viewer's eye-rape of female characters. The fact that a previous shot has revealed this to be "Bates High" and that the scene of Carrie in the shower quotes shots from *Psycho* can't help but remind us of voyeuristic Norman Bates (Tony Perkins), who stabs the Janet Leigh character in the shower. Thus De Palma's filmic allusiveness and his conspicuously "Peeping Tom" camera[4] counter the suggestion that this scene might be taken from a woman's perspective: The diegetic focalizer may be sympathetically and innocently female, but the extradiegetic eye seems distanced and predatorily male. The women characters in this scene are both sex objects and sexual innocents as the viewer's vantage shifts between Carrie as naive perceiver and Carrie as salaciously perceived. (One might compare Milton's presentation of Eden in *Paradise Lost*, first seen from Satan's cynical, destructive perspective but also alternately from that of prelapsarian Adam and Eve.)

De Palma's urge to identify with girlish innocence seems at odds with his fear of mature female sexuality as evil; the director's cynicism pulls back from idealism as if in horror at the prospect of being victimized along with women or by women. De Palma seems to participate in the dizziness of first love when he has Carrie and Tommy whirl wildly in their prom dance together, but the dancers begin to spin so fast that the viewer is made aware of their turning as technique or trope, as conspicuous metaphor fashioned by a director both within and outside the fantasy of first love, both identifying with Carrie in Tommy's arms and looking on as two actors revolve on a rotating platform.[5] Soon after, the shower scene's slow motion is resumed as Tommy and Carrie progress to the stage to be crowned King and Queen of the prom; as before, our entranced identification with Carrie is broken as the blood falls (this time pig's blood from a bucket overhead), and the film speed reverts to real time, befitting a postlapsarian world of female victimization. But this is also a world of bloody female revenge, of the "bitch goddess" and her "hormonal rage." The division in De Palma between a feminist sympathy for women's right to fight back and a patriarchal horror of the female sex as destructive is now spectacularly in evidence as a split-screen effect: On one side is Carrie, blood-spattered and blood-spattering; on the other, her victors turned victims. Like a visual trace of the director's schizophrenia, a line splits the screen, showing up identification as problematic—divided and unstable.[6] At one point Carrie's side slides from right from left: We are uncertain with whom to identify, by whom to be repulsed; victor and victim seem displaced, displacing each other, unplaceable.

The film's most lasting impression of formal division as ideological contradiction comes in its concluding dream sequence. As in the preceding shower and dance scenes, here viewer identification is ostensibly with another "good girl," Sue, whose barefoot, slow-motion progress in a white dress beside a white picket fence to Carrie's graveside seems another example of cinematic free indirect discourse, of a scene imbued with Sue's own sensibility: She sympathizes with the wounded innocent in Carrie and brings flowers in commemoration of that innocence to lay on her grave. But the soft-focus in this scene is strangely insistent; Sue's walk is peculiar and the movement of cars in the background seems odd; even the sunlight appears somehow unnatural. Suspicious spectators—viewers who know De Palma—watch with a cynical eye, somewhat distanced from Sue's perspective and from her idealization of Carrie. When Carrie's bloody hand reaches out from the grave to grab Sue's white arm as the film jolts back into the misogynist nightmare that is real time, we are shocked—but not entirely. Previous shocks—and De Palma's style-disturbing content, his identification-troubling technique—have partially prepared us. When the scene match-cuts from Carrie's grip on Sue's arm at the graveside to Sue's mother holding her in bed, we are only partially identified with Sue the victim; another part of us cranes up and away with De Palma the director who, in his coolly cynical self-control, knew better than to trust in female innocence. De Palma shot the dream sequence night for day, with special lighting and filters to simulate the sun, and he shot it in reverse, with the actress playing Sue walking backwards. In the final version, nothing is quite convincing (the movement of the cars seems odd because they're going backwards), just as for De Palma wish-fulfillment fantasies have lost much of their credibility: His film exposes their unreality.

King's comments on De Palma's film are interesting for what they reveal about the psychosocial and stylistic conflict registered by both auteurs. Arguing that "humor and horror exist side by side in [the movie], playing off one another," King notes that "Much of De Palma's film is surprisingly jolly, but we sense his jocoseness is dangerous" (*Danse Macabre*, 170). Both the humor and the horror seem particularly to do with the film's women:

The girls laboring over their calisthenics [in an amusing scene] were the same girls shouting "Plug it up, plug it up, plug it up!" at Carrie not long before. . . . [De Palma] sees this suburban white kids' high school as a kind of matriarchy. No matter where you look, there are girls behind the scenes, pulling invisible wires, rigging elections, using their boyfriends as stalking horses. . . . I think the film unconsciously takes the attitude that all men are cat's paws. (*Danse Macabre*, 171, 172; King, quoted in Underwood and Miller, 95)

Whereas De Palma would like to see women as a certain source of hope and leavening humor in the world, he is continually uncovering their other side: horrible, dangerous, violent, matriarchal—cats playing with their male victims. Like the film's divided tone of humor and horror, its female characters are two-faced, double-dealing, putting on an innocent, frolicsome front while secretly plotting behind the scenes to gain control over men. Or perhaps we should say that it is King and De Palma who are divided: between a conscious desire to identify with female innocence and an unconscious gynephobia. When King says that "De Palma's film is kind of light and frothy and he gets you at the end when you think it's all over," we see again Sue's white arm being grabbed by Carrie's bloody hand: the film's representational schizophrenia in regard to illusion and supposed reality, the dream of female innocence betrayed by shocking duplicity (King, quoted in Connor, 12).

The ideological tensions implicit in the split forms of the novel and film versions of *Carrie* became major rifts in the stage musical (1988). Because this dramatic version of *Carrie* is virtually unknown, some background information may be in order. Representing the first joint venture ever of British and American equities, *Carrie, the Musical*, ran for twenty-five performances at Stratford-upon-Avon before its transfer to Broadway. The director, some crew, and several cast members were regulars of the Royal Shakespeare Company, which hoped that *Carrie* would follow in the line of successful British imports like *Cats* and *The Phantom of the Opera*, helping to fund future plays by the Bard (Shakespeare, not Stephen King). *Carrie* made its Broadway debut on 19 May 1988 and closed just five performances after its opening night; the production lost $8 million, becoming the biggest flop in Broadway history or, as one outraged investor put it, "the biggest flop in the world history of the theater, going all the way back to Aristophanes" (Henry, "The Biggest," 65).[7]

Most of the reviews were enough to frighten prospective theatergoers away, with headlines like "Bloody Awful," "Blood and No Guts," "Getting All Fired Up over Nothing," "'Carrie' blazes, can't bring down the house," "Shakespeareans' fling with King disastrous," and "Staging a Horror on Broadway." Critical commentary certainly focused on the musical's horrible aspects, describing it as "dreadful," "hideous," "ghastly," "grotesque," "coarse," "disgusting," and "in the worst possible taste." The most phobic reaction to the show probably comes from the reviewer who wrote: "'Carrie' is not merely problematic. It is not simply a miscalculation. It is stupendously, fabulously terrible—ineptly conceived, sleazy, irrational from moment to moment, the rare kind of production that stretches way beyond bad to mythic lousiness" (Winer). Many critics thought that the whole thing was simply a terrible idea from the very beginning: "A show about a girl who discovers she has diabolical powers related to her menstrual cycle is not everybody's idea of a musical," warned one (Kissel), and the *New Yorker* critic commented, in inimitably fastidious fashion, that "Among those works one might consider adapting for the musical stage, I would have thought that a story whose plot is set in motion by the onset of the heroine's first menstrual period belonged pretty far down the list—only a notch or two above John Chadwick's 'The Decipherment of Linear B'" (Kramer, 85). Stephen King himself was only slightly more sanguine about the show's prospects, saying "Look, if they can do a musical about a dictator in Argentina and a barber in Fleet Street, this might work, too" (quoted in "Broadway"). It seems that this play will live on in memory, if at all, as a colossal mistake; the April 1991 issue of *Spy* magazine, for example, lists *Carrie, the Musical* among what the editors call "great lapses of common sense through history," ranking it up there with "Esperanto," "open marriage," and "the electric carving knife" (Collins, 48). *Carrie, the Musical*, was not videotaped; no cast album was made; the music and lyrics were never published.

Act I opens with a scene of the adolescent girls in calisthenics class, their aerobics exercises presumably intended as a sign of youthful exuberance and natural high spirits. At odds with this impression are the chorus-line high kicks, professional acrobatics, and towering human pyramid the girls build with their obviously twenty-five-year-old-and-up bodies, which continually remind those in the audience that they are attending a showy Broadway musical and not merely eavesdropping on an average high-school day in the gym. As one critic noted, "[Debbie] Allen's choreography isn't about joy or striving or aspiration, it's about T. & A.—a sort of sexualized aerobics: balletoporn" (Kramer, 85). The girls then strip down before hitting the showers and, in appraising themselves from an imagined male point of view, they sing of hating their bodies. But there are actual male spectators in the theater audience, and the girls' undressing is played less as introspection than as a striptease in the come-hither style of the hookers' line-up in *Sweet Charity* (the choreographer is a Bob Fosse veteran). Our identification with these girls' insecurity over their bodies is further hampered by the fact that, as one reviewer put it, "Since these young women have the world's greatest bodies, the show immediately leaps into a logical quandary" (Kroll, 73). As with the schizophrenic style of De Palma's film version, this "logical quandary" consists of a conflict between lyrics calling for a female-identified viewer and other insistent theatrical devices that hail the spectator as a male voyeur who will appreciate a burlesque-house ambiance, grind-show costumes, and peekaboo routines with towels and semitransparent scrims set up as shower stalls.

Even the set design prevents us from losing ourselves in the characters, distracting us both from feminist sympathy and from boys'-night-out lechery. Ralph Koltai's sets are neither here nor there, not a girls' gym and shower nor a burlesque show/bordello. Koltai's abstract design presents the "gym" as a black-and-white formica cube like a Mondrian box. As the set changes from "gym" to "shower," brilliant white enamel panels revolve smoothly under computer control. The stylized and depersonalized look of Koltai's design seems to set the play in some perfect future, far removed from the girls' adolescent angst or from their professional titillation of $50-a-seat theatergoers. As one reviewer remarked, "[The] sets are nervy, but their highly kinetic high-tech sleekness has little to do with establishing a realistic ambiance from which the supra-real goings-on could startlingly take off" (Simon, "Blood," 60).

The show casts black actor-singer-dancer Gene Anthony Ray from TV's *Fame* as bad boy Billy, thus inadvertently perpetuating the racist association of blackness with evil, and of interracial couples with devil's pacts (the play's Chris is white). (This unfortunate stereotyping is only partially counterbalanced by the casting of black singer Darlene Love—also from *Fame*—as the kindly gym teacher.) Composer Michael Gore and librettist Dean Pitchford, who won Best Song Oscars for the movie *Fame*, impede both audience identification with the sympathetic characters and spectator shock at their evil doings. The extraordinary conventionality of the music and lyrics keeps returning our attention to the fact that we are watching a Broadway musical, distracting us from our would-be involvement in Carrie's plight (she sings: "Was it his voice? Was it his smile?/I haven't felt so wonderful in quite a while") and severely mitigating the effect of the horror (the evil Chris sings: "It's a simple little gig./You help me kill a pig").

The most effective scenes in the musical are the Lulu-inspired operatic duets between Carrie and her mother, the latter played by Betty Buckley, who won a Tony for her performance in *Cats* (she sang "Memory"). Buckley's "haunting, burnt vibrato" (Winer) and "vinegar and molasses voice" (Barnes) work powerfully to convey maternal anguish, and we in the audience are drawn in. As Carrie, seventeen-year-old Linzi Hately, who "has a belter's voice in the reigning (and amplified) English rock-musical manner" (her only previous credit is as an orphan in *Annie*) (Rich, C3: 1), tends to be more alienating, but she does succeed in communicating her wonder at her female powers in a marvelous scene where she telekinetically animates her hairbrush, powder puff, party dress, and shoes, which come to life, dance, and help her get ready for the prom. (This

Disneyesque sequence is reminiscent of the sorcerer's apprentice scene from
Fantasia.)

Yet the play's climax pushes us away with the strenuousness of its
effort to draw us in, and it elicits cool derision where it wants to provoke active
fright. As Billy simply walks up to Carrie and empties a bucket of red confetti
on her head, we are not moved by pity or fear; underwhelmed, our attention
wanders to consider whether it is the director or the dramatic medium itself that
is inadequate to the staging of this scene. Carrie then ascends on a pedestal so
slowly that we have time to realize that it must be hydraulically powered. The
red laser beams that blast from her fingertips shoot out over our heads to points
at the back of the theater, a special effect that, probably because we are so
accustomed to lasers now, serves mainly to remind us that we are in an
electrically wired theater watching a "Broadway spectacular," not at a school
prom being terrified by Carrie's flame-throwing revenge. The crashing chords
and whizzing lasers seem as familiar and as retro as disco or a 1970s rock
concert, and, as characters below Carrie "tumble about confusedly behind a
smoke-screen scrim lighted in red to symbolize fire," we're so busy trying to
figure out what is happening that the veil between us and the characters'
emotions might as well be opaque (Kramer, 85). As one critic wrote, "the
gymnasium *Gotterdammerung* is all metaphor. It is just smoke and flashing
lights and lasers asking to be transformed by the audience's imagination"
(Henry, "Getting," 80). As in the novel and the film, the conspicuousness of the
Broadway musical's devices splits our attention between pity at female suffering
and fear of female revenge, ultimately distancing us from both. Rather than
resolve the ideological contradiction that divides "Thank heaven for little girls"
from "Ding! Dong! The witch is dead," each new patriarchal mediation of
Carrie seems to take us deeper into formal conflict, as if unsure about whether it
wants in or out of the girls' gym.

NOTES

1. All subsequent quotations from King's novel *Carrie* will be identified by
parenthetical page citations within the essay.

2. The identification of certain female body-types and athletic abilities with
feminism is one of many ways in which King's novel is a product of the historical period
in which it was written—the early 1970s.

3. Winter is one of the few critics who actually talk about *Carrie*'s form as if it were
something other than merely transparent.

4. Compare the opening sequence of De Palma's *Sisters*, the film on the basis of
which King recommended that De Palma be chosen to direct *Carrie*.

5. John Simon's negative reaction to the extravagance of this whirling scene may not
be too far from the mark insofar as it points out how De Palma's obtrusive style ends up
disturbing viewer identification with the characters: "Worst of all are the big effects,
drawn out to impossible lengths and shot with trashy blatancy, as when a couple whirling
about a dance floor are dwelt on with a monomaniacal insistence that gives the viewer an
acute case of nausea" (*Reverse Angle*, 280).

6. Compare Pauline Kael's comment about how this film device disturbs clear viewer identification with (or of!) character: "There are only a few places where the film seems to err in technique. . . . [T]he split-screen footage is really bad: the red tint darkens the image, and there's so much messy action going on in the split sections that the confusion cools us out" (212).

7. By contrast with the ill-fated musical, the De Palma film was an outstanding success, garnering Oscar nominations for Sissy Spacek (Carrie) and Piper Laurie (her mother), earning over $15 million in domestic film rentals, and establishing King's reputation as a bankable author (Wood, 38).

WORKS CITED

Barnes, Clive. "Musical 'Carrie' Soars on Blood, Guts and Gore." *New York Post*, 13 May 1988.

Beahm, George, ed. *The Stephen King Companion*. Kansas City: Andrews and McMeel, 1989.

"Broadway Goes for Blood." *Newsday* (New York), 8 May 1988.

Collins, James. "What Could We Have Been Thinking?" *Spy*, April 1991, 48.

Connor, Jeff. *Stephen King Goes to Hollywood*. New York: New American, 1987.

Henry, William A. "The Biggest All-Time Flop Ever." *Time*, 30 May 1988, 65.

——. "Getting All Fired Up over Nothing." *Time*, 23 May 1988, 80.

Kael, Pauline. *When the Lights Go Down*. New York: Holt, Rinehart and Winston, 1980.

King, Stephen. *Carrie*. New York: Doubleday, 1974.

——. *Danse Macabre*. New York: Everest, 1981.

Kissel, Howard. "Don't 'Carrie' Me Back to Ol' Virginny." *Daily News*, 13 May 1988.

Kramer, Mimi. "Bloody Awful." *New Yorker*, May 1988, 85.

Kroll, Jack. "Shakespeare to Stephen King." *Newsweek*, 23 May 1988, 73.

Rich, Frank. "'I Just Want to Set the World on Fire.'" *New York Times*, 13 May 1988, C3, p. 1.

Simon, John. "Blood and No Guts." *New York*, 23 May 1988, 60.

——. *Reverse Angle: A Decade of American Films*. New York: Clarkson N. Potter, 1982.

Underwood, Tim, and Chuck Miller, eds. *Bare Bones: Conversations on Terror with Stephen King*. New York: McGraw-Hill, 1988.

Winer, Linda. "'Carrie': Staging a Horror on Broadway." *Newsday*, 13 May 1988.

Winter, Douglas E. *Stephen King: The Art of Darkness*. New York: New American Library, 1984.

Wood, Gary. "King's Boxoffice Bite." *Cinefantastique* 21, 4 (February 1991): 38.

4

Rituals of Male Violence:
Unlocking the (Fe)Male Self in *Gerald's Game* and *Dolores Claiborne*

Theresa Thompson

[I]t is our impression that more constraint has been applied to the libido when it is pressed into the service of the feminine function, and that—to speak teleologically—Nature takes less careful account of its [that function's] demands than in the case of masculinity. And the reason for this may lie—thinking once again teleologically—in the fact that the accomplishment of the aim of biology has been entrusted to the *aggressiveness* of men and has been made to some extent independent of women's *consent.*

Sigmund Freud
"Femininity" (32)

Both sadism and masochism imply that a particular quantity of libidinal energy be neutralized, desexualized, displaced and put at the service of Thanatos [death].

Gilles Deleuze
Masochism (110)

By virtue of affirming the primacy of the phallus and of bringing it into play, phallocratic ideology has claimed more than one victim. . . . man has been handed that grotesque and scarcely enviable destiny (just imagine) of being reduced to a single idol with clay balls. . . . For, if psychoanalysis was constituted from woman, to repress femininity (and not so successful a repression at that—men have made it clear), its account of masculine sexuality is now hardly refutable: as with all the "human" sciences, it reproduces the masculine view, of which it is one of the effects.

Hélène Cixous
"The Laugh of the Medusa" (884)

Stephen King's *Gerald's Game* (1992) and *Dolores Claiborne* (1993) are written from the perspective of women victims of domestic violence. Both the Mahout family in *Gerald's Game* and the St. George family in *Dolores Claiborne* have three children at the time of the 1963 complete solar eclipse. They live in Maine. Joe St. George, his wife Dolores, and their children have no other visible affiliations with "Jessie Mahout, daughter of Tom and Sally, sister of Will and Maddy, wife of nobody" (*Gerald's Game*, 107). The main connection between the two families are the acts of domestic violence enacted before, during, and after the eclipse.

In *Gerald's Game*, Jessie understands sexual molestation from the point of view of a victim because her lawyer father sexually molested her during that eclipse thirty years before the events of the novel. Dolores Claiborne's narrative voice expresses the efforts of a mother driven to murder her husband in order to save herself from further domestic violence and to save her daughter from sexual abuse. These novels focus their central scenes during the 1963 solar eclipse, which cast its shadow over Maine like some dark cloud. King's use of the 1963 solar eclipse is intriguing for a number of reasons, but the date itself is significant for understanding the links between an eclipse and King's focus on domestic violence and incest. These two novels, both from a woman's point of view, explore the effects of our persistent cultural myth of female masochism, a myth that dominated the 1950s and 1960s cult of the domestic.

It may simply be a coincidence that these novels focus on the effects of what Betty Friedan identifies, in her 1963 landmark text of the same name, as the "feminine mystique." The feminine mystique, according to Friedan,

says that the highest value and the only commitment for women is the fulfillment of their own femininity. . . . But the new image this mystique gives to American women is the old image: "Occupation: housewife." The new mystique makes the housewife-mothers, who never had a chance to be anything else, the model for all women; . . . it simply makes certain concrete, finite, domestic aspects of feminine existence . . . into a religion, a pattern by which all women must now live or deny their femininity. (43)

The housewife constructed relying on this mystique was, in 1963, "the cherished and self-perpetuating core of contemporary culture" (Friedan, 18). Thirty years later when King published *Gerald's Game*, this "self-perpetuating core," as Susan Faludi argues in *Backlash* (1991), had regained much of the power it lost during the women's movement of the 1970s.[1] In *Gerald's Game* and *Dolores Claiborne*, King analyzes and attempts to disrupt the regenerative nature of the feminine mystique with its concomitant domestic paragon who— mother, wife, sister, or daughter—is "really not here at all" and never was (*Gerald's Game*, 5).

Efforts to expose the fallacies of the feminine mystique are more successful in the first novel primarily because *Gerald's Game* rejects what can only be described as the mystique of the happy middle-class family. This mystique supplies the professional class family with a privileged discursive space for popular notions of family life. For example, in the 1980s, *The Cosby Show* provided Gary Bauer, Ronald Reagan's "family-policy czar" with what Bauer felt was the perfect set of values for the American family (Faludi, 263). On *The Cosby Show*, the two parents are professionals (a lawyer and a doctor), the income is reliable and substantial, one parent is always at home, and their children receive quality day-care and educational experiences. The only significant difference between *Cosby* and popular 1950s and 1960s family sitcoms like *Father Knows Best* or *Leave It to Beaver* is skin color and the professional status of the wife/mother character.

In contrast, popular conceptions of the blue-collar family on shows like *Roseanne* and *The Simpsons*, with their many instabilities related to limited education and the necessity of living paycheck to paycheck, make the working-class family appear dysfunctional by definition. Certainly neither the Cosby family nor the Simpsons provide realistic family images. The number of African-American families that might identify with the Cosby's household is small, as are those white working class households who feel comfortable with the Simpsons for an icon. Yet both the Simpsons and the Cosby family reflect the white dominant cultural assumptions I call the middle-class mystique.

Popular recognition that feminine domesticity and its companion image of masochism are not the result of some natural disposition but are instead the result of a socially constructed, self-enforced ordering of female expressions of desire won't undermine the psychosexual discourses that enable patriarchal dominance and aggression to continue if that image is contained within the dysfunctional space of the working class. A recognition of the difficulties inherent in creating any shift in public perceptions about the middle classes might explain why King wrote two novels in which the American father emerges as the real monster-under-the-bed who terrifies wives and daughters. *Dolores Claiborne*, as if King wished to recant his earlier work, returns to the more acceptable paradigm of the working-class family as locus for domestic violence and incest in the cultural imagination.

The first-person narrative in *Dolores Claiborne* struggles to voice the concerns of an ill-educated woman forced by circumstances to commit murder. Dolores's harsh bitchiness does nothing to refute images of the dysfunctional working-class household wherein women can be, like Roseanne Barr, loud and strong. This reliance on the middle-class mystique permits the novel's discourse about sexual transgression and family violence to remain within acceptable parameters. It is always-already acceptable for the working classes to experience domestic violence. *Dolores Claiborne* has in consequence proven more acceptable, as Hollywood's willingness to make a film version in 1995 attests.

Movie moguls may have found the second novel more palatable than *Gerald's Game* for a number of reasons, most of which reconfirm the sacred cows of middle-class family life. First and foremost, unlike the Mahout family in *Gerald's Game* in 1963, the Claibornes offer no pretense to being *Cosby* or even *Father Knows Best* doubles. Dolores fights to earn a living as an abused housekeeper for an eccentric (often crazy) rich woman. Her husband Joe was a blue-collar alcoholic with little interest in the discourse of family values but who developed around 1963 a sexual desire for his budding young daughter. Joe's moves to seduce his daughter offer nothing unacceptable in the imaginary space enfolding the American working classes. The myths surrounding incest and well-cherished beliefs about domestic violence maintain that such horrors happen among the unwashed and ill-educated poor.[2]

Dolores also murders her husband in defense of her child, an act that simply reasserts the feminine mystique's image of powerful maternal instincts able to overcome woman's "natural" passivity.[3] In this case, the mother sacrifices her brutal husband so that her daughter, Selena, can grow safely into womanhood, get a good education, and perhaps become middle class. Dolores learns that Joe, no longer sexually capable with her, has "got inside [Selena's] life, and once in there, he must have finally noticed just how pretty she was getting, and decided he wanted something more from her than just to have her listen when he talked or hand him the next tool when he was head-down in the engine compartment of some old junk truck" (*Dolores Claiborne*, 79). Dolores learns what Joe has been doing to Selena, and his "days were numbered from that moment on" (95). Such images of maternal dedication and paternal sacrifice as necessary for entering into the middle class simply take the American myth of success to an extreme degree. Middle-class sacrifices to the rigors of advanced education, to sexual repression or inhibition, to jobs in the white-collar jungle are validated by contrast with this imaginary space of the dysfunctional working-class family.

Unlike *Dolores Claiborne*, *Gerald's Game* focuses on issues of domestic violence located firmly within the white middle class. The Mahout family, with its lawyer father and stay-at-home mother, its squabbling son and daughter, might appear recast from *Father Knows Best*, but the horrors Selena St. George experienced lie hidden beneath. In replacing the socially acceptable dysfunctionality of the blue-collar home with a professional middle-class family, King disrupts social narratives about the power of little sacrifices to prohibit domestic violence and heterosexual excess. *Gerald's Game* repositions assumptions of dysfunctional familial sacrifice and dominance onto a less palatable symbolic plane. This disruption of the class mystique creates horror in a story that might otherwise pass for American naturalism alongside Frank Norris's *McTeague* or Stephen Crane's *Maggie*. The novel reveals that in the middle-class and professional heterosexual white family, imbalances of social power encourage violent transgressions of sexual boundaries. These power imbalances create, in addition, a misconstruction of heterosexual desire. A patriarchal system of justice, which the focus in *Gerald's Game* on lawyers reveals, enables a false pattern of male sexual aggression and female sexual masochism as the heterosexual model for the American family.

Perhaps because its focus is heterosexual patterns of dominance and masochism, *Gerald's Game* at first glance appears more appropriate to backroom pornography where heterosexuality is often predicated on notions of bondage. It is a story about a middle-aged woman, Jessie Mahout Burlingame, whose husband Gerald, in his middle age, has become dependent on sexual fantasies of a sadistic sort. Jessie and Gerald go to their lakeside cabin one autumn day, "long after summer had run away for another year," because Gerald wants to use the new official handcuffs he has purchased (*Gerald's Game*, 5). Jessie, both wrists chained to the bed, changes her mind about the whole game. Unfortunately Gerald refuses to recognize her loss of enthusiasm; "pretending *into* ignorance . . . he meant to rape her" (15). In a terribly typical move on King's part, Jessie moves from passive participant who could let "him shoot his squirt" to aggressive assault weapon, kicking Gerald in the crotch (17). Gerald falls "over backward with his knees up and his head down" and dies, leaving Jessie naked and handcuffed in the middle of nowhere. The rest of the story rotates around Jessie's attempts to free herself from his handcuffs before dying of hunger or thirst or, worse, before the odd "man in the corner," who appears during the night, decides to kill her (123).

Although the initial critical response might be to assume that *Gerald's Game* is a work exploiting sadomasochistic fantasies to increase sales, a careful examination reveals the novel grapples more with the psychological and sociological reasons behind Jessie's current bound position. Of course, King does not ignore the horrible aspects of her bondage; every gruesome aspect of Jessie's current dilemma is explored for full horrific effect. But King's examination of the social scripting that lies beneath the heterosexual paradigm of masculine sadism and feminine masochism lift the book from these mundane levels of exploitation to a more complex status. Jessie is trapped on her marriage bed by official police Kreig M-17 handcuffs, a significant symbol.

Jessie must recognize the differences between the Kreig F-23s Gerald wanted to buy and the M-17s he actually purchased. She is chained in more ways than one: physically and socially. Shock and revulsion aside, for Jessie to free herself from the bonds holding her to Gerald's bed appears impossible; she is wed to his bed as she was legally bound to his life. Her chains are not just very real Kreig police handcuffs, they are substantial metonyms for the mystique itself, critical representatives of the legal and psychological systems that support myths of masculine dominance. As with other women raised in the 1950s and 1960s, the legally and socially validated mystique makes, for Jessie, "chains in her own mind and spirit. They are chains of mistaken ideas and misinterpreted facts, of incomplete truths and unreal choices" (Friedan, 31).

In 1985, Susan Faludi points out, the psychological term "masochism" itself almost became an official synonym for woman:

The "masochistic personality disorder" may have been the most regressive, and peculiar, of the three [APA] proposed diagnoses [that would affect women]. The APA panel had come up with nine characteristics to define masochism—and they were strangely broad indeed. . . . The APA panel had neatly summed up female socialization—and stamped it a private, psychiatric malfunction. (357)

This cultural misperception of the socialized woman (an image central to Gerald's sexual fantasy) as essentially masochistic is dislodged in Jessie's violent rejection of Gerald's bondage game. Her rebellion involves a belated assertion of a previously unsuspected identity, a self not devoted to preserving a June and Ward Cleaver image of the family. Significantly, rebellion involves Jessie in what, as Jessica Benjamin argues, must occur when sexual self-differentiation effaces the Other in the heterosexual script of male dominance: death.[4] Gerald lies dead on the floor, his rapidly chilling body gnawed occasionally by a wild dog named, ironically, Prince.

To expose the fallacies (or perhaps phalluses) of the middle-class mystique and dismantle the myth of feminine masochism, King tears away the boundaries between his readers and the intimate lives of his characters. He focuses solely on the explicitly heterosexual space wherein cultural assumptions of sadism and masochism are constructed and enforced: the heterosexual middle-class bed itself. *Gerald's Game* positions its domestic terror squarely within the parameters of heterosexual games and rituals. This focus occurs in part, as Magistrale says, because King's "awareness of the pervasiveness of evil" extends even to those institutions and beliefs society marks sacred and taboo (Magistrale, *Landscape*, 16). In imagining the taboo secrets of the middle-class bedroom, *Gerald's Game* makes explicit how the scientific discourse of sexuality shapes desire, to borrow from Foucault, into the "point of weakness where evil portents reach through to us; the fragment of darkness that we each carry within us: a general signification, a universal secret, an omnipresent cause, a fear that never ends" (Foucault, 69).

King reveals some of the underlying (unspoken) consequences of this sexual fear as it resides within the structure of the middle-class bedroom as Jessica works to free herself from her husband's handcuffs. Through Jessie's remembering of her experiences with her lawyer father and her lawyer husband, King explores the idea that Jessie's misleading masochistic posture may result from her privileged economic and social position, a reversal of psychological assumptions about the dysfunctional working class. The thousands of years of womankind's commodified association with the production and reproduction of domestic and societal worlds, upon which modern Western psychobabble visions of female masochism rely, create an intimidating cultural force within the middle-class household itself.

The following lengthy quotation from Gerda Lerner's *The Creation of Patriarchy*, establishes a necessary background for clarifying this point:

At any given moment in history, each "class" is constituted of two distinct classes—men and women. The class position of women became consolidated and actualized through their sexual relationships. It always was expressed within degrees of unfreedom on a spectrum ranging from the slave woman, whose sexual and reproductive capacity was commodified as she herself was; to the slave-concubine, whose sexual performance might elevate her own status or that of her children; then to the "free" wife, whose sexual and reproductive services to one man of the upper classes entitled her to property and legal rights. . . . Class for men was and is based on their relationship to the means of production: Those who owned the means of production could dominate those who did not. The owners of the means of production also acquired the commodity of female sexual services, both from women of their own class and from women of the subordinate classes. (215)

In patriarchal societies, female behavior in relation to reproductivity and sexuality has long been legislated to favor male privilege, regardless of the class or race of the woman involved. Power arises from control of sexuality and reproduction, and control over both arises from controlling the means of production.[5] White middle-class women participate in this system of oppression, certainly, but they are themselves co-opted, purchasing their power at a cost. One such cost can be the sublimation of their own desires into a willful submission to masculine sexual violence: feminine masochism.

Jessie Mahout Burlingame self-identifies through both her father's and her husband's names. Her sexuality, like her names, has been constructed by her father's explanations for his sexual transgression, which has in turn determined her later choice of a sexual partner. Jessie is not exactly a "nightmare image from some old TV commercial . . . a smiling woman in a fifties hairdo with a pair of blue rubber gloves on her hands" (*Gerald's Game*, 86–87). She is, however, nightmarishly handcuffed to her marriage bed through most of the novel with nothing concealing her from the reading/gazing eye but "a pair of bikini panties" (3). The lack of resemblance between her masochistic sexual posture and the domestic posture of the 1950s and 1960s suburban American housewife emphasizes the persistence of the "feminine mystique" in defining female heterosexuality within masochistic confines.[6] Yet the idea of perceiving Jessie's submissive posture—redolent with the masochist's "inability to express one's own desire and agency" (Benjamin, 79)—as a natural part of her heterosexuality becomes less and less plausible.

Unlike Dolores Claiborne, Jessie is not a mother, the only role within the feminine mystique that permits a woman to be a heroine (Friedan, 45). As she struggles against her bonds, Jessie fights only to save herself, again disrupting the notions of natural sacrifice. Correspondingly, Gerald is not a provider who symbolically sacrifices himself for any family, nor is he depicted as a completely depraved alcoholic. He is an aggressive bully who dies because he chooses to sacrifice his wife's body (just this once) to satisfy his own wish for dominance. His death is not the sacrifice Gerald intends at all, nor does he seem capable of understanding how raping his wife will cause her harm.

Jessie's nature is not what keeps her bound to her marriage bed. Gerald's handcuffs hold her to the bed(rock) of patriarchal fantasy. Jessie needs to remember something about the Kreig handcuffs holding her, but to remember is dangerous; it conjures horrible specters much as her cries for help attract that mysterious figure resembling Death. What she does not want to remember or think about at all is Tom Mahout's sexual molestation of her during the 1963 solar eclipse. Jessica, when she allows herself to think about that past at all, refers to his calculated and well-planned molestation as a "sexual accident about as serious as a stubbed toe" (*Gerald's Game*, 187). Yet what is abundantly clear throughout is that this event keeps Jessie bound emotionally and physically because she has never before questioned her father's construction of the incident. When she does, Jessie wonders how "many of the choices she had made since that day had been directly or indirectly influenced by what had happened during the final minute or so she had spent on her Daddy's lap, looking at a vast round mole in the sky through two or three pieces of smoked glass? And was her current situation a result of what had happened during the eclipse?" (179).

Tom Mahout, a lawyer, wields excessive verbal and financial power over the women in his home, and he permits that power to extend into the sexual arena. When Jessie, chained to Gerald's bed, finally confronts the paternal ghost, Tom appears so intimately connected to the person Jessie now perceives herself to be that her mind and body unfold as incarnations of a haunted site: Her mind is the house that Tom built, so to speak, and her body is the space he continues to haunt. Like many a haunted space, after one ghost opens the door, many ghosts follow. Jessie's mind houses ghosts of many social and cultural authorities from her childhood, authorities who upheld the foundations of Tom's patriarchal authority:

Mrs. Wertz, her first-grade teacher, starts to laugh. Old Mr. Cobb, their gardener until he retired in 1964, laughs with her. Maddy joins in, and Ruth, and Olivia of the scarred breasts. Kendall Wilson and Bobby Hagen are bent almost double, and they are clapping each other on the back like men who have heard the granddaddy of all dirty jokes in the local barber-shop. Perhaps the one whose punchline is *A life-support system for a cunt*. Jessie looks down at herself and sees that now she is naked, too. Written across her breasts in a shade of lipstick known as Peppermint Yum-Yum are three damning words: DADDY'S LITTLE GIRL. (*Gerald's Game*, 116–17)

"Daddy's" shattering of Jessie's own reflection, her sense of self as a child and as a sexual person, reveals the unspoken face of middle-class domesticity and female submission. Like many women during the 1950s and 1960s who were not allowed control over their own lives, Jessie remains stuck in childhood. Like the women whom Friedan describes, Jessica continues to feel "inferior, childish, helpless, with no possibility of happiness unless she adjusted to being man's passive object" (Friedan, 119). These feelings persist not because she still is weak or ever was inferior, but because Jessie has been forced to displace her sense of self as an active subject able to make choices freely. She has become, literally, a very specific object: Daddy's Little Girl.

Daddy's little girl may or may not envy what she cannot have: Daddy's power. What is certain, though, is that Daddy does desire what the patriarchal economics of production/reproduction intimate always-already belongs to him: his daughter's body. The power of the middle-class mystique, with its subtle narratives against divorce and instability, forces the young Jessie to believe that to tell will, at best, destroy the family, at the worst, it might kill her mother (113). So Jessie submits to the silence, believing that to arouse sexual pleasure for a man—the "heat in Gerald's gaze when he looked at her"—requires that she play the game according to Daddy's rules of dominance and submission and silence (18). To satisfy the rules of the game, the horror at the center of the middle-class myth must be kept a "desperate secret" (183).

When *Gerald's Game* reveals Tom Mahout's face as the grinning death's head beneath Jessie's smiling masochism, the middle-class mystique imbuing the middle-class structure with its social and political power becomes dislocated. As Carol Siegel points out in *Male Masochism*, female "[m]asochism as a concept seems particularly suspect when we consider that it rewrites the traditional love story into a tale of man's failure to achieve sufficient masculine mastery of woman to make them both happy" (15). The mystique of the middle-class family is a concept that also becomes suspect when we consider how it rewrites the image of a happy family into a tale of man's mastery of the domestic realm. Like Jessie's husband Gerald, Tom's actions arise from a perception of masculine domestic power. That power then links to the script of female masochism until, in the end, any assertion of masculine authority becomes permissible. Tom's actions do not reflect on "Punkin" or her adult counterpart, Jessie. The adult Jessie Burlingame is a sexually violated domestic figure, revealed as both a fatal woman (she kills Gerald) and a fatally bound woman. When Jessie remembers the past, she shatters the false mirror of the feminine mystique and remaps the territory of the American family.

The (un)reality of her submissive and masochistic sexual history with Gerald and with her father binds Jesse as firmly as the Kreig M-17. Both bonds of love, like the material reality of Gerald's handcuffs, have been designed by men for men: M stands for male, F stands for female. To escape a bond just a little bit too big for her, Jessie cuts a "wound across her inner wrist . . . creating a blood-caked chasm" (242). The wound lubricates the wrist enough to free her and, if she doesn't hurry, to kill her. Jessie's final act of masochism, like the seemingly impossible man who visits the bedroom where she lies handcuffed, is constituted in the symbolic as well as the material realm. Her freedom from bondage lies somewhere between both these arenas, as King demonstrates when Jessie's escape mandates she die (without dying) to escape the manacles of the present and the bondage of the past.

The haunting figure of the skeletal "man in the corner," whose "waxy whiteness" (*Gerald's Game*, 123) connects so readily to Jessie's and our own conceptions of female hysteria and hallucination, provides an apt symbol for the way the feminine mystique still controls the social scripts behind the legal system. The mystique, to quote Punkin, "it's real" (205), just like the stocks that hold Jessie's inner child—and so the skeletal man. Silence often encompasses the discrepancies between women's experiences and the myths of the middle-class family, and silence is advocated regarding the reality or fictionality of Joubert. Jessie, who takes over writing her narrative after her escape, says her friend Brandon suggests that Jessie "might be wiser not to mention this idea of an intruder in the house" (304). As with the lies about feminine masochism and middle-class stability, "all the men investigating what had happened out at the lake—had made certain assumptions" concerning Jessie and her behavior, all based "only from the fact that [she's] a woman, and women can be expected to behave in certain predictable ways" (305). The strange man is identified as Joubert, an escaped lunatic. He is just as materially real as he has appeared to be symbolically imagined.

Like Joubert, the consequences of patriarchally-determined sexual and social patterns shape the symbolic that constructs the literal world. Jessie's father, and the legal system he supported, makes her willing to submit to any torture or degradation if submission provides a way out of subjugation:

And do you know what haunts me most of all? I thought it was my father, that was my *Daddy*, come back from the dead to do what he'd wanted to do before. . . . I would have let him put his cock—the cock [Joubert] stuck down the throats of dead men—into me, if only he would have promised me I didn't have to die the dog's death of muscle-cramps and convulsions that was waiting for me. If only he would have promised to SET ME FREE. (*Gerald's Game*, 321)

What is recognizable from a distance—and not at all obvious from Jessie's subjective perspective—is the illogic of this capitulation. Jessie was not free as long as she was willing to be submissive. Only when Jessie takes her life into her own hands, literally and symbolically, does she escape. She sets herself free. The real power behind these two novels about domestic violence and transgression arises from their ability to subvert narratives of female masochism and middle-class stability. These cultural narratives reassert the imbalances of power by granting them the status of natural phenomena. Both *Gerald's Game* and *Dolores Claiborne* horrify because, as King has demonstrated since his publication of *Carrie*, the family provides a key imaginative site for our most cherished passions as well as our darkest cultural fears. *Dolores Claiborne*, because it supports the middle-class mystique, seems to indicate that King has not quite understood the power of the social narrative he deconstructs in *Gerald's Game*. *Gerald's Game* makes explicit the idea that money and power permit the violation of sexual taboos within the imaginative site of the middle-class family. Familial instability is not located only among the working poor, and the middle-class white woman is not by nature a masochist. Like Joubert, the depredations of unequal power take material forms, grinning "like a dangerous lunatic" (*Gerald's Game*, 14) from the dark corners of our deepest held beliefs. In the end, this is the lesson *Gerald's Game* provides.

NOTES

1. Susan Faludi argues in *Backlash: The Undeclared War Against American Women* that the

false feminine vision that has been unfurled by contemporary culture in the last decade is a sort of vast velveteen curtain that hides women's reality while claiming to be its mirror. It has not made women cocoon or become New Traditionalists. But its thick drapery has both concealed the political assault on women's rights and become the impossible standard by which American women are asked to judge themselves. Its false front has encouraged each woman to doubt herself for not matching the image in the mass-produced mirror, instead of doubting the validity of the mirror itself and pressing to discover what its nonreflective surface hides. (57)

2. In actuality, as shown in "Statistics, 1988, 1989," by the National Clearinghouse for the Defense of Battered Women, Philadelphia, in one out of six heterosexual marriages in the United States, there is a pattern of abuse, and in 96 percent of these cases, the abuser is the husband. In addition, as reported in "Rape in America, A Report to the Nation," most rape cases occur during adolescence and childhood: 61 percent when the victim was under seventeen years old, 29 percent when the victim was less than eleven years old. For more information, see *Women's Action Coalition Stats: The Facts About Women.*

3. Faludi notes that

The backlash shaped much of Hollywood's portrayal of women in the '80s. In typical themes, women were set against women; women's anger at their social circumstances was depoliticized and displayed as personal depression instead; and women's lives were framed as morality tales in which the 'good mother' wins and the independent woman gets punished. And Hollywood restated and reinforced the backlash thesis: American women were unhappy because they were too free; their liberation had denied them marriage and motherhood. (112)

4. Benjamin observes that in Bataille, the

body stands for boundaries: discontinuity, individuality, and life. Consequently the violation of the body is a transgression of the boundary between life and death, even as it breaks through our discontinuity from the other. This break, this crossing of boundaries, is for Bataille the secret of *all* eroticism; and it assumes its starkest expression in erotic violation. It should be noted, however, that the break must never *really* dissolve the boundaries—else death results. (64)

5. Also see Faludi who argues that the

1970s women's movement made its most substantial progress on the twin fronts of employment and fertility—forging historic and record numbers of equal employment and anti-discrimination policies, forcing open the doors to lucrative and elite "male" professions, and ultimately helping to legalize abortion. And now, once again, as the backlash crests and breaks, it crashes hardest on these two shores. (55)

6. "The mistake, says the mystique, the root of women's troubles in the past is that women envied men, women tried to be like men, instead of accepting their own nature, which can find fulfillment only in sexual passivity, male domination, and nurturing maternal love" (Friedan, 43).

WORKS CITED

Benjamin, Jessica. *The Bonds of Love: Psychoanalysis, Feminism, and the Problem of Domination.* New York: Pantheon, 1988.

Cixous, Hélène. "The Laugh of the Medusa." *Signs: Journal of Women in Culture and Society* 1, 4 (1976), 875–93.

Deleuze, Gilles. *Masochism:* Coldness and Cruelty *by Gilles Deleuze and* Venus in Furs *by Leopold von Sacher-Masoch*. New York: Zone Books, 1991.

Faludi, Susan. *Backlash: The Undeclared War Against American Women*. New York: Crown, 1991.

Foucault, Michel. *The History of Sexuality: An Introduction*. Volume 1. New York: Random House, Vintage, 1978; 1990.

Freud, Sigmund. "Femininity." *The Women and Language Debate*. Edited by Camille Roman, Suzanne Juhasz, and Christanne Miller. Rutgers: Rutgers University Press, 1994.

Friedan, Betty. *The Feminine Mystique*. New York: Norton, 1963.

King, Stephen. *Dolores Claiborne*. New York: Viking, 1993.

——. *Gerald's Game*. New York: Viking Penguin, 1992.

Lerner, Gerda. *The Creation of Patriarchy*. New York: Oxford University Press, 1986.

Magistrale, Tony. *Landscape of Fear: Stephen King's American Gothic*. Ohio: Bowling Green State University Popular Press, 1988.

——. *Stephen King: The Second Decade*. Twayne's United States Authors Series 599. Edited by Warren French. New York: Twayne, 1992.

"Rape in America, A Report to the Nation." National Victim Center and Crime Victims Research and Treatment Center, 1992.

Siegel, Carol. *Male Masochism: Modern Revisions of the Story of Love*. Bloomington: Indiana University Press, 1995.

Women's Action Coalition Stats: The Facts About Women. New York: The New Press, 1993.

Women and Genre

5

Repulsive Attractions:
"The Raft," the *Vagina Dentata*,
and the Slasher Formula

Leonard Cassuto

"Twice-told tales" occupy a time-honored place in American literature, but Stephen King's "The Raft" deserves attention as a twice-written one. King himself was so haunted by his own creation that he rewrote the story from memory in 1981, thirteen years after first devising it. (He had published it in an obscure skin magazine in 1968 as "The Float," but he never located a copy and later discovered that he had lost the original typescript.) From his brief account of the story's composition, it's clear that King rewrote it because he wanted to read it himself, presumably because—to use his own phrase—it pushed his "horror-button" as hard as it does those of his readers (*Danse Macabre*, 273).[1]

I want to consider the lingering power of "The Raft" in terms of its genre conventions and central symbol. The story is a simple one: Four reckless college students (two men and two women) decide to defy the onset of autumn by driving out to an isolated lake forty miles from campus and swimming out to the raft anchored there. They are followed in the water by a mysterious, floating black spot that lurks alongside the raft. The spot tracks their movements, lures them with flashing colors, and takes advantage of their carelessness to pull them into the water one by one and devour them with gory rapacity. The story ends with the last character, Randy, standing cold and alone on the raft, unable to sit or lie down (if he does, the spot will slide underneath the raft and grab him through the cracks between the boards). Exhausted and despairing, Randy is about to give up and allow himself to be drawn into the water to be absorbed. The black spot is never explained.

The plot and setting of "The Raft" closely follow those of the slasher film, an unsubtle genre of horror, very popular in recent years, that typically features a killer who punishes adolescent sexuality with hideous, unconscious-driven aggression (drills, knives, axes, chain saws). But unlike the invariably phallic killers of *Halloween*, *Friday the 13th* and their ilk, the punishing monster in this case has a distinctly female quality, and the final character it stalks is a young man rather than the woman who survives in countless movies. The black spot that mesmerizes Randy—and that will shortly kill him as it has killed everyone else in the story—is a potent, archetypal female symbol. It is the *vagina dentata*: the womb that devours. In the pages that follow, I consider "The Raft" as a slasher narrative with an unusual hero (a male), an unusual monster (a "female"), and an unusual outcome (everybody dies). In the end, I will argue that the story stands as Stephen King's obliquely self-conscious, unusually deep and honest commentary on the attraction of formula-driven horror.

"The Raft" and the *Vagina Dentata*

When asked in a 1982 interview about his greatest sexual fear, Stephen King replied, "The vagina dentata, the vagina with teeth. The story where you were making love to a woman and it just slammed shut and cut your penis off. That'd do it" (*Bare Bones*, 189). King's fear has a lot of precedent, for the toothed vagina is an image that is found in numerous myths across cultures. It appears in various accounts as a "barred and dangerous entrance" that nonetheless holds great allure for the men who seek to enter it. Defanging the toothed vagina has generally been depicted in myth as an heroic act of male courage, a brave risk taken to bring safe reproduction to society. Akin to the *vagina dentata* is the so-called "bottomless lake," the womb that swallows men and makes them disappear. This image too is a staple of myth and folklore; its connection to castration anxiety is clear if only from the fact that its victims are always male.[2]

The black spot in "The Raft" is a voracious *vagina dentata* that engulfs its victims and rips them apart. The death of Randy's roommate Deke, for example, is rife with sexual connotation. Literally pulled "into the crack" between the boards of the raft, his body becomes "hard as Carrara marble," a "big tree," that is "purple" and "bulging" as it "disappear[s]" (259–60). Deke's "swelled" face is that of "a man being clutched in a bear hug of monstrous and unknowable force" (260, 261). He screams with pain at first, but his final utterances are "thick, syrupy grunts" (260) that might, in another setting, signify orgasm. They are followed by an ejaculation of sorts: "a great jet of blood, so thick it was almost solid" that forces itself from his mouth (260). Deke dies after that, and his body "collapse[s] forward," as the spot makes "sucking sounds" from under the raft (261). Finally, as his dead torso is slowly forced through the crack, there comes "a sound like strong teeth crunching up a mouthful of candy jawbreakers" (262).

Freudian psychoanalysis is strangely silent about the *vagina dentata* and the fear of the castrating woman generally. Among the work of later psychoanalysts, Karen Horney's important 1932 essay, "The Dread of Woman," has provided a useful starting point for modern theorists to analyze the image. Horney argues that masculine desire of woman is intertwined with a deep fear of her, a fear that the man seeks to expunge by objectifying it. Horney suggests that even the male "glorification of women has its source not only in his cravings for love, but also in his desire to conceal his dread" (136). This dread, says Horney, does not lie solely in the fact that woman has been castrated (which is the basis for Freud's explanation). Instead, "there must be a further dread, the object of which is the woman or the female genital" (137).

Horney sees a key link between sexual desire and a desire to return to the womb: "Does the man feel, side by side with his desire to conquer, a secret longing for extinction in the act of reunion with the woman (mother)?" (139). In diagram form, her argument would look something like this:

In Horney's developmental equation, early castration anxiety (exemplified by the *vagina dentata*) can lead in adulthood to an uncanny fear of the mystery of motherhood.[3] This latter sense of mystery encompasses a desire to return to the womb (here, the bottomless lake), a re-union that necessarily implies a loss of individuation, or death. Horney suggests that this desire may provide the basis for Freud's death-instinct, the subject's desire for the ultimate unity to be found in self-extinction.

Horney's two central postulates, that the male dread of woman can spring from early fear of castration and then later from fear of motherhood, form the conceptual basis for Barbara Creed's interesting recent work, *The Monstrous-Feminine*. Building on Horney's work and applying it specifically to horror cinema, Creed describes the *vagina dentata* as the "mouth of hell" (106), an image of woman as castrator that embodies unconscious male fears and fantasies about the female genitals. She argues that Freud represses the possibility of the castrating female as a fearful object because of his desire to promote the phallocentric view of woman as frightening because she is castrated. To Creed, "woman also terrifies because man endows her with imaginary powers of castration" (87). She sees the castrating woman as playing a powerfully ambivalent role in the Oedipal equation, expressing the conflicting unconscious feelings that accompany the child's breaking away from the mother. Following Horney, Creed sees this conflict reflected in the simultaneous fear of castration by the mother and the desire for sexual union with her.[4] This combination of unconscious fear and desire is expressed in the consumption of horror, an urge that reflects a "morbid desire to see *as much as possible* of the unimaginable" (29). The nature of horror (that is, its traffic in death and dismemberment) "allow[s] for an explicit representation of man's castration anxieties" (155).

The *vagina dentata* powerfully embodies these anxieties, and "The Raft" gives affecting expression to them in a generic setting. The black spot is variously described as "humped up" and "stuffing the cracks" (263, 265). Its abundantly bloody killings support the mythical and psychological arguments for the uncanniness of menstrual blood. Yet for all of its gruesome appetites, the spot also allures; its colors reduce Rachel to "trembling wonder" before she succumbs to them, and they make Randy "loopy" (258).

On its most basic level, "The Raft" is an Oedipal nightmare of the castrating mother. The story enacts an elemental struggle between child and parent, with the spot representing the mother who reasserts parental authority over her children who have strayed from the correct path. On campus (where the story opens), the young people pursue their wanton and slovenly ways away from parental influence by drinking, having sex, and acting in otherwise undisciplined fashion. (The narrator comments on the poor housekeeping by the men, Randy and Deke, who let food fester in their refrigerator [247]; the women, Rachel and LaVerne, come over on a Tuesday afternoon to lie around and drink beer.) But when they leave their own surroundings and go to the "Terrible Place," the ancient order (the Parental Law) takes control and punishes all misbehavior.[5]

"The Raft" makes undisciplined sexuality into a capital crime. This notion is not new; in particular, there is important precedent in fairy tales for imagining it as one. "Little Red Riding Hood," for example, has been read by Bruno Bettelheim as a parable whose message is caution: Good children shouldn't leave the path before they're able to take care of themselves in the dark, sexual woods.[6] If they do, they'll get eaten. To Bettelheim, the tale enacts a "'deathly' fascination with sex" (176); he gives particular emphasis to the redness of the girl's hood and the hair of the wolf. (The cover illustration by Gustave Dore that adorns Bettelheim's *The Uses of Enchantment* is of a young girl—Little Red—in bed with a mean-looking wolf in a bonnet. The girl is apparently naked under the covers, wearing an equivocal expression.) Bettelheim's broad thesis is that fairy tales offer children a chance to work through their unconscious fears and desires in an imaginative setting that always leaves them "happily ever after" at the end. In the case of "Little Red Riding Hood," these unconscious thoughts center on the alluring menace of sexual awakening. Like virtually all fairy tales, "Little Red Riding Hood" can easily be framed as a horror story, and in fact has recently been filmed as one.[7] Moreover, Creed cites "Little Red Riding Hood" as a story that invokes the *vagina dentata*.[8] And finally, "The Raft" bears a strong structural resemblance to "Little Red Riding Hood": The characters go literally off the path (eight miles down a back road) in order to indulge their sexual urges, and as a result, they get swallowed up.

Bettelheim says that "Premature sexuality is a regressive experience" that causes the immature subject to fall back on Oedipal coping mechanisms (173). The ultimate Oedipal regression is a return to mother, a reunion fraught with mingled fear and desire. King puts this uneasy mixture of unconscious feelings on full display out on the raft. When Randy stands alone facing the black spot after all of his friends have died, he hears the spot whispering mother-love to him in a voice he hears in his mind, amidst his own wandering memories of cars and baseball games. It is the voice of (re)incorporation: "*I love do you love*" (269). Randy responds to the voice as a child, weeping and begging, "Go away, please, go anywhere, but leave me alone. I don't love you" (269).

But predictably, Randy's fear and aversion are interlaced with curiosity and desire. The spot hypnotizes with blending colors and "rich, inward-turning spirals" on its surface (253) that lure Rachel to her death, and which Randy resists only by literally punching himself in the face (258). Even after watching his friends die, when Randy looks at the spot squeezing up between the cracks between the boards of the raft, reaching for him, he "wonder[s] what the stuff would feel like when it flowed over his feet, when it hooked into him" (263). And when, at the story's end, Randy is near to giving in to the lures and long siege by the black spot, he hears the voice in his head welcoming him into an ultimate, fearful union: "*you* do *you* do *love me*" (269). A few moments later, Randy asks, "Sing with me," and he sings a child's song about the end of school. Then he allows himself to be drawn to the spot, letting his eyes follow the spirals that invite him into its depths: The fear of castration and extinction become one with the desire for sexual union.

Randy sees the world with the eyes of a child living in a safe, protected world, an updated version of 1950s family sitcom existence. Such a world is bounded and guarded by nurturing parents. Throughout "The Raft," King has Randy inwardly describe what he sees in terms of benign cultural icons and kiddie commercialism, a diverse collection of images that spans a couple of decades, including Sandy Duncan (as Peter Pan), Arthur Godfrey, PacMan, Rialto movie shows, Richard Nixon's "V for victory sign," the Yankees, the Beach Boys, and the Ramones. These emblems are part of Randy's emotional lexicon of assuring images of family life. Accordingly, he wishes for family safety when he gets in trouble. When he first suspects that the spot may be dangerous, for example, his immediate thought is that there is no one to look out for himself and his friends: "*No one knows we're here. No one at all.*" No one to take care of them, that is—no one to be a parent to them. When he looks in vain for lights in the windows of the vacated summer cottages surrounding the lake, he imagines a family on vacation: "[S]*omebody's got to be staying the week in his place, fall foliage, shouldn't miss it, bring your Nikon, folks back home are going to love the slides*" (262). What is happening to Randy needs to be understood in terms of his all-American family view. The happenings on the raft expose the deep fears that hold up this family idyll in his mind.

Seen thus, the black spot is not simply a monster that somehow appears in the summer setting when fall comes—it is an ancient presence that has been lurking behind Randy's *Leave It to Beaver* worldview all the time, a menace for all seasons that has necessitated the construction of that ideal family order to hide its own uncanny presence in his mind. Though the origins of the spots remain a mystery, we might consider it as a projection of Randy's own unconscious fear and desire—an expression of the complicated urges that led him to suggest the fatal swim in the first place. These mixed feelings include his wish to break away from parental authority even as he desires to live under its continuing protection (a conflict that college life helps to keep in suspension). Randy longs to impress the women and win their attraction away from Deke, his football hero roommate; he fights his mingled desire for and "jealousy" of Deke's virile vitality (which he admires even as Deke dies [261]); he desires LaVerne but resents her attraction to Deke enough to want to hit her (251); later, he wants to protect LaVerne after Rachel and Deke die, even as he wants to be protected himself. The lure of the spot is, among other things, the promise to resolve these conflicts by returning everything to primal, undifferentiated oneness. At the bottom of the desire for mother is a desire for reincorporation.

If horror is essentially about the return of repressed or surpassed childhood fears—as Freud says in "The Uncanny" and King in *Danse Macabre*—then "The Raft" argues that one can literally never escape these fears. All four characters in "The Raft" are clearly familiar with Cascade Lake, where the story takes place; Rachel and Randy have clear memories of childhood summer days spent there.[9] Rachel voices a common childhood fear attached to such places, recalling that the first time she swam out to the raft as a child, she was afraid to swim back (247). Rachel's fear returns to Randy, Rachel, LaVerne, and Deke as adults in this childhood setting. It comes back in familiar, but crucially changed and newly mysterious, form. This is Freud's uncanny: the return of repressed early fear, the familiar become unfamiliar.

The outcome of the opposition between child and castrating mother in "The Raft" is one that broadly denies the possibility of passage from childhood to adulthood. "The Raft" suggests that it's impossible to escape one's youth and move on, that the attempt to break the parent-child bond will end in death.[10] The characters in King's story move away from home and find themselves returning in search of it anyway—and the return leads to the end of them. They can never escape their childhood origin. It literally sucks them back in—but it has the opportunity to do so only because they have gone to meet it at the isolated place (isolated in geography, and also in memory) where it lies. The raft is "a little bit of summer" (247) that the four young adults try to claim in October, after summer is gone. They can't go back to the childhood past, but neither can they get away from it in their present. "The Raft" is in this sense a story about impotence writ large, symbolized by the inability to escape from the most powerful ruler of the child's early life: the mother. But at the same time, it's also about the wish not to get away at all.[11]

"The Raft" as Slasher

"The Raft" resembles *Halloween* and other movies like it in that the story is propelled by a killer's terrible retribution for illicit teenage sexuality.[12] The slasher setting is always empty of other people and usually isolated, but it is also typically American, and recognizably middle class, as Vera Dika points out in her 1990 study of the genre (58–59). The point is that the killer and the victims meet on ground familiar to both. Dika presents a lengthy descriptive plot analysis of the slasher film that begins with a past event that triggers present retribution: "[T]he killer's destructive force is reactivated. . . . [t]he young community takes no heed. . . . [t]he killer stalks [and] kills members of the young community. . . . the heroine does battle with the killer . . . [she] kills or subdues the killer" and survives (though she is "not free") (59–60, 136). This summary is perhaps too elaborately patterned, with the definition of "past event" particularly needing to be questioned.

"The Raft" offers no direct clue to any notable past happening that would awaken the monster, but as I suggested in my earlier discussion of Randy's desires, the past need not include a public drama in order to leave the unconscious residue that makes the present danger possible—in horror, all unconscious desires are potentially dangerous. In practice, slashers are categorized according to Creed's more basic paradigm, the presence of a group of teenagers looking for someplace to have sex, and paying the highest price for their immature, headstrong behavior (124). Carol J. Clover describes the slasher's victims as "sexual transgressors [who] are scheduled for early destruction" (33). In the standard scenario, the monster, gendered male and equipped with a phallic weapon, does them in, one by one. They are punished until there's only one left, leading to a staple of the genre: the face-off between the last survivor (almost always a woman who, unlike her friends, is not sexually active) and the killer.

"The Raft" contains clear elements of the formula-driven slasher film. The supporting characters in the story fit the standard types seen in most genre entries. Deke is the typical he-man recognizable to all who are familiar with these stories. He's a football player with "sniper's eyes" (245), and he drives a Camaro (which one of my female friends once called a "penis car"). As his name suggests, Deke is defiantly male and unabashedly sexual: He can take his pants off in a fluid motion that Randy admires, and even when swimming, "the muscles in his back and buttocks worked gorgeously" (246). Moreover, Deke flashes the assaultive, possessive sexual gaze that Laura Mulvey has identified as a pervasive and pernicious form of cinematic expression: "He was talking to Randy but he was looking at LaVerne. LaVerne's panties were almost as transparent as her bra, the delta of her sex sculpted neatly in silk, each buttock a taut crescent" (250). Deke's eye is overcome by a stronger one, for the spot possesses its own controlling gaze. He literally disappears into the "'insatiable organ hole' of the feminine."[13] Before he suffers this fittingly sexual death, Deke seeks, receives, and revels in the sexual attention of both women in the story. He laughs off Randy's fear in a way designed to impress them (at the expense of the more cautious Randy). According to slasher convention, Deke is doomed. Characters like him—Rachel calls him "Macho City" (249)—are among the earliest victims of sexually motivated killers in slasher stories. Following formula, Deke is the second to go.

The two women in the story are also stock victims. Rachel, Deke's girlfriend and the first to die, is a "sloe-eyed" sufferer who Randy compares to petite, vulnerable Sandy Duncan (254). LaVerne, "a big girl" (261), is less sympathetic. She comes on to Deke in front of Rachel; her triumph over her rival sounds like "the arid cackle of a witch" (253). When the black spot first shows what it can do by messily consuming Rachel, LaVerne dissolves into "mewling," self-absorbed hysteria, and Deke fulfills Randy's unvoiced wish to hit her. By assigning her such marked lack of appeal, even *in extremis*, King sets LaVerne up to die in a fairly standard way. She is the third to go.

The basic slasher plot is immediately recognizable in "The Raft": Four promiscuous, pleasure-driven college students go off by themselves and three of them get theirs, leaving a confrontation between the last one and the killer. But the positions of the two main characters (the killer and the survivor) are off-center. Just as the killer is gendered female rather than male, the survivor is male rather than female. And in an unusual ending, the survivor is clearly doomed. In the most comprehensive and nuanced analysis of gender and modern horror to date, Clover connects gender in the slasher film with the pain and suffering that is ritually imposed by the genre as part of a "masochistic aesthetic" that "dominates horror cinema" (222). She notes that slasher movies kill boys quickly and girls much more slowly and painfully (35); she argues, moreover, that this happens because males in the audience will be more comfortable identifying with suffering if they do so through a female character (the protagonist, whom she terms "the Final Girl").[14] Slasher films, she says, promote identification with suffering by linking it to women, who are at greater social liberty than men to express fear and pain. But the death of Deke in "The Raft" is a clear violation of formula: Pulled down through a crack between the boards of the raft and eaten alive from his feet up, he suffers at gruesome length. Furthermore, his death, by far the longest of the three in the story, gives way to the protracted suffering of another male, Randy.

Randy's status as final survivor merits special consideration of his suffering. The Final Girl, says Clover, is an androgynous figure whose lack of sexual activity contributes to her boyishness (40). Her femaleness is further qualified by the bravery (behavior gendered male, argues Clover) that she calls upon to defeat the killer at the end. This reversal finally makes the Final Girl into "a congenial double for the adolescent male" (51), a "male surrogate in things oedipal" (53), and in sum, a "characterological androgyne" (63).[15]

King makes Randy different from the array of slasher survivors. His maleness is not a major issue in this context; boys as well as girls can be androgynous, and the slasher genre has proved flexible enough to accommodate them in the exceptional cases in which they appear in the survivor's role.[16] At first, Randy seems to fit right into Clover's unisex mold. "A shy boy" (252), he appears as a stereotypical college nerd: When we see him for the first time he is "resetting his glasses on his nose" (244). To Deke, he's a "brain-ball" who takes "all the fucking science courses" (255). Randy is socially weaker than Deke; he accepts subordinate status as "Pancho" to Deke's "Cisco Kid." He is also more uncertain than Deke about his masculinity (significantly, his name is ungendered), and he is sexually insecure—and not without reason. He sees that his attraction to LaVerne is endangered from the start: "He liked her, but Deke was stronger" (246).

Essentially unsexed and feminized to the point that he possesses uncertain gender status, Randy fits the androgynous type that Clover would expect for a Final Boy (63). It is therefore highly significant that Randy understands pain. Looking at Rachel after Deke spurns her and accepts LaVerne's attentions, "Randy saw dull hurt on her face. . . . [H]e knew that expression . . . how that expression felt inside" (251). This sensitivity sets up Randy to suffer, basically because he knows how to do it. He knows pain because he's not so rigidly male as Deke, and because he's lost what he calls "his fear cherry" (257). This link between fear and sex is worth dwelling on in conjunction with the *vagina dentata*. Deke is sexually experienced, but in matters of fear, he's still a virgin until the spot changes that. Randy has less sexual experience, but he knows pain when he sees it—and significantly, he fears and avoids the spot even before it kills anyone.

Although Randy shows an affinity for the culturally feminized role of sufferer, he violates the qualifications for Clover's Final Androgyne in two important ways. First, going to the raft is his idea, not Deke's. Though "he never expected Deke to take it seriously" (245) and he feels guilty and regretful about putting the women on the spot as a result of it, the bold initiative is his own and the dangerous situation of his own making.

Second and most crucially, Randy has sex while he is on the raft. When he and LaVerne are the last two remaining, fear and desire combine to draw them together in a coital embrace that ends in her death when the spot seizes her hair trailing in the water. The sex "had never been like this" for Randy, and it touches off a succession of images in his mind just before the spot intervenes: "firm breasts fragrant with Coppertone oil, and if the bottom of the bikini was small enough you might see some (*hair her hair HER HAIR IS IN THE OH GOD IN THE WATER HER HAIR*)" (266, 267). The sequence of thoughts connects pubic hair to the suddenly vulnerable hair on LaVerne's head; following the associations, we see that LaVerne is ensnared by her own sexuality. The spot prevents sexual climax ("He pulled back suddenly" [267]), substituting the big death (loss of life) for the little one (orgasm). Randy's name takes on added significance in light of this grisly sexual interlude: It's a pun. And as a result of his action, he definitively masculinizes himself—at the cost of the death of a woman.

In Clover's slasher typology, the standard narrative feminizes the Final Girl through her suffering, and then masculinizes her by her courageous heroism (59). "The Raft" moves through these gender changes in sexually explicit fashion but with an important added regression at the end. Randy starts out sexually uncertain (the unsexed Brain in the shadow of the virile Jock [248]) and then proves his masculinity not by bravery, but more directly by copulation (specifically, by comforting and then seducing the Jock's would-be girlfriend after the Jock dies). But then Randy regresses to childhood, ending in a position of lonely, hopeless, terrified suffering at the hands of the castrating mother. The Final Girl is always chaste in slasher films, but Randy has sex at a time when the standard plot calls for him to start saving himself. The Final Girl "looks death in the face" and finds the strength to survive and resist (Clover, 35), but "The Raft" ends with Randy's capitulation to the seductive gaze of the black spot. In effect, Randy finds his masculinity rather than his wits in time of stress, and his emergent sexuality does him in.

The nature of the black spot also runs counter to generic expectations. Whereas the killer is almost always gendered male in slasher films, Clover notes that like the Final Girl, he too is unsexed, substituting phallic weapons for actual sexual function and thereby strongly qualifying his masculinity. (Rape doesn't happen in slasher films—dismemberment takes its place.) Sexually ambiguous, the monster makes up a matched pair with the Final Girl, supporting Clover's general contention that the slasher film "at every level presents us with hermaphroditic constructions" (55). But "The Raft" has a female-type monster that is all-powerful, ultimately victorious, distinctly nonphallic. Unlike the usual slasher, whose face is covered by a mask, the spot is naked and undisguised, open in its castrating depths.

It seems clear that Stephen King wants us to read "The Raft" as a slasher narrative. The story feels like a slasher—that is, the plot and setting evoke the kinds of narrative expectations that a slasher does. But it's just as clear that King flouts the conventions of the formula. Though a sexual killer, the black spot is a highly atypical slasher monster, and the character of Randy is a kind of red herring: The author appears to draw him along the familiar unsexed lines of the Final Androgyne, but then he sharply and unexpectedly shifts Randy's behavior towards the male side of the sexual spectrum. In effect, King invites us to read "The Raft" in a certain way, and then deliberately counters our expectations. Why?

"The Raft" and the Attraction of Formula-Driven Horror

King's pointed violation of certain slasher conventions does not simply unmask the killer—his manipulation of the formula effectively pulls the cover off the workings of the entire slasher genre. If (as Clover argues) the slasher film refracts the male experience of fear, vulnerability, and pain through the socially reassuring lens of femininity and femaleness, then "The Raft" removes the looking glass and forces the reader to face the light directly. That is, "'The Raft" offers no illusion of comfortable distance afforded by the conventional image of a screaming, crying woman who just manages to save herself; instead, King presents us with an immediate, culturally disturbing sight: a crying man (one who nevertheless leaves no doubt about his maleness) who cries and suffers right up to the moment of his death. By placing a female monster and a fully masculinized final character in the two key roles in his slasher story, King parts the curtain to reveal the writer at the controls, openly ordering the steps that make up the slasher ritual—and reordering the roles to remove the gender diversions. Beneath the "identificatory buffer" of the female protagonist, Clover says that the slasher is a growing-up story of "sex and parents," with the killer as "a materialized projection of the viewer's own incestuous fears and desires" (51, 49). This omnibus interpretation fits "The Raft" compellingly closely, further legitimating the story's position in the slasher category. In Clover's dissection of the slasher's gender-identity strategies, she argues that the genre elides sex difference so that "[t]he same female body does for both" male and female (59), allowing males to identify with suffering in an act of voyeuristic masochism that takes place during the consumption of horror. But in "The Raft," King decisively rearranges this anatomy. Males and females are fully distinct, and the role of sufferer is occupied by a fully masculinized character. There is no buffer, no relief, no getting away from confronting the masochistic attraction of the story. The reader identifies with Randy in order to suffer through a man.

Just as King moves Randy away from androgyny by definitively asserting his masculinity, so does he position the monster (also an uncertainly sexed character in the standard slasher) clearly within the category of the feminine. Again, King offers no prism to partially deflect unpleasant psychic realities. The monster is no masked man who substitutes killing for sex.[17] Instead, the black spot in "The Raft" is unalterably, potently female, with no masks to disguise its nature. It is a force that combines killing with sex and makes them equally dangerous. When the spot clutches Deke, the narrator calls it an act of "unbelievable reversal" (261). King presents us with this "reversed" monster, and then he stages a violent Oedipal drama in the most elemental form: Four young adults face the primal abyss from whence they came.

By using an unequivocally male character to dramatize male suffering at the hands of a female terror, King makes a minor departure from formula into a deliberately uncomfortable, highly charged exposé of the fears whose exploitation drives the slasher genre, and the narrowly gender-based expectations that frame the characters in horror narratives generally. Clover says that the sexually ambiguous quality of the hero and killer in the standard slasher represents an attempt to shield the male viewer from the nature of the masochistic identification that he undergoes. King exposes the cultural politics of this need for weakness by placing these characters at gendered poles and thereby calling attention to the uncomfortable desire in between. Randy's behavior thus becomes a trenchant commentary on the cultural expectations of male heroism. Clover argues with some justification that modern horror is very direct about its gender politics (calling attention to its own "feint" [229]), but King is even more direct in "The Raft," exposing male masochism where it lies—at the center of things—and in the process showing the feelings of fear and weakness that widespread cultural conventions of male heroism continue to hide.

It may be that "The Raft" must be seen first as a boy's nightmare, if only because of the way that King strips away the gender trickery to reveal the cold sexual truth: that it all comes down to a terrified, (almost) naked boy and his menacing mother. But even if this is so, one might ask why a story of literalized castration anxiety should attract women. More generally, if the horror genre is driven by male fears, then why would women be drawn to it at all?

I want to approach this set of questions elliptically, by first looking into a specific question of plot that bothered me when I read "The Raft": Why doesn't Randy get away from the black spot when he can? He has two clear opportunities: the deaths of Deke and LaVerne, during which the black spot is busy enough with its victim to allow for a quick swim to the shore. King even has Randy notice this odd blind spot in himself—he doesn't realize until "much later" that he could have escaped while Deke died (260). In between the two deaths, Randy wonders whether he should put down the unconscious LaVerne and swim for it. What stops him is "an awful guilt" (261).

George Romero, screenwriting for director Michael Gornick, provides an answer to my question in the short film they made of "The Raft."[18] In the movie, Randy actually does escape while the spot consumes LaVerne. Watching the film, I realized that Randy doesn't escape in King's story because if he does, then he can't suffer the way he's meant to, the way that the ritual of slasher consumption demands.

Romero, himself a noted director of horror films (including *Night of the Living Dead*), understands that "The Raft" corresponds to the slasher formula, and he makes subtle changes in plot and character that allow it to conform more obviously to the genre conventions in its screen version. He enhances the transgression imagery, for example: The young people smoke marijuana on the way to the lake, and the film's last image is a shot of a "No Swimming" sign that makes little sense in light of the raft's presence on the lake, but which is entirely consistent with the crime-and-punishment logic of the slasher film. The most important changes, though, are in the character of Randy. In particular, Randy's guilt and hesitation are gone, leaving only his desperate longing to be a stud. He acts as much like one as he can, and looks more like one too: He doesn't wear glasses in the movie. Even so, he's less successful in his romantic endeavors than in King's original story; when he and LaVerne are alone on the raft, he tries to seduce her as she sleeps. She partially rouses herself to refuse him, but the distraction leads to the black spot grabbing her hair and pulling her into its depths. In the movie then, LaVerne's death is entirely Randy's fault: He tries to have sex with her when he should be watching the spot according to their agreement to take turns. His self-centered sexual greed makes him a standard issue slasher male, not a Final Androgyne type.

In Romero's version, Randy finds his resourcefulness when LaVerne dies and tries to escape while the spot quickly devours her and then sets off after him. He races the spot to shore, and narrowly wins the race. He then taunts the spot from the edge of the shore ("I beat you!") instead of moving out of range, and is abruptly engulfed, done in by his own attempt to ascend to the vacant alpha male slot instead of feminizing himself (as sufferer instead of warrior) and getting away. As this climactic episode shows especially clearly, the film version of "The Raft" makes Randy more stereotypically male than the story does. Most important, the changes in his character keep him from being coded feminine at any time. In contrast to his portrayal in the story, his groping for sex and subsequent escape are consistent with a male slasher victim, not a survivor. Not surprisingly, the film lacks the segment in which Randy stands tortured and terrified, alone with the spot. In effect, the movie version of Randy lacks the understanding of pain or the capacity to suffer, so the movie ends without delivering much emotional impact, with only a surprise (Randy's quick and sudden death at the moment when we believe that he has delivered himself) that doesn't adequately substitute for what has been excised from the story.

Paradoxically, even though the "Raft" movie accentuates the standard slasher plot inherent within the story by adding the escape segment (a more predictable form of confrontation between the killer and the survivor than King's lonely conclusion to the story), the film's mechanical adherence to conventional sex roles (making sure that boys don't suffer the way that girls are supposed to) keeps the movie from feeling like a slasher. The loss in feeling is a loss of suffering: The shift in Randy's character short-circuits the masochistic component of the viewing mechanism that Clover identifies as so central to the horror genre—Randy doesn't suffer, and there's no Final Girl to do the honors in his place. The movie thus changes certain parts of the story to make it superficially more slasherlike, but in making these changes, Romero eliminates Randy's pain, precluding the particular form of viewer identification that needs to take place with the slasher protagonist.

So the problem is not that Randy escapes—it's that by having him do so, Romero's rewrite of King's story prevents the character from enduring the pain and fear that a slasher narrative conditions its audience to expect. Consequently, the film can't deliver its emotional payoff, despite its careful adherence to genre conventions. The difference between story and movie can thus be summed up in broad terms: The movie is conservative (arguably too conservative), whereas King's story is experimental (within a conservative genre). Whatever the film's entertainment value, it lacks the story's depth because it takes away the story's pain. Randy's role in the narrative can be filled by a boy or a girl, but whoever occupies it is required to suffer, irrespective of gender. King's story, especially when compared to the film, shows that the needs of the slasher ritual transcend the gender conventions that have grown around them.

All of which brings us back to the question of female attraction to slasher narratives. That gender is an issue in the reception of horror is scarcely disputed by those who have considered the subject, but there is no consensus about its role or effect. In her influential 1975 essay, "Visual Pleasure and Narrative Cinema," Laura Mulvey says that the cinematic gaze is gendered male, with woman as its object, and women can participate in the viewing only by adopting the male perspective (which is either sadistic or fetishistic). Although Mulvey's model may account for some female attraction to horror, the image of the castrating woman complicates her thesis. Writing partially in response to Mulvey's view, Creed argues that "The slasher film actively seeks to arouse castration anxiety in relation to the issue of whether or not woman is castrated" by presenting her as both castrated and castrator (127).[19] It is worth noting that the castrating black spot in "The Raft" has an appetite for males and females alike. Randy says twice that "It went for the girls" (250), and its first victim is in fact female.

The existence of female horror fans is beyond dispute, so horror—even slashers—must have something to offer them. Creed persuasively defines horror on a fundamental level as the artistically expressed desire for the liminal and disruptive (Kristeva's "abject"), a desire constructed according to primal paradigms that are neither restricted to nor defined by the male experience. These include birth, seduction, and castration—with only the last of these routing female identification through male-defined channels (153–54). In essence, the mystery of the "archaic mother" is not an exclusively male preserve, and the return to the womb not necessarily a purely male desire or an exclusively male fear. Indeed, Creed disputes the idea that the unconscious is socialized male or female, theorizing that horror addresses the unconscious fears and desires of "both the human subject . . . and the gendered subject" (156). Slashers clearly implicate universal fears (pain, death) with gendered ones (female fear of violation or—especially in the case of "The Raft"—male castration anxiety).

Lots of horror stories are about regressive sexuality (one need only look to the enduring vampire and werewolf film cycles for confirmation), and it follows that a fundamental component of the experience of horror is the desire to experience such fantasies, again and again. The slasher film cycle (which varies strikingly little from film to film) is one of the more obvious manifestations of this desire to repeat. Accordingly, Clover identifies the consumption of horror as a cultural repetition-compulsion, a ritual play with ancient fears that King alludes to in "The Raft" when he has Randy describe the black spot as being like something out of the "Halloween Shock-Show down at the Rialto" (255). In their reenactment of their early experience and confrontation with their early fear, the characters in "The Raft" are no different from the horror consumers who encounter them in King's pages: Like the readers and moviegoers with whom Randy groups himself and his friends, the characters use a ritual—swimming out to the raft to "say good-bye to summer" (248)—to re-experience their old fears and desires. For the characters, for King's readers, and doubtless for the writer himself as well, these feelings are a defining part of the self that needs regular indulgence.

Randy's memory of his trips to the horror movies is part of a series of self-references and formula twists that set "The Raft" apart from the other slashers with which it claims kinship. Though Romero may have overlooked the viewing dynamic of the slasher film when he scripted "The Raft," he, like Stephen King, has no illusions about what the black spot represents. As the film ends with the spot moving back to the center of the lake (after overwhelming Randy at the water's edge), the camera pulls back, taking in Deke's abandoned Camaro parked further up the shore. The doors are open and the car radio is playing a raucous heavy metal song with these lyrics, which we hear as the film ends:

> Tryin'
> To get her out of my mind
> All my friends said,
> "You better watch that girl
> She's a taker, a knife edge woman
> She's a dream breaker"

This "knife edge woman" is an unexpected, archetypally female monster who sets her sights on a likewise unexpected victim: a young man. King uses the spot's inevitable victory to show us why we choose to suffer through Randy's ordeal, and what we are buying into when we do so. "The Raft" thus stands as a slasher that deconstructs the slasher formula.

NOTES

1. Since becoming famous, King has frequently written brief compositional histories to accompany his shorter works, generally publishing them as headnotes or appendices. For his account of his unusual loss and recovery of "The Raft," see *Skeleton Crew* (509–10).

2. For a useful historical and ethnographic overview of the *vagina dentata* and related imagery, see Erich Neumann's Jungian study *The Great Mother: An Analysis of the Archetype* and especially Wolfgang Lederer's *The Fear of Women* (quotation at 47; "bottomless lake" is also Lederer's phrase). For a survey of *vagina dentata* jokes and castration humor generally, see G. Legman, *No Laughing Matter. An Analysis of Sexual Humor.* Monte Gulzow and Carol Mitchell provide an interesting specific case of the way that the *vagina dentata* became a repository for unexpressable anxiety among Vietnam war soldiers in "'*Vagina dentata*' and 'Incurable Venereal Disease' Legends from the Viet Nam War." (I am grateful to my former student Jane Hogan for bringing the latter two sources to my attention.)

3. Horney says that the dread of the vagina and the dread of the father are not mutually exclusive; instead, the former "often conceals itself behind" the latter, despite

the fact that "it is more deep-seated, weighs more heavily, and is usually more energetically repressed than the dread of the man (father)" (138). Her project includes bringing the dread of the woman into view and into the debate over the child's developmental stages. Accordingly, she traces the dread of women to the early, instinctive realization on the boy's part that "his penis is much too small for his mother's genital" (142). If "the grown man continues to regard woman as the great mystery," says Horney, "the mystery of motherhood" is the root cause of it (141). Horney's hypothesis suggests that Freud's admittedly incomplete list of categories of uncanny fear should be expanded to include the return of childhood fears of woman (see Freud's "The Uncanny").

4. Creed argues that in films like *Psycho*, *Carrie*, and others, monstrosity—in the form of castrating woman—is constructed out of the failure to make the break between mother and child (38).

5. Carol J. Clover uses this phrase to describe the killer's lair in slasher films; its feminine characteristics (enclosure, dampness, darkness) are striking in their consistency from film to film (30, 48). In the case of "The Raft," the watery scene fulfills the formula's apparent requirement of a female setting. For King's own discussion of the "Bad Place" (which he identifies more directly with monstrosity itself), see *Danse Macabre*, 263–94.

6. See *The Uses of Enchantment*, 167–83.

7. Neil Jordan's stylized, elegant *The Company of Wolves* (1985) is an adult version of "Little Red Riding Hood" that realizes the story's unconscious theme of sexual awakening through the overtly sexualized use of the werewolf transformation.

8. Creed notes "the reference to the red riding hood/clitoris and its emphasis on the devouring jaws of the wolf/grandmother" (108).

9. Rachel says, "It seems like I spent my life out at Cascade lake" (246).

10. Clover argues that the slasher heroine's defeat of the monster and passage to safety represents an ascent to phallicized maturity (*Men, Women, and Chain Saws*, Chapter 1, especially 49–50). One might argue that Randy matures when he chooses to care for the prostrate LaVerne rather than save himself (261), but his regression at the end of the story calls any such gains into doubt.

11. King's understanding of (and fascination with) the magnetic power (both attractive and repulsive) of the castrating mother is evident from his positioning of "The Raft" within the *Skeleton Crew* collection. The story is followed by "Word Processor of the Gods," in which an uxorious man, Richard Hagstrom, uses a magic word processor (a modern genie-in-the-machine, designed by his precocious nephew, that makes any typed command come true) to first render his virago wife childless (by making their bratty son disappear), and then to make his wife herself disappear. He replaces the two with his sweet-natured sister-in-law and his gifted nephew (both of whom had been killed in a car crash along with Richard's selfish brother shortly before the narrative begins). The magic word processor effectively allows Richard to reposition the branches of his family tree, rewriting the past to retroactively install his unthreatening relatives as his nuclear family. King's segue thus places a meditation on powerlessness ("The Raft") next to a fantasy of ultimate power ("Word Processor of the Gods"). The latter story grants dominion not simply over life and death, but also over the past. The castrating mother figure, Richard's shrewish wife, is not simply neutralized; instead, Richard is able to nullify her by "deleting" all evidence of her existence. This Oedipal fairy tale is the psychic opposite of

"The Raft." The two stories form a matched pair, two different answers to the same "What if?" question.

12. The slasher genre is a modern cinematic development that most critics agree is a narrow offshoot from Alfred Hitchcock's *Psycho* (1960) that suddenly began to sprout vigorously a generation later, starting with John Carpenter's influential *Halloween* (1978). Scores of slasher films were made during the 1980s, with the pace beginning to taper off of late.

13. See Clover (188), quoting Michele Montrelay in part; Clover surveys the ways in which the gazer in horror films is frequently sucked into a vaginal vacuum, emphasizing the consistency with which "horror presents us with scenarios in which assaultive gazing is not just thwarted and punished, but actually reversed in such a way that those who thought to penetrate end up themselves penetrated" (192). This is exactly what happens to Deke.

14. Clover argues on the basis of her own (admittedly informal) survey that young males make up the majority of the audience for slasher films (6–7), but this claim is disputed by Dika (142).

15. Clover points to the unisex names of many Final Girls (Stevie, Joey, Stretch, etc.) as further evidence for the character's sexually ambiguous status (40). Her contention that the Final Girl is an androgynous figure who enables the viewer to identify with suffering has touched off some interesting arguments with other theorists working on the slasher film (including Creed and Dika, the authors of the most detailed studies), but her list of the defining characteristics of the Final Girl has encountered no like opposition; Creed, for example, sees the Final Girl thus: "[I]ntelligent, resourceful and usually not sexually active, she tends to stand apart from the others" (124).

16. Clover says in a note that "we may expect horror films of the future to feature Final Boys as well as Final Girls (Pauls as well as Paulines)." Among the incipient examples she cites is Stephen King's *Misery* (novel 1987; film 1990), in which a broken-legged novelist takes the . . . 'feminine' or masochistic position" (63). See also her note on *The Burning* (1981), in which a "nerdish male" plays the part normally taken by the Final Girl (52).

17. Clover: "[S]lasher killers are by generic definition sexually inadequate—men who kill precisely because they *cannot* fuck" (186).

18. "The Raft" is one of three segments, all scripted by Romero and directed by Gornick, that make up *Creepshow 2* (1987).

19. In a brief analysis of the attraction of horror to the female spectator, Creed allows that it is "complex" (155).

WORKS CITED

Bettelheim, Bruno. *The Uses of Enchantment: The Meaning and Importance of Fairy Tales.* New York: Vintage, 1989.

Clover, Carol J. *Men, Women, and Chain Saws: Gender and the Modern Horror Film.* Princeton: Princeton University Press, 1992.

Creed, Barbara. *The Monstrous-Feminine: Film, Feminism, Psychoanalysis.* London: Routledge, 1993.

Dika, Vera. *Games of Terror. "Halloween," "Friday the 13th," and the Films of the Stalker Cycle.* Rutherford, NJ: Fairleigh Dickinson University Press; London and Toronto: Associated University Presses, 1990.

Freud, Sigmund. "The Uncanny." Translated by James Strachey. Vol. 17 of *The Standard Edition of the Complete Psychological Works of Sigmund Freud.* 24 Vols. London: Hogarth, 1986, 219–52.

Gulzow, Monte, and Carol Mitchell. "'*Vagina Dentata*' and 'Incurable Venereal Disease' Legends from the Viet Nam War." *Western Folklore,* 39 (1980): 306–16.

Horney, Karen. "The Dread of Woman." *Feminine Psychology.* New York: Norton, 1967, 133–46.

King, Stephen. *Bare Bones: Conversations on Terror with Stephen King.* Edited by Tim Underwood and Chuck Miller. New York: McGraw, 1988.

——. *Danse Macabre.* New York: Everest, 1981.

——. *Misery.* New York: Viking, 1987.

——. "The Raft." *Skeleton Crew.* New York: Putnam's, 1985, 245–70.

——. *Skeleton Crew.* New York: Putnam's, 1985.

Lederer, Wolfgang. *The Fear of Women.* New York: Grune, 1968.

Legman, G. *No Laughing Matter. An Analysis of Sexual Humor.* Bloomington: Indiana University Press. Vol. 1, 1968; Vol. 2, 1975.

Mulvey, Laura. "Visual Pleasure and Narrative Cinema," *Screen* 16 (1975): 6–18.

Neumann, Erich. *The Great Mother: An Analysis of the Archetype.* Translated by Ralph Manheim. Princeton: Princeton University Press, 1963.

6

The Power of the Feminine and the Gendered Construction of Horror in Stephen King's "The Reach"

André L. DeCuir

In "A Dream of New Life: Stephen King's *Pet Sematary* as a Variant of *Frankenstein*," Mary Ferguson Pharr attempts to draw parallels between Mary Shelley's great work and Stephen King's reworking of "the dream of new life . . . a dream both seductive and malefic, the stuff finally of nightmares made flesh" (116). Pharr seeks to show that "what King has done in *Pet Sematary* is not to copy Mary Shelley, but rather to amplify the cultural echo she set in motion so that its resonance is clearer to the somewhat jaded, not always intellectual reader of Gothic fantasy today" (118).

Needless to say, gallons upon gallons of scholarly ink have been spilled over Shelley's multi-layered text, but all critics of the novel seem to be indebted to Ellen Moers's discussion of *Frankenstein* as a "*woman's* mythmaking on the subject of birth" (93), "a hideous thing" (95). According to Moers, when Victor "runs away and abandons the newborn monster," Shelley, because of the "hideous intermingling of death and life in her own life" (96), is expressing a "revulsion against newborn life, and the drama of guilt, dread, and flight surrounding birth and its consequences" (93).

With Moers's ideas in mind, framing the biographical and textual similarities Pharr points out in Shelley's novel and King's *Pet Sematary*, I wish to show that the deep-rooted, intermingled themes of childbirth and horror in *Frankenstein* are more directly presented and the horror more specified by King in a little-known short story called "The Reach" (originally published as "Do the Dead Sing"") than in *Pet Sematary*. Not only does the story feature a woman as the main character, but it also contains King's attempt to represent a *self-suppressed* feminine consciousness. Through the main character of the ninety-five-year-old Stella Flanders and the *imagined* conversations she has with her great-grandchildren, King maps out the cultural suppression of the female voice, but also the subsequent and inevitable resurfacing of the feminine, when the voice is rendered inaudible, through the female body and its functions, mainly childbirth. David G. Hartwell correctly writes that in "The Reach" "the horror is distanced but underpins the whole [story]" (15). I wish to show that King specifies this horror as a horror experienced by the male when female power is manifested through the female body which, despite constant efforts, cannot be totally known, experienced, or controlled. For the female, King implies that horror stems from witnessing and experiencing the measures taken by the male, who deems his authority threatened by an overt demonstration of female "otherness."

Briefly, "the reach" in the title of King's story refers to the body of water between an island and the mainland and becomes the story's controlling symbol. The story begins in the summer before the death of Stella Flanders, who has never left her island home, Goat Island, even to visit the mainland, moves through the fall and winter with occasional flashbacks to the summer, and concludes in the summer after the winter of Stella's death. Though the story is related by a third-person narrator, this narrator, in the summer flashbacks, "turns the story over" to Stella in a sense, for it is in these flashbacks that Stella's consciousness is more pervasive and reveals her thoughts about her family, their lives, and those of the people of Goat Island. After her 95th birthday, Stella begins to see the ghost of her husband, Bill, who keeps asking her "when you comin' across to the mainland?" (17). In March, while the reach is still frozen, Stella realizes that the cancer which she had always suspected of growing inside her is getting worse and decides to cross the reach to the mainland. The drifting snow causes her to lose her way until she encounters Bill and ghosts of their friends. They lovingly take her hands and lead her across the reach where she dies.

Such a bare-bones plot summary, of course, ignores a complex narrative structure that implicates long-standing codes in the cultural suppression and even in the self-censorship of women's voices. A close examination of the summer flashbacks, which are italicized in the text[1] and which contain more of Stella's "voice" than the fall and winter sections, reveals a tremendous silence as apparently, Stella speaks only once during the visit of her great-grandchildren in the summer before her death: "*The Reach was wider in those days*" (15). When the children ask her to explain, the narrator replies: "*She only sat in her rocker by the cold stove, her slippers bumping placidly on the floor*" (15). The subsequent flashbacks consist of Stella's thoughts, framed by the narrator's implication that these thoughts are what Stella would express verbally "*if she could*": "*'Gram, what's the Reach?' Lona **might have asked** . . . although she never had. And she **would have given** them the answer any fisherman knew by rote: a Reach is a body of water between two bodies of land, a body of water which is open at either end*" (16–17; bold emphasis added).

Twice, the narrator interjects that Stella does not cry (16, 20), and perhaps the most graphic example of self-suppression, which also seems to serve as an indictment of male-centered heterosexual sex as repressive, occurs when

Stella is addressed by the ghost of her late husband, Bill: "She could say nothing. Her fist was crammed deep into her mouth" (22). Stella's silence, however, has subversive potential because her nonverbal recollections of herself and the women of Goat Island and their various experiences with marriage and childbirth in particular serve to "feminize" Goat Island as a primal, nurturing environment while they indict the mainland as a masculine sphere of industrialization that fosters greed and exploitation, and ultimately, spiritual death.

The mainland, Raccoon Head, is simply referred to by the residents of Goat Island as "the Head," and is surrounded by phallic, "split and fissured rock" (29). While Stella imagines that her great-granddaughter, Lona, will complain that Goat Island is *"so small"* and that *"We live in Portland. There's buses, Gram!"* and even catches herself in "real wonder" after contemplating how *"cars passing to and fro on the Head's main street . . . can go as far as they want . . . Portland . . . Boston . . . New York City"* (26), she more frequently recalls tragedies that have befallen Goat Island residents while on the mainland. For example, Stella remembers that George Havelock "had died a nasty death over on the mainland in 1967, the year there was no fishing. An ax had slipped in Big George's hand, there had been blood—too much of it!—and an island funeral three days later" (16). Goat Island is not immune to death, however, as Stella recalls that Bull Symes had a heart attack *"while he was out dragging traps"* (17), but for Stella and her neighbors, misfortune on the mainland can be exacerbated by practices arising from an existence based on cash nexus (e.g., lawsuits, foreclosures, liens).

When Goat Island resident George Dinsmore takes a job on the mainland "driving plow for the town of Raccoon Head," and gets "smashed on rye whiskey" and drives the plow through three power poles during a storm, Raccoon Head loses power for five days, and as George's "punishment," the electric company *"slap[s] a lien on his home."* (24). Stella's recollection of George's rescue from his financial straits by his Goat Island neighbors portrays the collective action of the Goat Island residents as directly opposed to that of mainland individuals who are in danger of becoming absorbed into a corporate machine as suggested by Stella's use of the third person plural possessive pronoun in reference to the company threatening George, *"the Hydro"*: "[I]*t was seen to it that the Hydro had their money"* (24). Stella would like to emphasize to her great-grandchildren that *"'we always watched out for our own'"* (24) and her consciousness shapes this "we," the collective body of Goat Island residents, not as a corporate force but as a sentient parental entity, willing to take its prodigal son back into the fold while recognizing his faults but also praising his attributes. Stella would like to point out that George was *"good for nothing when his workday was done"* but also to emphasize quickly that *"when he was on the clock he would work like a dray-horse"* (24). Like a desperate parent resorting to "He is a good boy," "This is his first offense," "He was just in the wrong place at the wrong time" arguments in order to defend a child facing a judge, Stella, through her consciousness, adds, "*That one time he got into trouble was because it was at night, and night was always George's drinking time*" (24). The more protective and nurturing environment of Goat Island is suggested by Stella's addendum that since George "now . . . worked on the island . . . he didn't get into much hurt" and that quality of life on the island results, not from being well paid, but from being "*kept . . . fed*" (24).

The "daughters" of Goat Island apparently would fare worse than its "sons" if they should attempt to exist on the mainland independently. According to Stella "*If you* [a woman] *had business on the Head, your man took you in the lobster boat*" (16–17), for if a woman should venture to the mainland on her own, she runs the risk not only of being exploited in the Head's economic system, but she is also in danger of being robbed of something innately and exclusively feminine:

[I]*f she stays* [on Goat Island], *she may be able to keep something of this small world with the little Reach on one side and the big Reach on the other, something it would be too easy to lose hustling hash in Lewiston or donuts in Portland or drinks at the Nashville North in Bangor. Am I old enough not to beat around the bush about what that something might be: a way of living—a feeling.* (24)

I would suggest that the cryptic nature of this segment of Stella's consciousness, which falls within a contemplation of the seven-month-pregnant Missy Bowie and her future on Goat Island as opposed to a future on the mainland, when examined within the context of the story's references to the bodily processes culminating in childbirth and when further magnified by contemporary feminist criticism, becomes an attempt to define what French feminist critics posit as a powerful difference stemming from and sustained by female sexuality. While the thought attempts to disclose a bleak picture of women's loss of dignity in an exploitive economic system, it also warns about the possible loss of something that cannot be defined by the dominant system of signifiers. Stella's concern for its loss if removed from Goat Island suggests that this quality she would like to explain has the potential to empower and to develop, perhaps into something "explosive" and "*utterly* destructive" (italicized in text; Cixous, 886), if nurtured within the environment of Goat Island and not on the mainland where it is subject to repression and perhaps obliteration "by the [Lacanian] Law of the Father" (Jones, 362).[2]

The "gender" of the parental force made up of the collective efforts of the Goat Island residents is suggested by its spokesperson, Stella, who happens to be the oldest person on the island, but who also takes pride in being the oldest woman on the island: "They were talking about Freddy Dinsmore, the oldest man on the island (two years younger'n me, though, Stella thought with some satisfaction)" (18). Incidentally, Freddy dies of the flu in February "before anyone could take him across to the mainland and hook him up to all those machines they have for guys like Freddy" (21). Stella's lack of contact with the mainland and her reiteration in different phraseology that Goat Island "*is my place and I love it*" establish her as the island's matriarch. "Most of the village" turns out for Stella's 95th birthday with a "tremendous birthday cake" (16), and she is still able to make the younger residents of Goat Island stare in wonder, "wide-eyed" (19), with her tales of unusual occurrences that transpired on Goat Island before her listeners were born. For example, in January, when Stella is asked if she "had ever seen such a winter," Stella relates that in February of 1938, the reach froze, allowing her husband, Bill, and his friend, Bull Symes, to walk across the reach to the mainland and back again (18).

Although she holds no political office that legislates the behavior of the island community, her unobtrusive authority, which undoubtedly stems at least partially from her longevity, also seems anchored in female sexuality as her silent reminiscences are punctuated by references to menstruation, conception, pregnancy, midwifery, deliveries and births, a miscarriage, and deaths of ill newborns. She recalls, for example, how her own mother "*conceived four times but one of her babies had miscarried and another had died a week after birth*" (20). At a post–memorial service reception, Stella notices that the widow, Missy Bowie, is "seven months big with child—it would be her fifth" (18). Even Stella's condensed version of her family history, which she would like to relate to her great-grandchildren, emphasizes not official titles, heroic, or even infamous deeds, but propagation:

She would say: "*Louis and Margaret Godlin begat Stella Godlin, who became Stella Flanders; Bill and Stella Flanders begat Jane and Alden Flanders and Jane Flanders became Jane Wakefield; Richard and Jane Wakefield begat Lois Wakefield, who became Lois Perrault; David and Lois Perrault begat Lona and Hal. These are your names, children: you are Godlin-Flanders-Wakefield-Perrault.*" (21)

King does not overtly define Goat Island as a feminist utopia "ruled by women" (Showalter, 191).[3] Curiously, however, he structures Stella's mental and therefore "silent" account of her family history without reference to formal marriage, thus demonstrating how Stella, at least in her mind, has ostensibly always minimized the importance society places on an institution in which women are often relegated to an inferior position. Also, we learn through Stella's memories that the only male child in her family to reach adulthood is her son Alden, whose "*slow brain*" and lifelong bachelorhood (20–21) conflate into a suggestion of male sexual impotence. Stella's consciousness does not reveal, however, a desire for more potent male progeny to carry on the family name, and nowhere does she express hope that her great-grandson Hal will grow up to sire more Perraults. A particular observation about Hal actually adds to Stella's silent disregard for prescribed gender-based behavior. To Stella, not Lona, but Hal, her male great-grandchild, is "*somehow more intuitive*" (20).

Whereas the "gender" of Goat Island has been suggested by that of its oldest-living resident, Stella, King more definitely sketches out the environment of Goat Island as a feminine realm by linking the Reach itself to the womb through Stella's explanation of the birth of the deformed Wilson infant:

*There was Norman and Ettie Wilson's baby that was born a mongoloid, its poor dear little feet turned in, its bald skull lumpy and cratered, its fingers webbed together as if it had dreamed too long and too deep while swimming that **interior Reach**.* (bold emphasis added, 24)

At the outset of this essay, I suggested that for King, horror, as experienced by the male in "The Reach," is generated by a confrontation with the changes undergone by the female body culminating in actual reproduction, changes he can never experience in a body he thought he controlled. In his terror, the male is "unmannned," pushed to drastic measures, or utterly destroyed. Stella recalls, for example, that after her husband, Bill, delivered their daughter himself, he went *"into the bathroom and first puked and then wept like a hysterical woman who had her monthlies p'ticularly bad"* (20). The images of Victor Frankenstein rushing out of his chambers after gazing upon his creation with "horror and disgust" and his later destruction of the unfinished female creature after contemplating how, if it should couple with his male creation, "a race of devils would be propagated upon the earth, who might make the very existence of the species of man a condition precarious and full of terror" (Shelley, 163), converge, in "The Reach," into an example of drastic measures taken by the male when a female bodily process does not transpire according to societal expectations and produces a terrible result.

Just as Victor destroys in order to protect the condition "of the species of man," Norman Wilson, the infant's father, takes drastic measures to eradicate any evidence of the "hideous progeny" (Shelley, 229) of that "interior Reach," which could "unman" him as confrontation with this "unknown" did Bill Flanders:

Reverend McCracken had come and baptized the baby, and a day later Mary Dodge, who even at that time had midwived over a hundred babies, and Norman took Ettie down the hill to see Frank Child's new boat and although she could barely walk, Ettie went with no complaint, although she had stopped in the door to look back at Mary Dodge, who was sitting calmly by the idiot baby's crib and knitting. Mary had looked up at her and when their eyes met, Ettie burst into tears. "Come on," Norman had said, upset. "Come on, Ettie come on." And when they came back an hour later the baby was dead, one of those crib-deaths, wasn't it merciful he didn't suffer. (24–25)

The infant's mother seems to be privy to the plan for her tearful outburst occurs when her eyes meet those of Mary Dodge who she knows is present to carry out her designated part, the actual killing of the infant, while she and her husband are out. Norman's urgings of "come on" would seem to indicate a creeping sense of remorse, but his choice of Mary Dodge to actually carry out the deed, a woman *"who had midwived over a hundred babies"* and who could probably make the baby's death look "natural," serves as his acknowledgment that this woman's "feminine knowledge" of the bodily processes surrounding childbirth and her experience in assisting in this process somehow empower her enough to take the life of the infant. Just as Victor runs away in revulsion from his "newborn," Norman "runs away" to Frank Child's boat, perhaps fearing that directly confronting the "hideous" product of a female bodily process himself would unman and weaken him.

By positing the reach as a metaphorical body of amniotic fluid produced by the feminine entity, Goat Island, King sets the stage for a demonstration of the "explosive, *utterly* destructive" return of the repressed or "silenced" power of the feminine that is particularly horrifying and devastating to the male who seeks to subdue this "female" body. The characters Stewie McClelland and Russell Bowie "trust the ice" of the presently frozen reach and take "Stewie's Bombardier Skiddoo" out onto the ice while "drinking Apple Zapple Wine, and sure enough, the skiddoo went into the Reach. Stewie managed to crawl out (although he lost one foot to frostbite). The Reach took Russell Bowie and carried him away" (18). The loss of Stewie's foot can be viewed as a symbolic castration, a "punishment," initiated by the Reach. Stella's later vision of the body of Russell Bowie, twisting and dancing beneath the ice covering the Reach, looks forward to her memory of the Wilson baby, "swimming that interior Reach," thus further establishing the reach as a metaphorical womb, that center of an exclusive feminine power, but also dramatizes what Gilbert and Gubar allude to as an historical male fear of the womb as a dark, suffocating, annihilating prison (93–95).[4]

The only example of a female character's experience of horror resulting in a reaction comparable to the responses of Bill Flanders and Norman Wilson is that of Ettie Wilson who bursts into tears at the understanding that, according to her husband's plan, her baby will no longer be alive when she returns from a diversionary outing. Though her reaction is certainly justified, if we are to understand King's gendered polarization of the constitution of the "horrible" and responses to it in "The Reach," we must recognize Ettie's intensely personal tragedy as an integral part of the story's paradigm of a female recognition of horror. If horror for the male is generated by a confrontation with female bodily processes altered through sexuality, then it follows that horror for the female is brought on by the extreme measures taken by the male when faced with this female "otherness."

As presented earlier, Stella alludes to a *"being and a way of living—a* feeling," a quality that she seems to ascribe exclusively to women. It apparently stems from and is sustained by female sexuality, but this essence can be drained by an existence on the masculinely-structured mainland that seeks to harness it. The events surrounding her own death not only further gender-identify the mainland but also characterize it as a haven for death itself. In Stella's consciousness, crossing to the mainland seems to be a euphemism for dying as the apparition of Bill asks her, "When you comin [*sic*] across to the mainland?" (17). When the reach is still frozen, Stella decides to cross over to the mainland where "*she had never once in her life been*" (16), but only after realizing that the cancer she had always suspected of growing inside her has "finally gotten around to . . . the '*pièce de resistance*' (23). She reasons that perhaps on the mainland, death will finally overtake her, thus ending "the griping pain in her stomach" and the spitting up of "bright red blood into the toilet bowl," "foul-tasting stuff, coppery and shuddersome" (23).

Sure enough, as Stella nears the mainland, she weakens and is supported by the ghosts of the Goat Island dead until "it is time":

They stood in a circle in the storm, the dead of Goat Island, and the wind screamed around them, driving its packet of snow, and some kind of song burst from her [Stella]. It went up into the wind and the wind carried it away. They all sang then, as children will sing in their high, sweet voices as a summer evening draws down to summer night. They sang, and Stella felt herself going to them and with them, finally across the Reach. There was a bit of pain, but not much; losing her maidenhead had been worse. They stood in a circle in the night. The snow blew around them and they sang. (29)

Despite the wholeness and wholesomeness suggested by the image of children standing in a circle, the narrator's revelation of Stella's final thoughts discloses her continuing effort to gender-identify the mainland and death itself that she associates with the mainland. The sensation Stella uses as a standard by which to measure the "bit of pain" experienced at the moment of death is not the pain of childbirth, a phenomenon that she recalled can unsettle the menfolk more than the women actually experiencing its accompanying pain, but that resulting from male-female penetration.

Throughout "The Reach," Stella's consciousness is rendered in italics, a method of representation that lessens as the story concludes, perhaps suggesting Stella's impending loss of consciousness and death. The last seven paragraphs, which carry the reader to the summer *after Stella's death*, curiously, are printed in italics, and the consciousness of Alden, Stella's son, who has now assumed the "matriarchal" position of entertaining Stella's great-grandchildren during their summer visits to Goat Island, is at the center of the story's conclusion. The focus on Alden, shaped in the same manner as Stella's silent acknowledgments of female empowerment, however, does not suggest that, with the death of Stella, Goat Island, will become "masculinized" as the mainland. Like Stella and other women, Alden, even though a biological male, is still a marginalized figure due to his "mental slowness" a condition that also presumes a sexual slowness or impotency or at least a lack of sexual knowledge, either of which would displace Alden from socially sanctioned masculine behavior (i.e., the wielding of phallic power). Whereas women may choose silence to avoid the sapping of their essences by an inimical socioeconomic system,[5] Alden, due to his disability, cannot coherently articulate, and thus exists in a deeper silence imposed by forces beyond his control. King's linking of Alden's and Stella's "silences" via narrative structure, however, suggests that what Alden keeps hidden can be just as subversive, namely a knowledge that the dead have the power to make themselves known in the realm of the living.

Alden recalls the looks in the eyes of two male characters, Larry McKeen and John Bensohn, when they recognize that the cap found on Stella's frozen body is not Alden's, but that of Bill, his dead father. This oddity has the potential to subvert any male-induced normalcy, just like childbirth in Stella's recollections (I use "male" because the only witnesses Alden remembers are male), and as a result of this "horror," the incident is stigmatized as one of those *"things that can never be told,"* something *"not exactly secret, that* [is] *not discussed"* (30). For Alden, however, it is something not to be completely obliterated from memory but *"made for thinking on slowly"* and *"at length, while the hands do their work and the coffee sits in a solid china mug nearby"* (30). His recognition of *"his dead father's cap, the look of its bill or the places where the visor had been broken"* (30) found on his mother's body allows him, in his own mind at least, and his consciousness is the prevailing one at the end of the story, to revise the finality of death feared by his mother in her narrative into death as the ultimate liberator from repression (Stella herself may have experienced this sense of release as, just before crossing the Reach, "she burst into tears suddenly—all the tears she had never wept"). He is able to comfort himself in his loneliness with an affirmation that the dead, who may have been verbally, intellectually, sexually, and spiritually repressed all their lives, do inevitably make their voices heard.

NOTES

1. Throughout this chapter, selected italicized passages from "The Reach" will be quoted without notation (for example, "italicized in text"), but any italicization utilized from other sources will be noted as such.

2. Critics such as Julia Kristeva, Hélène Cixous, and Luce Irigaray seem to have based their ideas on the psychoanalytic theories of Jacques Lacan, who suggests that the individual experiences two "systems" of language, the "imaginary" and the "symbolic." The former is a prelinguistic phase in which the individual is unaware of signs that express "difference," such as the signifiers "male" and "female." The latter is the present system of language that illustrates difference.

Kristeva translates the "imaginary" into the "semiotic" and associates this phase with the female body and the sensations experienced by both woman and child during pregnancy, birth, and infancy. The symbolic is associated with the father as the child is indoctrinated into a system in which the imaginary or semiotic is suppressed in favor of polarities and implied inferiorities. Cixous and Irigaray argue that if women are to express themselves completely, they must fracture, revise, or replace the present system of language with one stemming from "jouissance," a reclaiming of the female body and a rediscovery of its eroticism. I contend that what Stella may mean by "something" is like the concept of "jouissance."

For more complete summaries of these theories, see Ann Rosalind Jones's "Writing the Body: Toward an Understanding of *l'Écriture feminine*" and Raman Selden's *A Reader's Guide to Contemporary Literary Theory.*

3. Showalter, in a discussion of feminist novelists, refers to a group of nineteenth-century women writers who expressed some "very peculiar fantasies." Works by writers such as Lady Florence Dixie, "Ellis Ethelmer," and Charlotte Perkins Gilman portrayed "imagined worlds ruled by women, feminist revolutions, and virgin births" (191). Showalter attributes this tradition to a "horror" similar to the one experienced by Mary

Shelley in *Frankenstein*. According to Showalter, these novels reflected some women's "repugnance for the actual process of intercourse and childbirth" that perhaps stemmed from the increasing awareness of the "dangers in pregnancy, venereal disease and childbearing," but also the simultaneous need to share in the Victorian "veneration of motherhood and maternal love" (191).

4. In Chapter 3 of *The Madwoman in the Attic*, "The Parables of the Cave," Gilbert and Gubar assert that the womb is "the place of female power . . . one of the great antechambers of the mysteries of transformation" (95). Stella's mental image of what Russell Bowie might have experienced, writhing beneath a translucent barrier, frantically trying to break through its surface (which he may have tried to do before drowning), echoes and illustrates Gilbert and Gubar's premise of the Victorian (male) fear of the womb and association of it with the tomb, "the cavern confrontations and the evils they might reveal--the suffocation, the 'black bat airs,' the vampirism, the chaos of what Victor Frankenstein calls 'filthy creation'" (93–94).

5. Joyce Zonana, in a discussion as to why Safie's letters are not reproduced in the text of Frankenstein, concludes that their absence sends a strong "feminist message of resistance, rebellion" (181) as the letters cannot be appropriated and possessed by the male characters. Victor, Walton, and the creature "seek to 'know' or possess something outside of themselves" (181). Zonana supports her argument with Cixous's "The Laugh of the Medusa" and writes that women's self-silencing "actually asserts the integrity of female experience. Such silence resists and baffles the act of appropriation" and interpretation according to "patriarchal conventions" (Zonana, 180–81).

WORKS CITED

Cixous, Hélène. "The Laugh of the Medusa." Translated by Keith Cohen and Paula Cohen. *Signs: Journal of Women in Culture and Society* 1 (1976): 875–93.

Gilbert, Sandra, and Susan Gubar. *The Madwoman in the Attic: The Woman Writer and the Nineteenth-Century Literary Imagination*. New Haven: Yale University Press, 1979.

Hartwell, David G., ed. *The Dark Descent*. New York: Doherty, 1987.

Jones, Ann Rosalind. "Writing the Body: Toward an Understanding of *l'Écriture feminine*." *The New Feminist Criticism: Essays on Women, Literature, and Theory*. Edited by Elaine Showalter. New York: Pantheon, 1985, 361–77.

King, Stephen. "The Reach." *The Dark Descent*. Edited by David G. Hartwell. New York: Doherty, 1987, 15–30.

Moers, Ellen. *Literary Women*. New York: Doubleday, 1976.

Pharr, Mary Ferguson. "A Dream of New Life: Stephen King's *Pet Sematary* as a Variant of *Frankenstein*." *The Gothic World of Stephen King: Landscape of Nightmares*. Edited by Gary Hoppenstand and Ray B. Browne. Bowling Green: Bowling Green State University Popular Press, 1987, 115–25.

Selden, Raman. *A Reader's Guide to Contemporary Literary Theory*. Lexington: University of Kentucky Press, 1989.

Shelley, Mary. *Frankenstein or The Modern Prometheus*. 1818. Edited by James Rieger. Indianapolis: Bobbs-Merrill, 1974.

Showalter, Elaine. *A Literature of Their Own: British Women Novelists From Brontë to Lessing*. Princeton: Princeton University Press, 1977.

Zonana, Joyce. "'They Will Prove the Truth of My Tale': Safie's Letters as the Feminist Core of Mary Shelley's *Frankenstein.*" *The Journal of Narrative Technique* 21 (1991): 170–84.

7

Gerald's Game and *Dolores Claiborne*: Stephen King and the Evolution of an Authentic Female Narrative Voice

Carol A. Senf

Stephen King is a force to be reckoned with because the prolific novelist is so immensely popular: Though relatively young (born in 1947), he has already written thirty-two novels (including six under the pen name Richard Bachman and one, *The Talisman*, with Peter Straub), six collections of short fiction, one book of criticism, six screenplays, and hundreds of short works. Even more significant is his popularity, which is documented by Stephen J. Spignesi in *The Complete Stephen King Encyclopedia*, a work that details King's success up to 1990: "Of the top twenty-five *Publishers Weekly* fiction bestsellers of the eighties, Stephen King had seven titles on the list: *The Dark Half, The Tommyknockers, It, Misery, The Talisman, The Eyes of the Dragon*, and *Skeleton Crew*. The twenty-five titles on the list sold a combined total of 25,889,924 copies. Of that total, 7,269,929—or twenty-eight percent—were Stephen King titles" (5). That popularity continues.

Such popularity alone makes him a phenomenon that merits scholarly attention; and I agree with the observation of Gail E. Burns and Melinda Kanner in "Women, Danger, and Death: The Perversion of The Female Principle in Stephen King's Fiction": "Although critical and academic audiences . . . ignore, denigrate, or otherwise declare King's fiction as unworthy of serious consideration, the vast popularity of this body of popular culture suggests an area for investigation by the social scientists as well as the literary critic" (159).

No anthology that examines King's treatment of women can afford to ignore the fact that so many of these immensely popular works examine women characters. Of his twenty-nine novels, seven feature women (or girl) protagonists (*Carrie*, 1974; *Firestarter*, 1980; *Cujo*, 1981; *Misery*, 1987; *Gerald's Game*, 1992; *Dolores Claiborne*, 1993; *Rose Madder*, 1995); five have women as sidekicks, wives, or buddies (*The Dark Tower II: The Drawing of the Three*, 1987; *The Tommyknockers*, 1987; *The Dark Half*, 1989; *The Dark Tower*

III: The Wastelands, 1991; *Insomnia*, 1994); three feature large casts of characters that include women prominently (*The Stand*, 1978; *It*, 1986; and *Needful Things*, 1991); and finally, *The Shining* (1977) is a story of a woman's transformation from domination by her husband in the early portions of the novel to personal triumph at the conclusion. Assuming that readers return to King's fiction because something in it satisfies their needs, scholars who examine King's women characters may also discover new insights into both his popularity and social attitudes to women at the end of the twentieth century.

Though there is decidedly little agreement among them, a number of critics have already commented on King's portraits of women. At one end of the spectrum are critics who label King a misogynist, including Clare Hanson, who argues that his fiction is a means of working through the Oedipus complex. Thus Hanson argues that *Carrie* reveals King's fear of the female body, and *Misery*, King's most deeply misogynist text, presents Annie Wilkes as the "monstrous feminine, the castrating female" and adds that there are "*no* positive images of the feminine in this misogynistic text" (150).

Other readers, including fellow novelist Chelsea Quinn Yarbro and critics Richard Bleiler, Robin Wood, Jackie Eller, and Tony Magistrale, observe that King's women characters are weak—though they do not necessarily agree on the causes of this weakness. Yarbro, for example, observes that King is "not able to develop a believable woman character between the ages of seventeen and sixty" (65). Bleiler notes that King finds it difficult to make women and minority members believable: "He has candidly admitted that Mother Abagail and Hallorann, the cook in *The Shining*, are 'cardboard caricatures of super-black heroes, viewed through rose-tinted glasses of white-liberal guilt.' The self-criticism is justified. Nor are Frances Goldsmith and Nadine Cross, the two other women who figure prominently in *The Stand* any more believable" (1040). Wood explains that King is not a great creator of characters and that "his women are particularly colourless" because they fall into a limited number of stereotypes. He adds furthermore that there "are virtually no independent women in his work":

In the King world women are wives and mothers, and ideally they are much in need of male protection. . . . The books cannot attack the institutions of marriage and family to which they are committed (while demonstrating ad infinitum that they don't work); consequently, they repeatedly endorse bourgeois domesticity as right, natural, and inevitable while expressing the most intense resentment of it in vindictive fantasy. (305)

Eller agrees that King's women characters are stereotypes and argues furthermore that the stereotypes stem from King's limited view of women rather than from a general inability to create strong characters. Her paper, "Morality is the Message: Image-making of Female Characters in the Work of Stephen King," which was delivered at the International Popular Culture Association's 1987 meeting, argues that King's restricted perspective as a male is indicated by the fact that there are so few mature—much less powerful—women in his works. Instead, the numerous references to women's physical bodies, especially his preoccupation with anatomical details and the implication that feminine sexuality is inherently decadent and evil, reveals his sexist orientation (quoted in Magistrale, 93). Magistrale, who observes that King's focus in "dramatizing the human struggle between good and evil is centered exclusively on men or boys," agrees that "there are few complex women in his canon—women who are multidimensional blends of good and evil" (51). Nonetheless Magistrale concedes that King occasionally creates women characters who are "as strong as the supernatural forces they encounter and stronger than the men with whom they associate" (94). Among them are Beverly Marsh in *It* and Dayna Jurgens in *The Stand,* who "assert themselves against the violence that manifests itself in each respective book" (94).

At the other end of the spectrum are Mark Jancovich, who argues specifically that King is not a misogynist, and King's friend and former teacher, Burton Hatlen, who describes King as a feminist. Jancovich observes that King's novels often include strong women:

In fact, like *Carrie*, King's other novels also present . . . women, such as Susan Snell in *Carrie*, who are at least as intelligent, resourceful and compelling as men within the novels. Nor are these women simply idealized figures, but, as the feminist horror writer, Lisa Tuttle has argued, King's novels frequently "show insight into female characters." (101–2)[1]

Furthermore, Jancovich observes that King creates many male characters, including Larry Underwood in *The Stand,* who "begin as traditionally male characters, but pass through a process of feminization which is presented as positive" (102). Hatlen observes that many of King's strong women characters were inspired by a strong woman in his life, his wife and fellow novelist Tabitha King, and explains both that "the evolving presence of King's female characters owes much to his relationship with a feminist wife" (cited by Magistrale, 104). [2]

The purpose of this chapter is not to attack any of these other readers but instead to examine the women characters in two of King's recent novels, *Gerald's Game* and *Dolores Claiborne*, works that I chose both because they are recent and thorough examinations of women characters and because King's experiments with narrative suggest his interest in strong and assertive women as well as his movement toward more realistic depiction of character.

In both works, King takes upon himself several difficult tasks: to focus on a single character and to tell his tale through that single character, a character furthermore who is very different from the novelist himself. *Gerald's Game* is narrated first by a third-person narrator who sees the story through the eyes of the middle-class college graduate, Jessie Burlingame, and ultimately *by* Jessie herself, whereas *Dolores Claiborne* is narrated entirely by the elderly Dolores Claiborne in her own words and voice. Thus the narrative structure becomes King's version of femaleness, and the novels also give increasing power and articulation to those women's voices. Moreover, both dedications suggest that

King may have been thinking of women when he wrote them; *Dolores Claiborne* is the second novel King dedicates to his "mother, Ruth Pillsbury King," another woman that biographers agree was a major influence on King. She reared him and his older brother after King's father abandoned the family when the novelist was two years old; she encouraged King to submit manuscripts even when he was receiving more rejections than acceptances. *Gerald's Game* is dedicated "with love and admiration, to six good women: Margaret Spruce Morehouse, Catherine Spruce Graves, Stephanie Spruce Leonard, Anne Spruce Labree, Tabitha Spruce King, Marcella Spruce" (King's wife and five other women in her family).

In the two novels, King examines the social forces that intrude on women's lives and help to shape them until each woman discovers her own power—in these novels, literally her own narrative voice. Jessie Burlingame had been more or less silenced by her traditional family and husband until the events in the novel take place. She had spent her entire life repressing the fact that her father sexually abused her when she was a child, and she had married a man who continued to dominate her life. Now middle-aged, she is a literal prisoner of her husband's sexual desires. She is handcuffed to the bed at their summer house when the novel opens and remains trapped there for most of the novel, for Gerald has a heart attack and dies in the first chapter. Thus King has her confront the truth about herself before she can escape to tell her own story; and King's narrative strategy literally reveals his version of female empowerment, for the novel begins with traditional third-person narration and concludes with Jessie's telling her own story in her own voice and with her own words.

Dolores Claiborne, the sole speaker in the novel of that name, has already come into her own, though she must convince others that she is telling the truth. Her self-knowledge and control are evident in the fact that hers is the only voice in that novel. Accused of murdering her husband over twenty-three years earlier and her employer earlier that week, she concludes her story by looking inward: "I've done my part, n I feel at peace with myself. That's all that matters, I guess; that, n knowin exactly who you are. I know who *I* am: Dolores Claiborne, two months shy of my sixty-sixth birthday, registered Democrat, lifelong resident of Little Tall Island" (301). Her willingness to tell her story to a disbelieving community is evidence of her self-awareness.

In addition to helping us to understand these novels, I hope that examining King's narrative strategy in these two works will also provide insights about how King's attitude to women affects his popularity. Though anyone who has ever taught knows that readers are capable of egregious misreadings, I assume that most readers will not totally miss the point that a novelist is trying to make. In other words, most readers will not mistake the villain for the hero even if they come from cultures in which the criteria for one or the other differs significantly. The reason for this degree of consistency is the narrative voice. Even though novels lack the community who listened to the bard relate the adventures of Odysseus or the spectators who responded to the tragic life of Hamlet, the presence of a unifying narrative voice tends to mediate between writer and readers. Thus, if King is celebrating strong and independent women, most of his readers should understand that fact. Such a reading would tend to confirm that King is a feminist, a person who advocates that women receive social, political, and economic rights that are equal to those of men. On the other hand, if King is a misogynist, one who hates, dislikes, or mistrusts women, he would tend to advocate boundaries that keep women in roles where they can do little damage.[3] This view might correspond to the widely held view that horror genres are conservative, that they reinforce the status quo, and that they tend to punish those who step outside traditional boundaries. Indeed, some of King's own comments might be read as confirmation of this view. For example, in *Danse Macabre*, he notes that the "final truth of horror movies" is that they are basically conservative:

They do not love death, as some have suggested; they love life. They do not celebrate deformity but by dwelling on deformity, they sing of health and energy. By showing us the miseries of the damned, they help us to rediscover the smaller (but never petty) joys of our own lives. They are the barber's leeches of the psyche, drawing not bad blood but anxiety . . . for a little while, anyway. (194, King's ellipsis)

On the other hand, the same critical study examines the movie *The Stepford Wives*, which King observes has "some disquieting things to say about the American male's response" to women's desire for greater equality (164). Certainly, King's novels are conservative in that they celebrate fairly traditional values, including life and health and love. They are also radical in that they condemn both men and political institutions who use the power of patriarchy against women and children, and they celebrate women who manage to carve out positions for themselves. In this chapter I examine the relative strengths and weaknesses of the women characters in *Gerald's Game* and *Dolores Claiborne* and attempt to discover the source of their strengths and weaknesses. If there are strong women in his fiction, do their strengths lie in stereotypical roles—in their roles as mothers, for example? Or does King leave room for new, more autonomous roles for women? The latter would, of course, ally King more closely with members of the feminist camp.

Point of View in *Gerald's Game* and *Dolores Claiborne*

King is certainly not the first male novelist to tell his tale from a woman's point of view, for I can cite Samuel Richardson, Daniel Defoe, Henry Fielding, Gustave Flaubert, and James Joyce among his predecessors. Indeed, looking at the earliest English novels (*Pamela*, *Clarissa*, *Moll Flanders*, *Amelia*) makes me wonder whether the novel originated as an attempt on the part of men novelists to understand women. In King's case, however, the movement from third-person narration (the narrative strategy most frequently used by King) to first person and the shift from limited omniscience to individual consciousness are a significant accompaniment to King's apparent interest in women and women's issues. Looking at King's experiments with point of view, I agree with Wallace Martin who describes the importance of point of view: "Rather than being added as an appendage that will transmit the plot to an audience, narrative point of view creates the interest, the conflicts, the suspense, and the plot itself in most modern narratives" (130–31). Thus King's decision to have his women characters tell their own stories in their own voices is an important part of experiencing the novels as a whole. Moreover, in these works, King moves away from the supernatural horror fiction that established his reputation and toward mainstream realistic fiction. Although there is no room in this chapter for a discussion of King's evolution as a novelist or for a full definition of realism, I should note here that my thinking on the subject of King as a realist has been influenced by a wide range of critics, including George Lukacs and George Levine, who have emphasized natural causality and believable characters. The main point I wish to make here is that neither *Gerald's Game* nor *Dolores Claiborne* includes the supernatural figures or paranormal forces that King often included in earlier novels. Instead, they depict ordinary human women with ordinary human problems, including child abuse, bad marriages, and institutions that favor men over women. Furthermore, instead of telling those stories through the "voice" of a neutral third-person narrator, King creates plausible women characters who relate their own stories. It is as though King wants the reader to believe that he as novelist has turned the stories over to his women characters.

Gerald's Game begins with fairly traditional third-person narration, the narrator having access to Jessie's mind: "Jessie could hear the back door banging lightly, randomly, in the October breeze. . . . She thought of telling Gerald to go back and shut the door. . . . Then she thought how ridiculous that would be, given the current circumstances. It would ruin the whole mood. *What mood?*" (1). The italicized "What mood?" is a means of entering more directly into Jessie's mind, to see her response to the situation in her own words rather than have it filtered through the language of an author or implied author. The entry into Jessie's mind also suggests that, although Jessie is not interested in Gerald's bondage games, she is reluctant to say so. Thus, the reader might conclude correctly that Jessie is trying to cater to Gerald's needs rather than gratify her own.

King interrupts his third-person narration throughout the novel both to dramatize scenes in the present (Gerald's death, Jessie's ultimate escape from the handcuffs, and her confrontation with the psychopathic Raymond Andrew Joubert) or in flashback (scenes from her childhood, college days, and marriage) and to let Jessie speak directly. At the end, however, he turns over the novel to Jessie, who is writing about her experiences to Ruth Neary, her former college roommate and a woman from whom Jessie had earlier run because Ruth had asked her to be more introspective and to face the truth about her life: "And I want to tell you something else. . . . I'm going to be okay. . . . You and your tough talk were a big part of saving my life last October. . . . I love you so much" (331). Although King returns briefly to third-person narration to reinforce Jessie's ultimate survival, he nonetheless allows her voice to dominate the final fifth of the novel.

In *Dolores Claiborne*, King totally turns over the narration to Dolores, as can be seen in the novel's opening: "*What* did you ask, Andy Bissette? Do I 'understand these rights as you've explained em to me'? . . . No, *you* never mind—still your jawin and listen to me for awhile. I got an idear you're gonna be listenin to me most of the night, so you might as well get used to it" (1). Although King makes it clear that three people (Police Chief Andy Bissette; Frank Proulx, a policeman; and Nancy Bannister, a stenographer) are listening attentively to Dolores's story, he doesn't provide the reader with their voices. In fact, Dolores's voice is the only voice heard in 301 of the novel's 305 pages, and King even turns over the narration of dramatic scenes to her, as he does in the following scene where she describes what precedes the death of her husband Joe:

"Dolores!" his voice come driftin up. "You can have the money! All of it! And I'll never touch Selena again, I swear before God Almighty and all the angels I won't! Please, honey, just help me get outta this hole!"

I got up the last board—I had to yank it outta the blackberry creepers to get it loose—and tossed it behind me. Then I shone the light down into the well. (204–5)

Only in the final pages do other "voices" intrude to provide additional commentary to Dolores's version of the story. A local newspaper account indicates that Dolores is cleared of murdering her employer; another newspaper account reveals that Dolores leaves Mrs. Donovan's inheritance to charity; and an account from the local gossip column indicates that Dolores's daughter Selena is returning home for the first time in over twenty years.

King's Continued Interest in Women's Issues

Not only does King tell these women's stories primarily through their own points of view, but he also focuses on issues that have been important to women in the latter part of the twentieth century, the time period covered by both novels. One of the most important is women's quest for autonomy, and King indicates that Jessie had been angry at Gerald for making her quit a job that gave her a sense of worth:

Ten years ago she had reluctantly given up her job as a substitute teacher, finally giving in to the pressure of Gerald's persistent . . . logic. He was making almost a hundred thousand dollars a year by then; next to that, her five to seven grand looked pretty paltry. . . . teaching, even on a part-time basis, filled her up in some important way, and Gerald didn't get that. Nor had he been able to get the fact that subbing formed a bridge to the life she had lived . . . when she'd been a full-time English teacher . . . a woman on her own who was working for a living, who was well-liked and respected by her colleagues, and who was beholden to no one. (102–3)

Although Jessie identifies the job as an important indicator of her identity, King also reveals that she had, prior to her ordeal at the cottage, not had a strong sense of personal identity. For example, she had allowed herself to be defined by certain stereotypical roles, for she keeps saying that "Jessie Mahout Burlingame, wife of Gerald, sister of Maddy and Will, daughter of Tom and Sally, mother of no one, was really not here at all" (4–5).

King also suggests that her lack of identity stems from the fact that she has been listening to the opinions of others rather than looking at herself, and his observation about her lack of identity connects in interesting ways to his narrative strategy. For example, while handcuffed to the bed, she engages in a kind of internal dialogue: "She had always heard voices inside her head . . . and most of them were old friends, as comfortable as bedroom slippers. This one, however, was new . . . and there was nothing comfortable about it. It was a strong voice, one that sounded young and vigorous. It also sounded impatient" (3–4). This assertive voice is, of course, her own, and she recognizes that she must listen to it, for the alternative is death in the remote cottage. Right before she takes the drastic step of cutting her wrists to slide out of the handcuffs, she "decided she had done all the praying she intended to do. Now she would depend on her voices . . . and on herself" (234, King's ellipsis). Like Donna Trenton in *Cujo*, another woman who decides that she cannot wait for a white knight to rescue her, Jessie determines that she must save herself.[4] Unlike Donna, who waits too long to act and thus loses her son, however, Jessie acts in time.

Moreover she finally recognizes that both the voices in her head[5] and her contempt for herself began when her father sexually abused her:

I spent two years sharing space in my head with . . . dozens of voices that passed judgment on my every word and action. Some were kind and supportive, but most were the voices of people who were afraid, people who were confused, people who thought Jessie . . . deserved every bad thing that happened to her. . . . For two years I heard those voices, Ruth, and when they stopped, I forgot them. . . . if I let nice, kind Brandon Milheron have his way, I'd end up right back where I started—headed down Nuthouse Lane by way of Schizophrenia Boulevard. And this time . . . I have to do it myself, just as I had to get out of Gerald's goddam handcuffs myself. (323–24)

These observations, including Jessie's decision to listen to her own inner voice rather than to the voices that she hears around her and her decision to take charge of her life, come at the end of the novel and indicate Jessie's growing realization of her own strength. Listening to others is a form of madness and victimization. Having allowed herself to be victimized by both her parents and her husband, she decides that she will not continue to be a victim. That sense of self-assurance means that she will need to come to terms with the men in her life, including the father who had abused her and the husband who had failed to listen to her, and with a patriarchal culture that still expects women to be inferior to men.

While she is still handcuffed to the bed, Jessie wakes up to find a stranger in the room with her. Because her traumatic experience at the cottage has allowed Jessie to remember the childhood experience that she had repressed and also because Jessie is beginning to understand how that one episode of sexual abuse had established the pattern for her life, Jessie sees the stranger as her father: "Before her, the figure's face . . . seemed to wrinkle upward in a grin. There was something horribly familiar about that grin, and Jessie felt the core of her sanity . . . begin to waver. 'Daddy?' she whispered. 'Daddy, is that you?'" (129).

It doesn't take Jessie long to realize that the stranger is a true monster rather than simply a weak man who takes advantage of the power that patriarchy gives to fathers: "It wasn't her father; compared with the evil and the lunacy she saw in the face of her visitor, she would have welcomed her father, even after twelve years in a cold coffin" (132). The stranger, Raymond Andrew Joubert, is a monster of the realistic and plausible variety: Murderer, grave robber, burglar, ghoul, and necrophile, he had killed and scalped his stepmother and her common law husband and had, like Jeffrey Dahmer, eaten parts of his victims. It is interesting that Joubert is also the victim of childhood sexual abuse (by his father, stepmother, and stepfather). Though the theme of child abuse in King's novels is definitely a subject for another paper, its presence here is one more indication of his preoccupation with ordinary human problems rather than with supernatural monsters.

Fortunately, Joubert leaves the cottage, allowing Jessie to escape before he returns. When she tells her story about an intruder at the cabin, the police refuse to believe her, a situation that Jessie also sees in gendered terms:

I suddenly understood that all of them—all the men investigating what had happened out at the lake—had made certain assumptions about how I'd handled the situation and why I'd done the things I'd done. Most of them worked in my favor . . . but there was still something both infuriating and a little spooky . . . that they drew most of their conclusions not from what I'd said or from any evidence they'd found in the house, but only from the fact that I'm a woman, and women can be expected to behave in certain predictable ways. (305)

Accustomed to seeing women as weak, the police don't believe that Jessie was capable of killing Gerald, and they see the entire situation she endured in terms of gendered stereotypes. By the end of the novel, Jessie has come a long way in terms of ridding herself of those same stereotypes and in both recognizing who she is and what social and personal forces had kept her from arriving at that view earlier. Even at this relatively late point in the novel, however, Jessie believes that she cannot make herself heard by men (hence the confessional letter to Ruth Neary and the plan to return to the woman therapist she had seen several years before). In his next novel, however, King creates a particularly strong voice, one that ultimately makes herself heard by the entire community.

Not only are Jessie and Dolores connected by King's experimentation with point of view, but their lives are connected in numerous other ways.[6] Key episodes in both stories happen during a total eclipse of the sun that takes place on July 20, 1963; both novels depict fathers who abuse their daughters sexually; both protagonists suffer from marriages to men who refuse to see them as human beings; both protagonists ultimately kill their husbands; and both protagonists refer directly to the other. For example, Jessie sees Dolores on the day of the eclipse, "a skinny woman in a housedress with her salt-and-pepper hair put up in a bun. . . . Who are you? Jessie asked the woman, but she was already gone" (167). Because the day of the eclipse is the day that turns Jessie into a victim for part of her life, it is perhaps even more important that she sees Dolores as role model, as someone who can take charge of her life, for the day of the eclipse is the day that Dolores rids herself and her family of the husband who had been abusing all of them: "And the knowledge that something sexual had happened between her husband and her daughter very likely would have caused her to stop thinking about leaving and actually do it" (178). Jessie, however, will not be able to liberate herself until almost thirty years later.

Dolores also sees Jessie on the day of the eclipse:

I took one of the reflector-boxes from the bag . . . and when I did I had the funniest thought: That little girl is doin this, too, I thought. The one who's sitting on her father's lap. . . . I saw somethin else, as well, somethin that made me think of Joe: her Daddy's hand was on her leg, way up high. Higher'n it ought to've been, maybe. (183–84)

The connection occurs again thirty years later, when Dolores glimpses the adult Jessie and realizes that she is in terrible trouble: "She's all grown up now, almost Selena's age, but she's in terrible trouble" (255). Responding to Jessie's anxiety, Dolores is herself in terrible trouble, for she hears Vera Donovan's scream announce the fall that will result in her death and in Dolores's being accused of murder. Such overt connections suggest that King continued to see the two novels together.

More important to the issue here, King's presentation of women, however, is that the time framework links the two women and suggests that King may have been thinking about the changes that women as a whole experienced during his life. In 1963 when the eclipse takes place, Jessie is a preadolescent girl while Dolores is a mature married woman, and the most recent wave of the feminist movement hasn't yet started.[7] In fact, the period immediately before would be discussed by Betty Friedan, whose immensely popular *The Feminine Mystique* also appeared in 1963.[8] By 1991 and 1992, when the novels conclude, women have made significant strides in their move for greater political power, economic equality, and personal autonomy. The female voices with which he had experimented in *Gerald's Game* and honed in *Dolores Claiborne* are also much more strong and assertive.

Both novels focus on women's issues, though obvious differences stem from the ages of the protagonists as well as from their different social classes and personal experiences. Although both women kill their husbands (Jessie accidentally and Dolores quite deliberately), the deaths enable them to escape bad marriages. The husbands, however, are quite different: Gerald Burlingame, the corporate lawyer, is an assertive man at home as well, but his physical domination of Jessie is obviously a fantasy, a game that requires handcuffs and other "props." On the other hand, Joe St. George is physically abusive, and Dolores admits that she tolerated his abuse for a while—just as her mother had tolerated similar physical abuse: "Later on I put up with it because I thought a man hittin his wife . . . was only another part of bein married—not a nice part, but then, cleanin toilets ain't a nice part of bein married, either" (59). Dolores, who has lived through the feminist movement of the 1960s, 1970s, and 1980s, indicates that ideas about the relationship between husbands and wives have changed since she was a young married woman: "Times were different back then . . . but that didn't mean I had to take it . . . just because I'd been enough of a goose to marry him in the first place. . . . and in the end I decided I wasn't going to take it from the likes of Joe St. George, or from the likes of any man" (71). Even before the Women's Liberation Movement of the 1960s and 1970s encouraged women to stand up for themselves, especially when they were involved in abusive relationships, Dolores has the courage to stand up to Joe and stop the hitting:

Of course I knew he had a yellow streak in him; I never would have dared hit him . . . in the first place I hadn't felt I had a pretty good chance of comin out on top. Besides, I realized somethin as I sat in that chair after he hit me, waitin for my kidneys to stop achin: if I didn't stand up to him then, I probably wouldn't *ever* stand up to him. So I did. (70)

Standing up to Joe, however, doesn't eliminate the power he has over her and their children, for King reveals that patriarchal institutions give legal power to husbands and fathers.

When Dolores learns that Joe had been abusing their daughter Selena, she plans to take the children and leave him; and she hopes to take the money she had saved to start a new life. At this point, she discovers that banks support the power that men have over their wives and children, for Joe had put all their money, including money she had saved for their children's education, in his name:

Because Joe was the man of the house. . . . And the reason nobody'd bothered to tell *me* was because I was just his wife. What the hell was *I* s'posed to know about money, except how to earn some down on my knees scrubbin floors n baseboards n toilet-bowls? If the man of the house decided to draw out all his kids' college money, he must have had a damned good reason, and even if he didn't, it didn't matter, because he was the man of the house, and in charge. His wife was just the little woman, and all *she* was in charge of was baseboards, toilet-bowls, and chicken dinners on Sunday afternoons. (126)

Dolores even has the courage to stand up to a representative of the bank, one of many patriarchal institutions that help husbands hold power over their wives, though her courage doesn't get the money back: "If it'd been the other way around," I says, "if *I'd* been the one with a story about how the passbooks was lost and ast for new ones, if *I'd* been the one who started drawin out what took eleven or twelve years to put in . . . wouldn't you have called *Joe*?" (125, King's ellipsis). The situation at the bank reveals that Dolores is trapped in a bad marriage from which there is seemingly no legal escape.

King, however, has Dolores take another route when she finally kills Joe by luring him to an abandoned well on their property on the day of the eclipse. As she confesses, she got the idea to murder Joe from Vera: "You just want to remember that what's yours is his and what's his is yours. If he had an accident, for instance, the money he's holding in his bank accounts would become yours. It's the law in this great country of ours" (147). It later becomes clear that the wealthy Vera had also killed *her* husband, though the motive in Vera's case seems to have been jealousy rather than a desire for independence:

But sometimes men, especially drinking men, *do* have accidents. They fall downstairs, they slip in bathtubs, and sometimes their brakes fail and they run their BMWs into oak trees when they are hurrying home from their mistresses' apartments in Arlington Heights. (149)

This brief observation suggests that troubled marriages and abusive relationships are not simply a problem of working class families like the Claibornes and the St. Georges. Bad marriages impact women of all classes.

In fact, much of *Dolores Claiborne* focuses on the similarities that join all women into a sisterhood that includes Vera, Dolores, Selena, Nancy, and Jessie. One of these is the power of love.[9] King has Dolores observe: "You mightn't think a hard-talking old bitch like me believes in love, but the truth is it's just about the only thing I *do* believe in" (56). Indeed, love is something that King seems to believe in as well.

According to Dolores, maternal love is especially strong: "That's the strongest love there is in the world. . . . There's no bitch on earth like a mother frightened for her kids" (298). Dolores observes that mother love was the main reason that she was compelled to kill Joe: "What I did was mostly done for Selena, not for the boys or because of the money her Dad tried to steal. It was mostly for Selena that I led him on to his death" (229). Dolores, however, indicates that mother love is not the only kind of love when she confesses her love for her former employer, a love that she notes would be difficult for men to understand:

So I guess I didn't *have* to go live with Vera, no. But by then her and me was used to each other. It's hard to explain to a man. I 'spect Nancy . . . understands. . . . I guess in the end I stuck with her because she didn't have nobody else; it was either me or the nursin home. (9–10)

It is clear that, by the end of Vera's life, Dolores has become both a friend, a sister, and a mother to the older woman, as she cleans up the incontinent Vera and soothes her when she is frightened.

If Dolores observes that men cannot possibly feel the love that women feel, she also repeatedly talks about something else that men won't understand, the work that links women of all classes and ages (Dolores, Vera, and Nancy) in sisterhood: "Hangin sheets in deep cold is a kind of torture. Nobody knows what it's like unless they've done it, and once you've done it, you never ever forget it. . . . it's all a part of woman's work no man knows about or wants to know about" (20–21). In addition to the drudgery of hanging sheets, the novel is full of the sights, sounds, and feel of women's work: the sound a vacuum cleaner makes, a sound that Dolores observes Nancy will recognize but the men won't, and the creative pleasures of knitting and sewing. For example, Dolores is most proud of the afghan that Vera had knit for her and still keeps it on her bed, another connection between the working class woman and her wealthy employer. What divides the women of this generation (the period immediately following World War II) is merely the amount of money that they have to spend, for *Dolores Claiborne* reveals that even wealthy women are not particularly empowered.

If patriarchal institutions keep women from gaining power over their own lives, however, women can achieve personal identity and a sense of self-worth. For example, Dolores regains her sense of personal identity when she takes back her maiden name six months after Joe's death: "I was damned if I was gonna drag St. George around behind me the rest of my life. . . . but I didn't get rid of *him* as easy as I got rid of his name" (252). In discussing her decision to use her maiden name, Dolores further suggests that she is thinking of a sisterhood of women when she identifies herself as "Patricia Claiborne's daughter Dolores" (29).

Obviously quite comfortable with her rather limited existence, Dolores has made peace with her own life. Given the possibilities available to her (because of her lack of education, her poverty, and the place where she lives), she is a strong character with a confident and self-assured voice. More troubling to me is her daughter Selena, a woman who has stepped outside the traditional roles established for women. Dolores paints a brief portrait of Selena as a professional woman, a writer:

She writes for all those magazines and still finds time to write me once a week . . . but they feel like duty-letters, just like the phone-calls twice a month feel like duty-calls. I think the calls n the chatty little notes are the way she pays her heart to be quiet about how she don't ever come back here, about how she's cut her ties with me. Yes, I think she paid, all right: I think the one who was the most blameless of all paid the most, and that she's payin still. She's forty-four years old, she's never married, she's too thin (I can see that in the pitchers she sometimes sends), and I think she drinks. (250, King's ellipsis)

Selena's drinking and her guilt suggest that the nontraditional woman is somehow less fulfilled than the traditional woman, the mother and caregiver who does everything for love.

As a reader, I am sometimes tempted to step back from King's novel and admit that the confident voice he gives Dolores and the fact that Selena remains silent do argue that King puts women into certain stereotypical roles and that he celebrates women who remain in well-defined traditional roles. Certainly he has Dolores, the traditional mother and caregiver, worrying about the fact that her daughter has chosen a different role. However, as a reader who has chosen to look carefully at his narration, I must also evaluate the narrative voice, including certain characteristics inherent in first-person narration.

First and foremost among these characteristics is the fact that first-person narrators are limited by time, space, and experiences. In other words, they cannot be other than who they are. Thus, King makes Dolores a strong and convincing character but not especially imaginative. Because she has not lived Selena's life, she doesn't have enough information to imagine what that life might be like. Therefore, even though she has witnessed at least three bad marriages firsthand (her own, Vera's, and her mother's), she is still a product of her own historical period, a period that saw marriage and motherhood as women's primary responsibilities.

Furthermore, because first-person narrators can be particularly convincing, King, like Charlotte Brontë (in *Jane Eyre* or *Villette*) or Twain (in *The Adventures of Huckleberry Finn*) is caught in the trap of his own making: He has created such a strong and convincing narrative voice that it is difficult to go beyond it, to suggest that other possibilities exist. For that reason, he must change narrative strategy in the last few pages and step outside his first-person narrator:

Dolores Claiborne will be shopping for one extra this week! She knew her son Joe . . . was coming home with his family . . . but now she says that her daughter, famous magazine scribe Selena St. George, will be making her first visit in over *twenty years!* Dolores says she feels "very blessed." When Nosy asked if they would be discussing Selena's latest "think-piece" in the *Atlantic Monthly,* Dolores would only smile and say, "We'll find lots to talk about, I'm sure." (305)

Thus, the conclusion suggests a real reconciliation of mother and daughter and also suggests that Selena may learn to accept herself as well, that she will no longer feel guilty for the decisions she has made or for the decisions that were made for her. Like Jessie Burlingame and her own mother, she may be able to accept herself. As Jessie writes to her friend Ruth, "survival is still an option. . . . sometimes it actually feels like victory" (331).

The conclusions to the two novels may not be as strong and affirmative as a modern feminist reader might want (for that matter, I often find myself wishing that George Eliot had created one woman character who was as strong and interesting as the novelist herself). Though I occasionally find myself wishing for something more, I also find myself applauding King for the risks he has taken in *Gerald's Game* and *Dolores Claiborne*. Not only do *Gerald's Game* and *Dolores Claiborne* move away from the horror genre that first made King a best-selling author, but they also move away from some of the magical solutions inherent in that form.

Whereas characters in King's early novels might use magic to overcome the monsters with which they were confronted, Jessie Burlingame and Dolores Claiborne are ultimately forced to rely only on themselves. Having chosen to write mainstream realistic fiction, King has accepted the limitations of that form. Having eliminated chance, fate, or supernatural intervention as well as the idealized characters found in romantic literature and chosen to use the conventions of realistic fiction, he must stick to natural causality, plausibility, and to characters whose lives seem authentic to readers. (He returns to magic and supernatural intervention in both *Insomnia* and *Rose Madder*, however.) Just as it is appropriate for Nancy Bannister to remain silent during the novel because both her job and her experiences demand it, it is appropriate that neither Jessie nor Dolores Claiborne step outside the believable characters that King has created or outside the current social environment for women that, though more congenial for women than the environment was in 1963, is still far from ideal. Thus, their courage—their willingness to take charge of their own lives and their willingness to tell the truth—are perfectly plausible kinds of heroism.

One would hope that King's own ability to tell the truth and his willingness to celebrate ordinary women are at least partially responsible for his continued popularity. At this point, I cannot answer for other readers though I confess that his shift in perspective and his ability to create strong, plausible women characters are two reasons that I continue to be interested in his novels. As King's character Dolores notes, times have changed, and the economic and political climates for women are better than they were in 1963 and before.

NOTES

1. Lisa Tuttle's observations are cited by Jancovich from the "Introduction" to *Skin of the Soul: New Horror Fiction by Women* (London: Women's Press, 1990, 5).

2. King, in addition to dedicating several novels to his wife, is often known to speak highly of her abilities as he did in the following interview with Michael J. Bandler of *Parents Magazine* (January 1982) in "The King of the Macabre at Home":

When Tabby isn't pecking out the plot of her second novel on her typewriter, she sits on several committees at the University of Maine, notably on issues involving women. Recently she was involved in preparing a directory of women in various professions in the locale. "I think someday she'd like to get a place on the board of trustees," her husband suggests. "She doesn't talk about it, but I think she's laying the ground for a career in public service of some sort—not politics, but something close to it, something between being a Tupperware lady and being a senator." (222)

3. Hanson, for example, argues that horror fiction seems to be designed for men and that "it offers a way of repassing through abjection and of distancing oneself once again

from the power of the mother. Horror fiction works in this sense as a kind of obverse of romance" (153).

4. For a discussion of Donna Trenton as a strong heroine, see my essay, "Donna Trenton, Stephen King's Modern American Heroine." See also Robin Wood who observes that "*Cujo* has a particular relevance to women's concerns: it is the one King novel to center on an adult woman, and it combines very interestingly certain thematic concerns of the woman's melodrama (sexuality and the family, mother love, adultery, transgression, and punishment) with those of the horror film ('normality' threatened by 'the monster')" (303–4). There are other connections between the two novels. Both women see their lives in terms of literary conventions. For example, Donna contrasts herself to the heroines of romance and realizes that no knight is coming to save her. Jessie, on the other hand, keeps referring to her experience at the lake house as real life. In some ways, Jessie is a more realistic heroine, for she comes to accept relatively early that no one else will be responsible for her.

5. There is no place in this chapter for a discussion of the fact that childhood sexual abuse often triggers schizophrenia, including the presence of multiple personalities. Nonetheless, King's use of voices in Jessie's head and the ultimate dominance of her own articulate voice seems connected to a phenomenon often noted in psychiatric discussions.

6. Part of the reason for these connections may come from King's experience as a novelist. Although he was already committed to write *Dolores Claiborne*, the idea for *Gerald's Game* came to him when he fell asleep on an airplane (told to interviewer W. C. Stroby and recorded by Beahm in *The Stephen King Story*, 244).

7. In many ways 1963 is a pivotal year for the feminist movement, as Sara M. Evans observes in *Born for Liberty: A History of Women in America*: It was the year that saw the publication of the final report of the Presidential Commission on the Status of Women, a report that documented in great detail "problems of discrimination in employment, unequal pay, lack of social services such as child care, and continuing legal inequality. Though the committee paid careful obeisance to the centrality of women's traditional roles, it also spelled out the realities of inequality" (275).

8. That King is interested in the feminist movement should come as no surprise, for other overtly political novels reveal his interest in American politics: *The Stand*, for example, begins when a virus escapes from a secret government depository and destroys most of the population of the United States, and the rest of the novel examines what happens when the survivors attempt to reorganize; *The Dead Zone* features a right-wing candidate for the Presidency and John Smith's decision to prevent his further campaigning; *Firestarter*, like *The Stand*, also looks at the government's connection with scientific research; volumes 2 and 3 of *The Dark Tower* series feature an African-American woman who had been active in the civil rights movement as well as a character whose brother had been psychologically damaged by his experiences in Vietnam; and *The Tommyknockers* looks at public utilities and their relationship with government. Although these novels are the most obvious examples of King's interest in politics, one might observe that most of his novels look at human beings as social and political animals.

9. Love is important in most of King's novels, and the characters who manage to overcome the monsters are generally those who are capable of unselfish love. For example, Dick Hallorann in *The Shining* returns to the Overlook Hotel when he hears Danny Torrance's call in his mind. Jim Gardener in *The Tommyknockers* saves the world

by piloting the spaceship away from the earth. Even in *Pet Sematary*, where parental love is clearly perverted and selfish, it is the single most important force in the novel.

WORKS CITED

Beahm, George. *The Stephen King Story*. Kansas City: Andrews and McMeel, 1992.

Bleiler, E. F. "Stephen King." *Supernatural Fiction Writers: British Writers of the Interbellum Period*, Vol. VIII. Edited by E. F. Bleiler, Vol. 2: A. E. Coppard to Roger Zelazny. New York: Scribner's, 1985.

Burns, Gail E., and Melinda Kanner. "Women, Danger, and Death: The Perversion of The Female Principle in Stephen King's Fiction." *Sexual Politics and Popular Culture*. Edited by Diane Raymond. Bowling Green: Bowling Green State University Popular Press, 1990, 158–72.

Evans, Sara M. *Born for Liberty: A History of Women in America*. New York: Macmillan, 1989.

Hanson, Clare. "Stephen King: Powers of Horror." *American Horror Fiction: From Brockden Brown to Stephen King*. Edited by Brian Docherty. New York: St. Martin's, 1990, 135–54.

Jancovich, Mark. *Horror*. London: Batsford, 1992.

King, Stephen. *Danse Macabre*. New York: Everest, 1981.

——. *Dolores Claiborne*. New York: Viking, 1993.

——. *Gerald's Game*. New York: Viking, 1992.

Magistrale, Tony. *The Moral Voyages of Stephen King*. Mercer Island: Starmont, 1989.

Martin, Wallace. *Recent Theories of Narrative*. New York: Cornell, 1986.

Senf, Carol. "Donna Trenton, Stephen King's Modern American Heroine." *Heroines of Popular Culture*. Edited by Pat Browne. Bowling Green: Bowling Green State University Popular Press, 1987, 91–100.

Spignesi, Stephen. *The Complete Stephen King Encyclopedia*: *The Definitive Guide to the Works of America's Master of Horror*. Chicago: Contemporary Books, 1991.

Wood, Robin. "Cat and Dog: Lewis Teague's Stephen King Movies." *Gender, Language, and Myth: Essays on Popular Narrative*. Edited by Glenwood Irons. Toronto: University of Toronto Press, 1992, 303–18.

Yarbro, Chelsea Quinn. "Cinderella's Revenge—Twists on Fairy Tale and Mythic Themes in the Work of Stephen King." *Fear Itself: The Horror Fiction of Stephen King*. Edited by Tim Underwood and Chuck Miller. New York: Signet, 1982, 67–71.

IV

Evil and Female Essence

8

"OH DEAR JESUS IT IS FEMALE":
Monster as Mother/Mother as Monster in Stephen King's *It*

Linda Anderson

Stephen King has been quoted as saying that in *It* he was attempting to create a monster that would be a synthesis of all of the great monsters of American popular culture: "[I]t's like a monster rally—everything is in this book, every monster you could think of" (Winter, 184). King scholars differ as to the literary value of this "monster rally": Michael Collings declares *It* a "masterpiece" (*Phenomenon*, 13), and Burton Hatlen likes it "a lot," although finding it "imperfect in certain ways" (146); Don Herron's assessment is scathing (216–17). Clearly, what King aimed to create in *It*—and in It—was what Georgie Denbrough imagines (rather exceptionally for a six-year-old) as "the apotheosis of all monsters" (*It*, 7). Whether King succeeded in his attempt must ultimately depend on each reader's taste, but it is certainly the case that King's monster, even if not exalted to divine rank, is unusual.

Instead of appearing in a single, gruesome, terrifying form, It manifests Itself as many different avatars. Its incarnations include such classic monsters as the Mummy, the Creature from the Black Lagoon, Dracula, a teenaged werewolf, and Frankenstein's monster. Less traditionally, It appears as a leprous hobo, Paul Bunyan, and Buddy Holly. It can possess the bodies of living people, as it does that of Beverly Marsh's father, and It can take the form of dead acquaintances of the other characters, such as Belch Huggins and Victor Criss. Its most frequent avatar, however, is Pennywise the Dancing Clown. One common element of nearly all of Its manifestations is that they are explicitly defined as male.[1] Though King as narrator is careful to refer to It Itself as gender-neutral, his characters sometimes refer to the avatars as male. On more than one occasion, It even defines Itself as male, saying that Its name is Bob Gray, or even Mr. Bob Gray. Ultimately, however, and this is presented as the ultimate of Its horrors, It is discovered to be female and pregnant—not It at all, but She and Mother.

Eventually, of course, It is defeated, first and temporarily in 1958 by children, and finally in 1985 by adults (themselves unable to have children) who are able to "become children" again. The principal battle of the book is between a group of six boys/men (and one token girl/woman) and a (literally) devouring mother-figure who is made more monstrous because, as the book makes clear, She does not kill merely for food or to support Her young: Her creative and bleakly humorous use of children's popular culture suggests that She enjoys terrorizing, mutilating, killing, and devouring children, primarily male children, whose only rational response is to destroy Her. The female character who is part of the victorious group (known as "the Losers") is ostensibly established as a virtuous mother-figure, in contrast not only to It but also to the novel's real human mothers. However, her part in the defeat of the monster is problematic. Only the group's boy-men, with advice and limited help from their fathers, father-figures, and other male characters, can defeat the monstrous mother. Despite all of the apparent male violence—human and inhuman—throughout the novel, *It* is ultimately about resolving pre-Oedipal conflict, the attempt to erase the "primary experience" of the link between mother and child and to "release the hold of the *maternal* entity" through male language (Irigaray, 14; Kristeva, 13).[2]

Whether or not readers agree that the revelation of It as She and Mother constitutes the ultimate horror, those familiar with King's other novels and stories should not be surprised at encountering a monstrous mother because such figures are common enough in his works to constitute a motif.[3] Even readers not familiar with King's other works should not be too surprised at the revelation of It as the monstrous mother because the idea of mothers as monstrous is established well before the book's climax. Human mothers in *It* are not entirely unsympathetic: Many of them are poor, often working in hard, sometimes hazardous, dead-end jobs, and some of them are struggling to raise children by themselves (among the Losers, only Beverly has a father who is a dominant figure). Nevertheless, *It* is largely written from a child's viewpoint, and as mothers these women are seldom more than ineffectual at best and often fail to rise even to that depressed and depressing level.

The best mother in the novel is probably Jessica Hanlon, but even she is represented as somewhat repressive, particularly when compared to Mike's father, Will.[4] Jessica is the parent who keeps Mike at his chores, while Will is the one who tells her a boy needs time to play. Jessica is the parent who enforces discipline, to such an extent that even Will avoids her anger. Jessica tries to keep Will from giving Mike information that he needs to combat the monster. Jessica is somewhat humorless: When Mike and his father were having "great fun" watching *Rodan* on TV, she "popped her head in and told them to hush up before they gave her a headache with the noise" (275). Toward the end of the book, It reveals that the reason Mike sees It as a monstrous bird is that the infant Mike was attacked in his cradle by a crow when his mother left him in the yard while she was hanging out laundry. Although Jessica Hanlon is a loving mother, she is clearly represented as stricter and less fun than her husband, although still unable to protect her son, or even, at times, to comprehend the dangers of the world he lives in.

Richie Tozier's is the only other family in the book that is other than gravely dysfunctional. (King offers almost no information about Stan Uris's family.) Maggie Tozier, however, again in contrast to her husband, is represented as being no fun. She reproves her husband for "vulgarity," refers to Richie's beloved horror movies as "awful junk," and "like Bill Denbrough's mother" is "death on rock and roll" and is "traumatized" by seeing Jerry Lee Lewis on TV.[5] She becomes "furious" with Richie when his glasses are broken by a bully (662). She is described as being likely to "have a bird" if she finds out that Richie has been riding double on Bill's bike, but she is completely unaware that her son is plotting with Bill to kill It and is shown as cheerfully pouring out iced tea for the boys as they plot their dangerous mission (363). Shortly after this episode, we hear her thoughts about the boys:

I don't understand either of them, she thought. *Where they go, what they do, what they want . . . or what will become of them. Sometimes, oh sometimes their eyes are wild, and sometimes I'm afraid for them and sometimes I'm afraid of them. . . .* A pretty little girl she could have understood. (King's ellipses, 366)

Ben Hanscom's mother is affectionate and supportive. She is a single mother and works hard to raise her son, although even that virtue causes Ben anguish, as he worries about what her job in a textile mill is doing to her health. She is "a hard woman," who usually insists on having her own way, and Ben is rarely capable of standing up to her (185–86). She knows little about her son's life, particularly about his friendlessness early in the book, and he feels unable to talk to her about this or his other worries. Although Ben loves her, he doesn't trust her. When he is pursued by It, he gets home to find that his mother, exhausted from work, "had not, in truth, much missed him" (215), and after being knifed by the murderous Henry Bowers, he thinks of his mother not as a comforter or protector but as someone who is "going to give him sixteen different flavors of holy old hell" or put him in the emergency room for ruining his clothes (216). Worst of all, she stuffs him with food, even after he is obviously grossly obese, and it isn't until Ben is in high school—and then only after having "a hell of a fight" with her—that he is able to lose weight, and then only with her fighting him every step of the way. His weight, Ben suggests, was "a kind of security thing with her" (496).

And these are the good mothers.

The remainder of the mothers in *It* are almost worse than the title character. Devastated by their younger son's death, both of Bill's parents withdraw into themselves, leaving Bill feeling that they blame him for George's death and no longer love him, but Bill's mother is the parent represented as least functional, most repressive, and most to blame for the failure of both parents. She is the parent who reproves the boys for making noise and who refuses to allow Bill to have a rifle. She is the parent whom Bill wants to please, but whom he never can please. And, like Maggie Tozier, she is the parent represented as being confused and frightened by children, including her own son.

Eddie Kaspbrak's mother is the most thoroughly described and in many ways the most monstrous in *It*. She is, in fact, described as "something nearly monstrous"—because she weighs 406 pounds—as well as "crazy" at the time of her death (90, 95). She is racist, anti-Semitic, anti-Irish, and homophobic, hugely fat, stupid, frightened, but also "implacable" (88). Eddie "in a sense, [marries] his mother," and his mother is obviously the cause of Eddie's marrying her epigone, Myra (85). Eddie's mother consciously uses tears as a weapon, is responsible for Eddie's psychosomatic asthma, and turns him into a lifelong hypochondriac. When Eddie is hurt or in danger or contemplating doing something as harmless as playing baseball, his principal concern is not his own feelings but his mother's reaction—always conceived of as strongly negative. Even after his mother is dead, he can still hear her voice inside his head, warning him of imaginary perils. She is terrified that he will grow up, move away, and get married, thus leaving her alone, and when he shows signs of independence, she becomes afraid of him. Sonia Kaspbrak is explicitly associated with It in several ways. When she tries to drive all of Eddie's friends away, Eddie sees It capering with glee and finally pretending to kiss Sonia's cheek. When Eddie sees her most clearly, he associates her with the incarnation of It that has frightened him most: Her eyes, he realizes, are "almost predatory, like the eyes of the leper that had crawled out of the basement at 29 Neibolt Street" (789–90). Horrified at his own realization, he succeeds only in further extending the comparison when he tries to tell another character, "*She's not the leper, please don't think that, she's only eating me because she loves me*" (790). Finally, It even takes the shape of his mother.

In addition to being manipulative, oppressive, ignorant, and afraid of their children, the human mothers in *It* all demonstrate a more immediate shortcoming: They are unable to protect their children. Occasionally, mothers in the book are actually the ones to inflict violence, intentionally or not: Tom Rogan's mother, a single parent with four small children, often beats young Tom with a stick, thereby turning him into a wife-beater. An unnamed mother accidentally drops her baby into the Derry Standpipe, where it drowns.[6] Sometimes, children become victims of It when their mothers (never, it seems, their fathers) fail to watch them carefully enough. Three-year-old Matthew Clements is taken when his mother briefly leaves him outside alone to attend to her laundry. Five-year-old Laurie Ann Winterbarger is in her mother's sole custody when she disappears. Patrick Hockstetter's parents both fail to realize that their five-year-old son is a psychopath, but it is his mother who is home asleep when Patrick murders his infant brother Avery. More commonly, though, the failure to protect children is due to a lack of understanding, although even this is represented as the mothers' fault because the children, reasonably, given the mothers they have, do not feel that they can talk to their mothers.[7] The mothers are not, for the most part, uncaring: They try to protect their children against falling off bicycles, contracting contagious diseases, or becoming victims of what they assume to be a sex maniac who preys on Derry's children. They fail, however, to understand not only the threat posed to their children by It but even the more obvious dangers of schoolyard bullies and domestic violence (at least some of which dangers are inspired by It).

Worse than the lack of understanding, however, is the fact that mothers in *It* fail to protect their children against domestic violence by men. Young Henry Bowers is driven insane largely by having to live with his crazy and abusive father, whose wife leaves him after he nearly beats her to death. Why she abandons their son to be abused by Butch Bowers is not explored. On occasion, mothers even protect abusive and violent men rather than their own children. Beverly Marsh's mother, like so many others in the book, is loving and concerned, but too busy with her job and her husband to be involved in her daughter's life or even to be aware of Beverly's lack of friends. More important, she seems to be unaware that Beverly's father is physically abusing their daughter, or, if she is aware, unwilling or unable to do anything about it. The mother of four-year-old Dorsey and ten-year-old Eddie Corcoran allows her husband, the boys' stepfather, to physically abuse both of her sons and defends him even after he kills Dorsey and Eddie disappears. She subsequently has Eddie, one of Its victims, declared legally dead so that she can "enter into possession of Edward Corcoran's savings account," which consists of $16.00 (255).

The inability or unwillingness of mothers to protect their children is particularly important because It preys primarily upon children, mostly boys. Although there are a few mass killings that must have involved girls—the disappearance of approximately 340 people in 1741 (153) and the explosion of the Kitchener Ironworks during an Easter egg hunt arranged for the town's children (157)—only a handful of Its more than twenty named or described child-victims are girls. When It chooses older victims, they are almost invariably men; although adult women sometimes die when It stages a mass killing—the fire at the Black Spot (463–69), the massacre of the Bradley gang (641–55)—the death toll is always much higher among men than women, and there are some mass killings in which the victims are exclusively men—the 1879 lumber-camp slaughter (157), the mass murder at the Silver Dollar in 1905 (883–93). Often, in fact, these mass incidents seem to occur in places where a largely or exclusively male population would be expected—an army base, a lumber camp, a disreputable saloon. Furthermore, King suggests that knowledge about It drives several men to suicide (including Stan Uris, Branson Buddinger, and Richard Macklin); women, apparently, either lack such insight or fail to be so horrified that death seems preferable to life with such terrible knowledge. In fact, there is no evidence that It ever singles out a female character over the age of eighteen for Its attentions. Adult women seem almost immune to Its attacks, except as incidental victims. The maternal monster rarely preys on Derry's monstrous mothers.[8] As Georgie Denbrough presciently imagines, It is "a creature which would eat anything but which [is] especially hungry for boymeat" (7).

The fact that It eats Its victims is central to the horror It evokes. Again, the eating seems confined almost exclusively to young male victims. Although girls, women, and adult men are killed by It, there is rarely a suggestion that they are devoured.[9] Its appetite is one of Its two defining characteristics, eating and sleeping: An alien life form that arrived "from a place much farther away than another star or another galaxy," It likes Earth because the "*quality of imagination made the food very rich. . . . Upon this rich food It existed in a simple cycle of waking to eat and sleeping to dream*" (758, 1007). It is described as a "homicidal endless formless hungry being" (1054), and describes Itself to Bill as "*the Eater of Worlds*" (1052). Bill comes to understand that It is a being that "only ate" (1054). When It becomes fearful of the Losers, Its response is defined in terms of eating: "*It hated the fear, would have turned on it and eaten it if It could have*" (1015).[10]

But it is not merely the physical fact of being devoured by It that is terrifying. More horrific is the suggestion that children who are killed and eaten by It continue, in some sense, to live not only with It but within It. Betty Ripsom's mother tells her husband that she heard "'a whole slew of voices, all of them babblin together' speaking from the drain of her kitchen sink: 'Who the hell are you?' she calls. 'What's your name?' And all these voices answered back, she said—grunts and babbles and howls and yips, screams and laughin, don't you know. And she said they were sayin what the possessed man said to Jesus: 'Our name is Legion,' they said" (154). Mr. Ripsom goes on to tell Mike that he himself later heard his daughter's voice "screamin and laughin down there in the pipes" (155). That these voices and Its repeated assertions that Its victims all "float" down where It dwells are not merely illusions or lies is strongly suggested during the Losers' first battle with It, when It tells Bill, "*wait for the deadlights! you'll look and you'll go mad . . . but you'll live . . . and live . . . and live . . . inside them . . . inside Me*" (King's ellipses, 1055). During his ordeal, Bill becomes confused as to whether "It wanted to eat little kids . . . or suck them in, or whatever It did" (1055). The answer, apparently, is that It both eats little kids and sucks them in. They are eaten but somehow remain alive within the monstrous mother.[11] As Jungian myth-scholar Erich Neumann explains,

The mysteries of death as mysteries of the Terrible Mother are based on her devouring-ensnaring function, in which she draws the life of the individual back into herself. Here the womb becomes a devouring maw and the conceptual symbols of diminution, rending, hacking to pieces, and annihilation, of rot and decay, have here their place. (71–72)

It is not until the end of the book (the ends of both battles with It being narrated in alternating sections) that Its true identity as female and mother is revealed. Whether or not this revelation shocks the reader, it certainly has a profound effect on the two characters who first (in terms of the book's somewhat skewed chronology) make the discovery. Tom Rogan drops *"dead of shock . . . his eyes filling with the blood that had squirted out of his brain in a dozen places"* (1016). Audra Denbrough puts *"out one powerful, horrified thought—OH DEAR JESUS IT IS FEMALE,"* before *"her mind [is] utterly destroyed by her first sight of It as It really [is]"* (1016, 1015). Though it is possible that we are supposed to believe that these characters' reactions are provoked by Its spider-avatar, that appearance had no such effect on the children who saw Its "true" form during the 1958 battle. Granted that the children know, as Tom and Audra do not, that they are about to face a monster, and granted that King emphasizes the toughness of children's minds, the power of the spider-avatar is later denigrated by the boy Bill, who thinks that "once seen, Its physical form was not so bad and Its most potent weapon was taken away from It. They all had, after all, seen spiders before. They were alien and somehow crawlingly dreadful. . . . But a spider was, after all, only a spider" (1074–75). Audra's last thought, in particular, suggests that Its femaleness, not Its arachnid form, is what causes death and madness.[12]

How that femaleness is recognized (not, one might imagine, a recognition easy to arrive at with regard to a bug, however large) is suggested when the Losers confront It in the final battle, although in a passage that raises at least as many questions as it answers:

Its belly bulged grotesquely, almost dragging on the floor as It moved. . . .
   That's Its egg-sac, Ben thought, and his mind seemed to shriek at the implication. *Whatever It is beyond what we see, this representation is at least symbolically correct: It's female, and It's pregnant. . . . It was pregnant then and none of us knew except Stan, oh Jesus Christ YES, it was Stan,* Stan, *not Mike,* Stan *who understood,* Stan *who told us. . . . That's why we had to come back, no matter what, because It is female, It's pregnant with some unimaginable spawn . . . and Its time has drawn close.* (King's ellipses, 1048–49)

Its swollen belly identifies It as pregnant, and therefore female, and the "grotesque" bulging of Its belly links It with the monstrously fat, devouring mother Sonia Kaspbrak.[13] The realization that It is pregnant adds to Ben's horror, and because he and his friends are in immediate danger of death and worse than death, only a powerful horror could increase his fear. Unfortunately, Ben fails to specify what Stan told the rest of the Losers during or after the first battle with It, since the book provides no other evidence that Stan realizes that It is female and pregnant. Richie does suggest that It is female during the first attack, but this suggestion puzzles Ben: *"Her?* Ben thought stupidly. Her, *did he say?"* (1051). Ben's befuddlement is understandable, as there is no indication of how Richie comes to recognize Its gender, although this recognition is immediately echoed by Bill, who begins referring to It as *"bitch"* (1052). Though there is no clue given as to how they do so, the boys recognize the undisguised It as She and Mother and that recognition makes It far more horrible than Its earlier assumed male or gender-neutral avatars.

In contrast to It and the human mothers of the book, one female character is represented as a positive maternal figure, even though she has no children. Late in the novel, after the first battle with It, Beverly invites each of her six comrades to have sex with her, which all of them do, one after the other. Some critics find this episode to be both an effective narrative device and a breakthrough for King, suggesting that the scene not only presents a positive female and maternal presence in the novel but also operates as a rite of passage, with an emotional rather than physical emphasis.[14] Clearly, King is trying to establish Beverly as a positive maternal figure[15]—Eddie, the first of the boys to have sex with Beverly *"comes to her . . . the way he would have come to his mother only three or four years ago, to be comforted"* (1080).

Nevertheless, though tastes, of course, will differ, there is no question that many readers are likely to find this episode disturbing or absurd or both. Although King is careful to establish the sex scene as Beverly's idea, it is irresistibly reminiscent of gang-rape. The children have faced their greatest fears, and ultimately death, together to defeat It, albeit only temporarily. Sexual intercourse seems unlikely to deepen the emotional bond they have already forged or make them more mature, even if maturity were a fate to be wished for in Derry, a place in which all of the adults are violent, corrupt, ignorant, or ineffectual.

Because of the structure of the group, each of the boys has sex individually with Beverly, who becomes less a character than a link between the boys, all of whom are saved by "doing it" with the same girl. If the physical aspect were not paramount, one might be tempted to suggest that a stronger "link" might be forged by group members having sex with each other regardless of gender, but this would violate the book's heterosexual-male perspective. The role of female characters is to be there for male characters, as either mother-enemy or mother-comforter. From this heterosexual-male perspective, having (as they think) killed mother, the male characters are now able to have sex with mother; in both instances, of course, there is displacement: The mother is not the *real* mother. Although this episode is intended to contrast Beverly as good mother with It and the book's other monstrous maternal figures, the contrast leads to the conclusion that the bad mother devours boys and therefore must be destroyed, to be replaced by the good mother, who encourages boys to have sex with her and thus become "normal" men.

Even if accepted as "good mother," Beverly is a severely limited character. It is defeated by the male members of the Losers' Club, all of whom take an active part in the 1958 battle. The four men who are present for the 1985 battle are also active in destroying It and Its offspring. Beverly, on the other hand, has to be rescued from Its clutches by Ben in the first battle and in both battles tries to prevent Bill from confronting It. Like the other human mothers in the book, she acts as an inhibiting force in the necessary male battle against the monstrous mother. In the earlier struggle, she heroically interposes herself between Bill and the monster, but she seems unable to attack It in Its final, feminine form, and her part in both battles is limited to encouraging and comforting her male companions. Her apparent inability to engage with It is not merely physical because the most important aspects of these fights are intellectual and imaginative. Bill, Richie, Stan, and Eddie all use their knowledge of It and their imaginations to hurt the monster. Although there seems to be no reason why Beverly could not do the same, she does not do so. Her only significant contribution occurs after the first battle, and it consists of offering sex and comfort. The necessary conclusion is that even the ideal girl/woman/mother is unable to be of much help in defeating the monstrous mother.

That killing the monstrous mother is a male task is also emphasized by the fact that the Losers defeat It with the advice and help of male characters, often fathers or father-figures. As Tony Magistrale has pointed out, "Mike's father and [male, army] friends unconsciously serve as models of inspiration for Mike and his friends" (*Moral Voyages*, 111). In addition to what he learns from his father, Mike gets his information about the history of Derry and the cycle of Its depredations from male authorities, mostly elderly men, but occasionally male children. (One of Mike's informants, Norbert Keene, suggests that Mike could get information about the massacre of the Bradley gang from Charlotte Littlefield, as well as five men he names, but there is no evidence that Mike avails himself of this opportunity.) Stan's father teaches him about birds, knowledge that he uses to ward off Its attacks on both himself and the group. Bill's father advises him that Derry's sewers are dangerous and (unwittingly) provides the workshop in which the children make the silver slugs with which they attack It on Neibolt Street. Bill also gets some good advice from a male child—"You can't be careful on a skateboard, man" (1126).

No one gets (or seeks) useful advice about It (or much else) from women or girls. Mothers, in fact, seek to prevent their children from getting information and tools they need to defeat It: Mike's mother doesn't want him to hear about the Black Spot, Richie's mother discourages him from learning about rock music and horror movies, and Bill's mother refuses to let him have a rifle. More significantly, the Turtle—Its most obvious opposite, if not exactly adversary, because the Turtle seems too passive to function in that capacity—is identified as male and is crucially important, because he not only encourages and advises Bill in his first battle with It, but also, at least in Mike's estimation, is responsible for awakening Mike to the possibility of Its return. The Turtle is large, old, kind, and more powerful than It, but, despite his apparent good intentions, cannot or will not act directly against the mother-monster: "*I take no stand in these matters,*" the Turtle tells Bill when the boy begs for help against the monstrous mother (1053). Clearly, however, the Turtle is a father-figure, because he repeatedly refers to Bill as "son" (1053, 1054, 1056, 1057, and so on).[16]

In a further suggestion that the boy-men attacking It must assume the role of the adult male who is, however, more capable than the book's inadequate fathers, King describes how Bill successfully recites his magic formula: "Dropping his voice a full register, making it not his own (making it, in fact, his father's voice)" (1056).[17] Finally, It is defeated only after Bill and Richie are able to bite into Its tongue, an attribute that "always possesses a phallic character" (Neumann, 169).

The book ends on a note of comparative happiness. Although Stan and Eddie have died in the attempt, the surviving adult males have "killed the bitch" (1098). Stan's and Eddie's deaths are themselves symbolic because Stan, unable to face a second battle with the monstrous mother, commits suicide in a kind of return to the womb, locking himself in his bathroom, removing his clothes, and cutting his wrists to bleed to death while sitting in a tub of water. Eddie, who does face the second battle, dies when It bites off his arm, a symbolic castration (in the sense that Freud uses that term to mean amputation of the penis) by the *vagina dentata*.[18] The word continually applied to the monster throughout both battles neatly represents the power gained by correctly naming the enemy, who is discovered to be not neutral, but female—not IT, but bITch. The monstrous mother, which could not be killed by boys, even though they recognized her as the source of evil in their world, is destroyed by men. The *"fucking BITCH"* (1049), who threatened to seduce and devour male children is no longer a danger. Furthermore, although the Losers are only thirty-eight at the time of the last battle, it seems that none of them still has surviving parents, or at least not parents worth mentioning. Thus, not only It, but apparently all of the real (inadequate or monstrous) mothers are dead as well. The ending suggests that, having defeated the monstrous mother, the surviving protagonists will now repress the memories of their titanic struggle and get on with their lives as adults.

In her analysis of *Carrie*, *The Shining*, and *Misery* in light of theorist Julia Kristeva's discussion of abjection, Clare Hanson concludes that "Horror fiction . . . seems to be designed to work for the masculine subject as an exorcism: It offers a way of repassing through abjection and of distancing oneself once again from the power of the mother" (153). From this perspective, *It* clearly does function as King's *"magnum opus"* (Winter, 183), not only providing the "gross-out" elements for which his work is notorious but also associating them with the huge, seductive, devouring mother as the ultimate horror. Despite critics' suggestions that It and Beverly Marsh are the novel's only significant female characters, it is clear that It is an objectification of the book's many monstrous mothers, who are powerful but un-nurturing.[19] For the boys in the book to survive, as many do not, to prevent themselves from being engulfed and devoured, and to become men (heterosexual and potentially fathers themselves), they must kill the monster who stands for all of their monstrous mothers, a task in which they can expect only limited help—advice and tools from their fathers and encouragement and sex from a young female figure. The devouring bITch-mother can only be destroyed by masculine force, knowledge, and language in an exorcism of pre-Oedipal anxiety.

NOTES

Thanks are due to Terri Whaling for her invaluable help with this chapter.

1. It does occasionally appear as female, briefly as the dead Greta Bowie and more significantly as "Mrs. Kersh" who turns into a witch. It also sometimes appears in nongendered incarnations, such as "the Crawling Eye," and as animals such as a giant bird, the shark from *Jaws*, and a gigantic Doberman Pinscher in a clown suit.

2. Many of the ideas underlying this chapter rely on the work of such literary theorists as Luce Irigaray and Julia Kristeva, who have identified a variety of cultural constructions as stemming from male anxiety about maternal power, and, in particular, the maternal body. For a more strictly psychoanalytic discussion of such issues, see Chodorow (106) and Horney.

3. Mothers who are religious fanatics, treacherous toward their sons, or in other ways monstrous appear in *Carrie*, *The Dead Zone*, *The Running Man*, and *Rage*, the last of which even provides a foreshadowing of *Its* mother-as-collection-of-monsters in a description of Carol Granger's mother. The mother in *The Shining* allows her son to be abused by his father, and mothers in *Cujo*, *The Stand*, *Pet Sematary*, and "The Boogeyman" are unable to save their children's lives. See Collings, *Stephen King as Richard Bachman* (26) and Pharr (26–27). For a contrasting view, see Magistrale, *Moral Voyages* (95–103). On monstrous women in *It*, see Collings, *Phenomenon* (21). On monstrous women in King's other works, see Collings, *Phenomenon* (108) and *Facets* (75); Hanson; Magistrale, *Landscape* (70); and Winter (53).

Fathers in King's works, of course, are also frequently abusive or ineffectual: See Collings, *Stephen King as Richard Bachman* (25–26 and 134) and Magistrale, *Landscape* (72). On dysfunctional families in *It*, see Davis (95). On the failure of parents and other adults in *It* to protect their children, see Magistrale, *Landscape* (111–13). On inadequate and abusive parents in King's other works, see Collings, *Facets* (74), *Phenomenon* (16), and *Stephen King as Richard Bachman* (16–17, 25, and 62–63); Collings and Engebretson (89); Heldreth (65–66); Magistrale, *Landscape* (92); and Newhouse (51–55).

4. One of the few good mother-figures in King's works is "Mother" Abagail of *The Stand*, but her virtue may have more to do with her race than with her gender or maternal qualities because King himself has described her, along with Dick Hallorann (who plays a major role in *The Shining* and a small role in *It*), as "cardboard caricatures of superblack heroes, viewed through rose-tinted glasses of white-liberal guilt" (Underwood and Miller, 47). This suggests that the fact that the Hanlons are African-American may have something to do with the fact that they are the happiest and most loving family in *It*, despite their comparative poverty.

5. That Maggie Tozier should so detest rock and roll is particularly ironic because her son grows up to become a famous disc jockey (343, 582, 720).

6. This is Eddie Kaspbrak's version. Ben says that he "had heard that it was actually a kid, a little girl of about three" (417).

7. A suggestion of how ignorant mothers in *It* typically are about their children's lives occurs in the case of sixteen-year-old Cheryl Lamonica, unusual among Its victims not only because she's female, but because she is a mother, having borne a daughter at thirteen. The authorities originally assume that Cheryl is the victim of one of her many boyfriends: "'They were nice boys, most of them,' Cheryl's mother said. One of the 'nice boys' had been a forty-year-old Air Force colonel with a wife and three children in New Mexico. Another was currently serving time in Shawshank for armed robbery" (180).

8. It claims to have killed Barbara Starrett, a librarian who was "fifty-eight or -nine" at the time of her death (548). Because, however, It makes this claim in the course of terrorizing Ben, who was fond of Mrs. Starrett, and because she reportedly died of a stroke, rather than being killed by violence, like the rest of Its victims (many of whom are also mutilated and entirely or partially eaten), the truth of this claim may be doubted. As Bill comes to understand late in the book, "*much of Its talk is nothing but a bluff, a big shuck-and-jive*" (1056).

9. Betty Ripsom is said to have been "ripped wide open" and "mutilated" (155, 180) and both she and "the Albrecht girl" are mentioned, along with three young male victims, when Mike is thinking about the word "haunt" as meaning "a feeding place for animals" (159). Mike recalls that "the bodies of the children that were found back then and now weren't sexually molested, not even precisely mutilated, but partially eaten" (702), but there is no explicit description of It actually eating Her female victims, although It is apparently preparing to eat Audra Denbrough and the adult Losers. It is described as having "*fed on [only] a few of the older ones over the years*" (1016).

10. Bosky sees It as having "five basic faces: eating, excreting, sex (including procreation), fighting or killing, and dying. These are, in other words, all of the universal activities of the animal body, except for sleeping and being born. In a sense, It *is* the body, a devilish body that tempts us with its appetites and betrays us into death" (147). In fact, however, excreting is never mentioned with regard to It, nor is sex—how It can have become pregnant is a question the novel does not invite us to ask. Until the end of the book, It is unaware that It could face an adversary requiring fighting, or that It could die. Killing is merely part of Its feeding cycle, and when It finally does have to fight, It does so by eating, both physically, by biting off Eddie's arm and swallowing it, and mentally, by "feeding on [pain]" (1056). Sleep is the other half of Its cycle: It sleeps for twenty-seven years (the approximate length of a human generation), awakes to feed on a new generation of children, and goes back to sleep: "*It wanted only to eat and sleep and dream and eat again*" (1008).

11. The horror of being "incorporated in [It] alive" is noted by Bosky, who sees this as an image that "presents a horror of corporeality, a duality of mind trapped inside flesh. In conjunction with Its pregnancy, the image also suggests a fear of the female body, which shelters yet engulfs, within the womb or through a hungry sexuality" (150). Because the mind of Audra Denbrough is described as being "*with It, in It*" (1015) while Audra is still alive, it is apparently possible for It to devour the mind without devouring the body, although what this means is not really explained or explored. Audra's mind apparently remains where It is even after Its death, until she is saved and restored by a bicycle ride. Also unclear is whether It is telling the truth when It tells Beverly that "No one who dies in Derry really dies" (571); if true, this statement may suggest that all of Derry's dead are somehow Its victims.

12. Abraham discusses the spider as symbolic of the "angry," "wicked," and "dangerous" mother, and cites a case in which a spider killing its victim by sucking his blood "served as a castration symbol" for a patient whose "phantasies were concerned with the danger of being killed by his mother during incestuous intercourse." C. W. Wahl also associates the spider with mother-son incest (Abraham, 326, 332, 331; Slater, 87 n., 65). Neumann notes that the spider symbolizes the "Terrible Mother" in various cultures (66, 177, 184, 233).

13. Its body is later referred to as "bloated" (1092). On obese female characters, particularly mothers, in King's works, see Bosky; Collings, *Facets* (75 and 81), and

Stephen King as Richard Bachman (17); Collings and Engebretson (28 and 147); and Wornom (158).

14. See Magistrale, *Landscape* (117–18) and *Moral Voyages* (94–95); and Collings, *Phenomenon* (24–25). In contrast, Don Herron finds the episode degrading to women, ridiculous in its content, absurd as one of the book's climaxes, and feeble stylistically (216–17). Collings points out that sexual intercourse is "also referred to as doing 'it,' with connections to the monster that are anything but accidental" (*Phenomenon*, 24).

15. Pharr describes Beverly as "earth mother," as does Magistrale (*Moral Voyages*, 95) and King himself (quoted in Magistrale, *Second Decade*, 7). Pharr also describes Beverly as "high priestess of heroism itself," a "living icon," and "the Jeanne d'Arc of the Losers," even while recognizing that Beverly "is no one's peer" and "fits a male-designed mold" (30, 31).

16. After the deaths of both the Turtle and It, the "Other," which is apparently more powerful than either of them, also refers to Bill as "son" (1094). The Other is not explicitly gendered, although its words and attitude would seem to align it with the male Turtle.

17. Bill's mother gives him this formula to help him control his stuttering, and it is perhaps the only useful piece of information given by a mother in *It*. Of course, it is Bill, not his mother, who realizes that the formula can be used as a weapon against It. Mike also emphasizes the importance of his father's voice (452).

18. Bosky describes this episode as "perhaps" a "symbolic castration." She also notes the parallel between Sonia Kaspbrak and It as devouring mothers, and makes interesting points about Bill's final attack on It, which "suggests both sexual violation and a kind of reverse, forced birth" (150).

19. Pharr suggests that It is "the only other significant 'female'" (besides Beverly) in the book, although she describes It as essentially asexual (31). Magistrale's insistence that "Beverly Marsh is the only human female in *It*" (*Moral Voyages*, 94) and that "[Beverly] and It are essentially the only females in the book" (*Second Decade*, 6) is simply inexplicable.

WORKS CITED

Abraham, Karl. *Selected Papers of Karl Abraham*. Translated by Douglas Bryan and Alix Strachey. Brunner/Mazel Classics in Psychoanalysis, 3. 1927. New York: Brunner/Mazel, 1979, 326–32.

Bosky, Bernadette Lynn. "Playing the Heavy: Weight, Appetite, and Embodiment in Three Novels by Stephen King." *The Dark Descent: Essays Defining Stephen King's Horrorscape*. Edited by Tony Magistrale. Westport, CT: Greenwood, 1992, 137–56.

Chodorow, Nancy. *The Reproduction of Mothering: Psychoanalysis and the Sociology of Gender*. Berkeley: University of California Press, 1978.

Collings, Michael R. *The Many Facets of Stephen King*. Starmont Studies in Literary Criticism, 11. Mercer Island: Starmont, 1985.

——. *Stephen King as Richard Bachman*. Starmont Studies in Literary Criticism, 10. Mercer Island: Starmont, 1985.

——. *The Stephen King Phenomenon*. Starmont Studies in Literary Criticism, 14. Mercer Island: Starmont, 1987.

Collings, Michael R., and David Engebretson. *The Shorter Works of Stephen King.* Starmont Studies in Literary Criticism, 9. Mercer Island: Starmont, 1985.

Davis, Jonathan P. *Stephen King's America.* Bowling Green: Bowling Green State University Popular Press, 1994.

Hanson, Clare. "Stephen King: Powers of Horror." *American Horror Fiction: From Brockden Brown to Stephen King.* Edited by Brian Docherty. New York: St. Martin's, 1990, 135–54.

Hatlen, Burton. Interview. *Stephen King's America.* Edited by Jonathan P. Davis. Bowling Green: Bowling Green State University Popular Press, 1994, 141–60.

Heldreth. Leonard G. "Viewing 'The Body': King's Portrait of the Artist as Survivor." *The Gothic World of Stephen King: Landscape of Nightmares.* Edited by Gary Hoppenstand and Ray B. Browne. Bowling Green: Bowling Green State University Popular Press, 1987, 64–74.

Herron, Don. "The Summation." *Reign of Fear: The Fiction and the Films of Stephen King.* Edited by Don Herron. Novato: Underwood-Miller, 1992, 209–47.

Horney, Karen. "The Dread of Women." *The International Journal of Psycho-analysis* 13 (1932): 348–60.

Irigaray, Luce. "Body Against Body: In Relation to the Mother." In *Sexes and Genealogies*, translated by Gillian C. Gill. New York: Columbia University Press, 1993.

King, Stephen. "The Boogeyman." *Night Shift.* Garden City: Doubleday, 1978, 98–107.

——. *Carrie.* Garden City: Doubleday, 1974.

——. *Cujo.* New York: The Mysterious Press, 1981.

——. *The Dead Zone.* New York: Viking, 1979.

——. *It.* New York: Viking, 1986.

——. *Pet Sematary.* Garden City: Doubleday, 1983.

——. (as Richard Bachman). *Rage.* New York: New American Library, 1977.

——. (as Richard Bachman). *The Running Man.* New York: New American Library, 1982.

——. *The Shining.* New York: Doubleday, 1977.

——. *The Stand.* Garden City: Doubleday, 1978.

Kristeva, Julia. *Powers of Horror: An Essay on Abjection.* Translated by Leon S. Roudiez. New York: Columbia University Press, 1982.

Magistrale, Tony. *Landscape of Fear: Stephen King's American Gothic.* Bowling Green: Bowling Green State University Popular Press, 1988.

——. *The Moral Voyages of Stephen King.* Starmont Studies in Literary Criticism, 25. Mercer Island: Starmont, 1989.

——. *Stephen King: The Second Decade, "Danse Macabre" to "The Dark Half."* New York: Twayne, 1992.

Neumann, Erich. *The Great Mother: An Analysis of the Archetype.* Translated by Ralph Manheim. Bollingen Ser. XLVII. 1963. Princeton: Princeton University Press, 1970.

Newhouse, Tom. "A Blind Date with Disaster: Adolescent Revolt in the Fiction of Stephen King." *The Gothic World of Stephen King: Landscape of Nightmares.* Edited by Gary Hoppenstand and Ray B. Browne. Bowling Green: Bowling Green State University Popular Press, 1987, 49–55.

Pharr, Mary. "Partners in the *Danse*: Women in Stephen King's Fiction." *The Dark Descent: Essays Defining Stephen King's Horrorscape.* Edited by Tony Magistrale. Westport, CT: Greenwood, 1992, 19–32.

Slater, Philip. *The Glory of Hera: Greek Mythology and the Greek Family.* 1968. Boston: Beacon, 1971.

Underwood, Tim, and Chuck Miller, eds. *Bare Bones: Conversations on Terror with Stephen King.* New York: McGraw-Hill, 1988.

Winter, Douglas E. *Stephen King: The Art of Darkness.* 1984. New York: New American, 1986.

Wornom, Howard. "Terror in Toontown." *The Stephen King Companion.* Edited by George Beahm. Kansas City: Andrews and McMeel, 1989, 155–60.

9

It, A Sexual Fantasy

Karen Thoens

> Smells of dirt and wet and long-gone vegetables would merge into one unmistakable ineluctable smell, the smell of the monster, the apotheosis of all monsters. It was the smell of something for which he had no name. . . . A creature which would eat anything but which was especially hungry for boymeat.
>
> Stephen King
> *It* (7)

It, Stephen King's epic gender fantasy, commemorates the androcentric world order of the 1950s. Nostalgia, a wistful yearning for past glory, validates the pursuit of male mastery over a menacing female sexuality. Rooted in half forgotten memories of childhood conquests, *It* exploits male longing for lost hierarchical power structures, a hunger for the authority of master narratives. Interwoven within the narrative, the myth of female ascendance is symbolically supported by twenty-seven year cycles of bloody violence, cycles that correlate with female menstrual patterns. In 1958, the novel's heroes, social outcasts united in a ritual male bonding ceremony, unearth the evil that spawns the violence. Their childhood adventures remain unnoticed, forgotten even by themselves, until the cycle of terror recurs.

In the summer of 1958, during the last reign of It, seven children attacked and wounded the monster. Brought together by their status as "Losers" and as victims of the bullying tyranny of Henry Bowers, Belch Huggins, and Victor Criss, each of them was marked in a physical, identifiable sense as an outsider in the social hierarchy of the 1950s. Bill Denbrough, unofficial leader of the group and brother of the first victim, was marked by his stutter; Ben Hanscom, by his obesity; Eddie Kaspbrak, by his asthma and his hovering mother; Richie Tozier, by the glasses he wore and his "trashmouth" (318); Mike Hanlon, by his race; Stan Uris, physically marked as a fastidious bird watcher, less obviously marked but clearly recognized in the closed world of Derry as Jewish; and Beverly Marsh, by the marker indicating the greatest difference, being female. Intentionally united by a power beyond their comprehension, they heroically battled the monster and vowed to return if It resurfaced. In 1984, the terror returns.

Hanlon, who had in the interim become the town librarian, compiled a history of Derry's violent anomalies. It, the Loser's name for the monster, awakened and stalked Derry every twenty-seven years, give or take a year; its reign marked by gory murders. The victims, usually children, were frequently bloodied and mutilated. In 1958, the first victim was six-year-old George Denbrough, whose arm was ripped from his body. In 1984, it was Adrian Mellon, a gay man, beaten and thrown off a bridge by the current generation of Derry bullies. It was waiting under the bridge to feast on him.

This change in victims, from a young, innocent child to a gay man, is a signifier of social change, indicating deterioration in a place already inhabited by evil. Mellon, like his boyfriend Hagarty, is marked and judged by voices carefully distanced from the author. Presented in opposition to violent homophobic voices, reasonable statements of male heterosexist privilege attain a central position. The graffiti in Bassey Park, "STICK NAILS IN EYES OF ALL FAGOTS (FOR GOD)!" and the violence of the queer bashers toward Mellon locate the statements of the investigating officers centrally, marginalizing the victim's voice (29). To Officer Gardener, a fair, decent man, Hagarty is a subspecies: "This man—if you want to call him a man—was wearing lipstick and satin pants so tight you could almost read the wrinkles in his cock" (17). Pronouncing social judgment on Hagarty and his dead companion, Adrian Mellon, Gardner[1] concludes that, "he was, after all, just a queer" (17).

The positioning in the narrative of the 1985 murder of Adrian Mellon immediately after that of little Georgie Denbrough serves to graphically illustrate social change read as deterioration. References to AIDS[2] and to Mellon as a "little queer," "fruit," "a fucking faggot," a "bum puncher,"[3] position sexuality as defined in contemporary terms in opposition to nostalgic versions of clearly defined sex roles. Linking male homosexuality with being female, and by oppositional definition less than male, Hagarty and Mellon are belittled for their resemblance to females: "Garton saw the two of them, Mellon and Hagarty, mincing along with their arms about each other's waists and giggling like a couple of girls. At first he actually thought they *were* a couple of girls" (21). The subtext of *It* links male homosexuality to female sexuality in a hierarchical structure privileging the heterosexual male.

In 1958, there was no recognizable gay community in Derry; the Falcon, a gay bar, opened in 1973. In 1977, the clientele shifted to gay men, a fact that the owner, Elmer Cutrie, failed to notice until 1981. As did the Black Spot, the Negro nightclub that burned down during the reign of It in 1930, the existence of the Falcon marked a change in the social order in Derry, a reflection of a change in America, a change that was also, perhaps, not noticed at first. In the world of *It*, change is frightening. Resistance to a confusing, demanding present is evidenced by a glorification of a simpler past.

In *It*, the past is not irretrievable. As Eddie Kaspbrak travels north toward Derry in 1985, he remembers the summer of 1958: *"Not going north. Because it's not a train; it's a time machine. Not north; back. Back in time"* (102). According to Stephen King, *It* represents an attempt to "reenter the world of childhood" (Magistrale, 5). He describes the return to childhood by the adult as the completion of a wheel. Intended as journey backward in time, according to King, this quest has the power to heal: "The idea is to go back and confront your childhood, in a sense relive it if you can, so that you can be whole" (Winter, 185). King proposes recapturing a "mythic power" that connects childhood to adult imagination (Magistrale, 5). This mythic power derives from the strategies used by Stephen King as a nostalgic writer.

In *Nostalgia and Sexual Difference*, Janice Doane and Devon Hodges examine nostalgia as a "rhetorical practice" (3), which they define as "a retreat to the past in the face of what a number of writers—most of them male—perceive to be the degeneracy of American culture brought about by the rise of feminist authority" (xiii). Nostalgic writers describe reality as a "system of oppositions that is at the same time a system of dominance and subordination" (8). These oppositions are hierarchical by nature: "[O]ne term is degraded, the other is exalted" (9). Past and present become oppositions in which past is privileged. In the male/female opposition, male is the privileged term.[4] "Nostalgic writers are entrapped by the illusion that their strategy of opposition creates: their mythic pasts become real" (9).

Analyzing modern male texts, Ellen Friedman notes a yearning for the influence of the master narratives evidenced in "the profoundly nostalgic conviction that the past has explanatory or redemptive powers" (241). She proposes that this notion is revealed in "the futile desire to stop time or to understand, recoup or recreate the past, summoning it into the present" (241). Nostalgia forms the subtext of *It*, in which the past wields power over the present, merging inseparably with it at some points. The overwhelming celebration of the past—its music, lost youth and innocence—combines with the fear of a monster that lurks in the past, a monster that has not been vanquished, a female monster. *It* resists the forces that have propelled society into the present, seeking out the glory days of the past, hoping to reestablish the lost paternal order. King uses Bruce Springstein's lyrics to suggest a connection between lost youth and women, a significant theme of *It*. "Glory days . . . gone in the wink of a young girl's eye" (63). For Stephen King, change is unpredictable, uncomfortable, undesirable. "Our lesson for today, boys and girls, is the more things change, the more things change. Whoever said the more things change the more things stay the same was obviously suffering severe mental retardation" (1003). The Losers travel back in time to their own childhoods, but, as adults, they all remain childless, symbolically castrated. *It* is not about childhood, *It* is about longing for the past, going back and finding that it is still inhabited by the same demons. In *It*, Stephen King's focus is clearly "frozen in the oedipal backward glance" (Friedman, 241). Stephen King's glance is revisionary; however, his authorial power allows him mastery over the bullies of his youth and over the ravages of time.

In "Creative Writers and Daydreaming," Freud describes fantasies as wish-fulfilling day dreams that are ambitious, erotic, or a combination of both. "A strong experience in the present awakens in the creative writer a memory of an earlier experience (usually belonging to his childhood) from which there now proceeds a wish which finds its fulfillment in the creative work" (Freud, 655). For King, *It* satisfies both ambitious and erotic fantasies. Bill, the horror fiction writer, goes back in time to champion King's childhood memories, rescuing "the Losers" from identification as intimidated victims and outcasts to those who dared to challenge evil incarnate. King re-creates the past and summons it into the present.[5] Significantly, Bill, an obvious substitute for the author, relives his youthful triumph only to surpass it, potent wish fulfillment for a middle aged author who must himself be experiencing the effects of time and age.

Within the nostalgic framework of *It*, mothers play a significant role. In "Women, Danger, and Death: The Perversion of the Female Principle in Stephen King's Fiction," Gail Burns and Melinda Kanner note that "Female reproductive potential, sexuality and death are forged by King in a manner that invariably locks his female characters into particular sexually defined roles" (160). Observing that King links female sexuality with death rather than life, Burns and Kanner conclude, "Women who do manage to give birth generally fail their children in the most fundamental ways" (161). This maternal failure is evident in *It*; the members of the Losers' Club are losers in many cases because of their mothers. Even the relatively benign mothers in *It* function as limiting and controlling agents in relation to their male children.

Mothers and Monsters

When six-year-old Georgie Denbrough went out to play in the rain with the newspaper boat his brother Bill had helped him make, the terror began again. Something lurking in the sewer lured Georgie over, grabbed him and ripped off his arm. While little Georgie was being murdered, his mother was inside, playing *Für Elise* on the piano. The piano playing, significant due to the frequency of references to it,[6] is linked forever in Bill's memory to his brother's death. Their mother, a former Juilliard piano student, detested rock and roll: "She didn't merely dislike it; she abominated it" (9). Rock and roll signifies the 1950s era to King in a deeply nostalgic way; it is significant that Bill's mother along with several other of the Losers' mothers opposes it. Restrictions placed upon rock and roll music exemplify the limits imposed upon the boys by their mothers. Bill's mother is symbolically linked with rigid, formal classical music. Her piano playing implies a negligent participation in her son's murder.

Before Georgie's death, Bill and George are careful not to disturb their mother. Even so, she stops long enough to scold George from her seat at the piano for slamming a door. Then, when the piano stops again, the brothers are "listening for the piano bench to scrape back, listening for their mother's impatient footsteps," but she resumes playing (10). As they work on the boat, Bill warns George that if he gets any paraffin on the blanket "Mom'll kill you," and if he doesn't put everything away, "Mom'll have a bird" (11). Never portrayed as nurturing, their mother is at best distant and restrictive, possibly negligent and perhaps worse.

At the age of three, Bill was "knocked into the side of a building" by a car (10). According to Bill's mother, the accident, which left him unconscious for seven hours, caused his stutter. "George sometimes got the feeling that his dad—and Bill himself—was not so sure" (10). What did they think caused the stutter? An ambiguous link exists between Bill's mother and the stutter that marked him as a Loser. Both Bill and George Denbrough were involved in life-threatening situations as young children, one of which was fatal. King's strategy of insistent repetition emphasizes their mother's piano playing on the day George was killed. This repetition shifts the interpretation from "he was killed *while* she played the piano," to "he was killed *because* she played the piano." Locating the stutter/car accident story in the middle of this chapter tends to substantiate charges of careless mothering that King is careful never to utter. Their mother bears the burden of guilt for pursuing her own interests and, by implication, neglecting her children without ever being explicitly accused.

Eddie Kaspbrak's weakness is his asthma; this physical infirmity marks Eddie for membership in the Losers' club. Mr. Keene, the druggist, tells Eddie that his aspirator contains a placebo. The druggist insists that Eddie does not have asthma and that Sonia, Eddie's mother, is the real problem: "Your mother is determined you are ill" (776). Eddie's throat tightens. He knows it isn't in his head; he isn't crazy: "Your asthma is the result of a nervous tightening of the diaphragm that is ordered by your mind . . . or your mother" (777).

The dynamics of their relationship becomes evident later, in the clash over Eddie's friends. Eddie, aware of his mother's manipulation of him, explains to his friends: "She had a way, a way of working on a guy" (766). Sonia feels uncertain, almost fearful when Eddie confronts her about sending his friends away. Picturing herself as a self-sacrificing, devoted mother, she refuses to acknowledge other motives. Eddie sees through her: "You're not going to steal my friends just because you're scared of being alone" (797). Sonia, adept in the use of emotional weapons, rationalizes her control of Eddie by calling it protection: "She felt safer in her tears. Usually when she cried Eddie cried, too. A low weapon, some might say but were there really any low weapons when it came to protecting her son?" (797). The emotional turmoil concerning the Losers continues until Eddie proposes a compromise; he will not question his asthma if she doesn't interfere with his friends. As Sonia carefully hugs Eddie sealing their agreement, she thinks, "What mother would kill her son with love?" (802). Emotionally devouring Eddie, Sonia's mothering creates an invalid.

Sonia's carnivorous love synthesizes the mother/monster, monster/mother opposition. During his stay at the hospital as he was slipping out of consciousness, Eddie confuses Sonia Kaspbrak and the monster. He thinks he has told the nurse, "*She's not the leper, please don't think that, she's only eating me because she loves me*" (790). The leper, the form of It that appears to Eddie, represents his maternally induced asthma. In a dream, when Sonia chases his friends away, Eddie sees the monster in many of its forms; the last form is his own mother: "But just before the clown washed out completely, he saw the most terrible thing of all: his ma's face" (792). In *It*, mothers are often monsters. Sonia Kaspbrak consumes Eddie as *It* devours children.

Sonia Kaspbrak is a widow. Arlene Hanscom is a single mother: "[R]aising a boy by herself had put a mark on her" (183). Like the Kaspbraks, the Hanscoms are portrayed by feeding imagery. Whereas Sonia feeds on Eddie emotionally, Arlene overfeeds Ben physically: "[W]hen there were leftovers from supper she would often bring them to him while he was watching TV and he would eat them, although some dim part of him hated himself for doing so" (185). Ben could not bring himself to acknowledge his mother's ulterior motives. "Ben's deeper thoughts—suspected her motives in this constant feeding. Was it just love? Could it be anything else? Surely not" (186). Embarrassed by his size, Ben wore baggy sweatshirts to hide his body when he was in fifth grade in Derry. His mother spoke of his size euphemistically. "She never called him 'fat,' she called him 'big'" (185).[7] Later, he recalls, when he was in high school, he was changing after gym when the other guys "fat paddled" him, chasing him and slapping his naked body. This incident led to his determination to diet. His greatest obstacle was his mother: "And nights when I went home and would only eat half of the stuff on my plate my mother would burst into tears and say that I was starving myself, killing myself, and that I didn't love her anymore, that I didn't care how hard she worked for me" (496). Being fat made Ben a Loser; like Eddie Kaspbrak, Ben's physical problem originates with his mother. Like Sonia Kaspbrak, Arlene Hanscom engulfs her son within a dangerous devouring motherhood.

In response to the murders in Derry, Ben's mother gives him a new Timex watch and tells him to be home by six o'clock every night during the summer. She warns him that if he is late she'll call the police and report him missing immediately. Emphasizing the need for caution, Arlene explains that she understands how boys like to spend their time. During their conversation, Ben realizes that his mother doesn't know that he has no friends: "If she didn't know he had no friends, she probably didn't know anywhere near as much about his boyhood as she thought she did" (184). Ben is touched by the concern that the Timex signifies because "She could be hard, his mama. She could be a boss" (185). Ben's mother is unaware of the essential facts of his life, assuming friendships where there are none.

Setting limits on Ben with the watch and the curfew, Ben's mother assumes that she has protected him. Did she really imagine that being home by six was sufficient protection from a murderer? Was warning Ben to come home early and go places accompanied by his friends a serious defense? Arlene Hanscom, like the other Losers' mothers, acts to set limits for her son but remains essentially uninvolved with him. Ben, astute enough to question her motives, struggles with ambivalent feelings for his mother. "Ben Hanscom would not have dared to hate his mama" (185). The chasm in their communication causes Ben's silence regarding the murders in Derry: "the thing which he hadn't quite been able to tell his mother" (208). The protection that the watch signifies is undermined by her disinterest in his life.

Richie Tozier's flaw, the mark of the Loser, is wearing glasses. Richie's mother's association with his glasses is established when a bully pushes Richie into the gutter breaking his glasses: "[H]is mother was furious with him about it, lending very little credence to Richie's explanations" (662). His mother's anger over the broken glasses compounded by her lack of sympathy over Richie's pounding by a bigger boy wounds Richie less than the knowledge that she didn't believe his story. "This failure to make his mother understand hurt much worse than being slammed into the gutter" (662). Conjuring up pictures of Richie's father working late, she suggests Richie's guilt in incurring the cost to replace the glasses. "You think about it. . . . Her voice was curt and final—worse, it was near tears" (663). Her lack of compassion and manipulation of Rich with guilt mark her as a mediocre mother, but even more deadly, at least in Stephen King's hierarchy, she didn't approve of rock and roll: "Like Bill Denbrough's mother, she was death on rock and roll" (582). Still, to the other Losers, Richie's parents seemed the most normal. When the Losers were looking for an adult to confide in, they asked Richie about his parents. Although Richie rated them as okay, he knew "they'd never believe something like this" (663). His mother's inability to believe Richie about the glasses isolates him and the other losers in dealing with It.

Stan Uris, who encountered It as the corpses of drowned children in the Standpipe, believed in an orderly universe, a universe of natural laws. "God had given the earth a final tilt on its axis. . . . He had done that and He then had said, in effect: 'Okay, if you can figure out the tilt you can figure out any damn thing you choose'" (429). Stan signifies nostalgia for those reliable master narratives, a past you could trust, the Great Chain of Being, a hierarchy in which God was on top and God was male. Before going out that night, the night he almost died, the night that preordained his suicidal death twenty-seven years later, "His mother made him promise to keep the hood of his slicker up," certainly a valid precaution when there are murderers about (418). Stan is an outcast in Derry because he is Jewish. Marginalized even in the novel, he commits suicide, rather than return to Derry with the others to face It again.

Like Ben Hanscom's mother, Mike's mother rationalizes that Derry is safe until dinner time, so when Mike was late for dinner one day, she was angry, "she had been nearly hysterical. She took after him with a dishrag, whopping him with it. Don't you ever scare me like that!" (274). Mike was surprised that his father didn't intervene and control her "wildcat anger" (274). But, now Mike knew his limits, his mother had made them clear: "Home before dark. Yes ma'am, right-o" (274). Mike's father, Will Hanlon is the benign patriarch in *It*, suggesting places for Mike to visit, telling him about the past. When Mike Hanlon eventually recovers and writes Derry's history, he is searching for a master narrative, the events that led into his father's story. Mike is an outcast in Derry because he is black, and Beverly Marsh is even on the margin within the Losers Club: She is the only girl.

When Al Marsh beat Beverly, he justified it as his duty as a parent to correct her behavior. "*Daughters*, Al Marsh said, *need more correction than sons*. He had no sons, and she felt vaguely as if that might be partly her fault as well" (398). Elfrida Marsh routinely dismissed her husband's physical abuse of Beverly. "Did you get your dad angry at you last night, Bevvie?" Then, voicing her true concern, she asked "Bevvie, does he ever touch you?" (403). Aware of an incestuous undercurrent to Al's violence, Elfrida Marsh neither confronted him nor protected Beverly. Warning Beverly to be home before dark, her mother implies concern about Beverly's safety, masking her crucial failure to protect Beverly at home.

Beverly's mother's failure was the inability to control her father. In *It*, mothers limit and control their sons. Limits were justified by male behaviors that were labeled risky. Richie's mother forbade him to ride double on Bill's bike, but even safety conscious Eddie recognized that life cannot be lived risk free. "Some stuff has to be done even if there *is* a risk. That's the first important thing I ever found out I didn't find out from my mother" (723). Some mothers in *It* are monstrous; others are negligent, distracted, incapable. Burns and Kanner conclude that in King's fiction "Mothers fail their children, witness their abuse, and stand helpless to prevent their deaths" (Burns and Kanner, 171). The failure of the mothers in *It* is so basic, they mirror the monsters their children combat.

Gender Myths

Victimized by her father's battering, Beverly Marsh substantiates myths about violence against women. Her father's rage is fueled by incestuous desire for her as Beverly's visit with It in the guise of the witch from Hansel and Gretel confirms. "I beat you because I wanted to FUCK you, Bevvie, that's all I wanted to do" (572). Surviving her father, Beverly intentionally chooses men like him for lovers, men who hit women. Tom Rogan recognizes this in Beverly from the start, he knows that she wants to be hurt, "And it might even be possible that some antelopes—and some women—*want* to be brought down" (105). Testing his theory, Tom smashes Bev across the face noting her reaction with interest. "Then the pain. Then the (nostalgia) look of a memory . . . of some memory" (108). He tells her he hit her for smoking in front of him. As a stunned Bev struggles to absorb the blow, her reaction—tearful and hurt, confirms his initial evaluation of her. "She was trying to find a tone, an adult rhythm of speech, and failing. He had regressed her. He was in this car with a child" (108). Before it was over, he intended to humiliate her, to make her apologize to him. Her eyes seemed to plead with him to stop, but he knew to persist "because that was not the bottom of her wanting, and both of them knew it" (109). Tom Rogan had established himself in Beverly Marsh's life.

This episode plays to myths about abused women, confirming that they intentionally choose violent men and stay with them, implying that the battering is really the victim's fault. She wants it. This unfortunate stereotype degrades the only female character who could have been noble. Significantly, though Beverly has the same kind of financial success as the other adult Losers, she is the only one who remains emotionally battered as an adult.

King does not present Tom Rogan as a model of male behavior. Tom's drinking and Beverly's ultimate violent resistance to the beatings do not serve to excuse his behavior, only to amplify it. Even his childhood is no excuse. Tom came from a violent family where he was the victim of an abusive mother: "*Tom, you been bad!* his mother had sometimes said—well, 'sometimes' was maybe not such a good word; maybe 'often' would have been a better one. *You come here, Tommy! I got to give you a whuppin*" (112). When his father, Ralph Rogan killed himself with a lye and gin cocktail, Tom was burdened with the care of the other three children and frequently beaten. "His life as a child had been punctuated by whuppins" (112). He decided that it was "Better to be the whupper than the whupped" (112).

Describing Bev's feelings toward Tom, King corroborates myths that support violence: "But that did not preclude her fear of him . . . her hate of him . . . and her contempt of herself for choosing him for dim reasons buried in the times that should be over" (118, 119). When Tom used the belt on Beverly, she knew that she wanted it: "[W]hat hurt worse was knowing that part of her craved the hurt. Craved the humiliation" (120). As Beverly searches her motives for marrying Tom, she wonders: "Why would a person go back into the nightmare of her own accord?" (930). She acknowledges her guilt to Bill admitting: "He hits and he hurts. I married him because . . . because my father always worried about me, I guess. . . . And as long as someone was worrying about me I'd be safe. More than safe. *Real*" (929). She wanted to be beaten, it made her feel loved. In this statement, Beverly accepts the blame for her own victimization, supporting an unfortunate stereotype of battered women. Tom Rogan, the batterer, meanwhile, performs the same function that the homophobic bullies serve in the Adrian Mellon incident. Tom's extreme cruelty, his manipulation of Beverly, becomes a border marker, centering and elevating the other men in the novel.

The battering serves another nostalgic function. It warns women that other women cannot, or will not, protect them from male aggression. After the fight that precedes her trip to Derry, Beverly goes to her friend Kay McCall for help. King, again distancing himself from applying the label, carefully marks Kay as feminist when Tom refers to her as "that titsy women's-lib bitch" (111). Later, Kay withstands a battering by Tom until he threatens to cut up her face. Terrified by the threat of mutilation, Kay tells Tom where Beverly has gone. Not only does the "women's-lib bitch" fail Beverly as a protector, she betrays her when threatened with loss of her own beauty. Kay's failure, significant in terms of the nostalgic world view of male/female, dominance/submission, serves to warn women that other women are not to be trusted.

Blood and Sex

Beverly Marsh first experienced It as blood gurgling out of the drain in the bathroom, splashing up around the room, blood that her father did not see. Beverly's impending puberty, the blood, the bathroom, and Al's anger masking his barely controlled incestuous desire are conveyed in sexually laden imagery. The evening ends with Beverly listening as her parents "did their sex-act thing" (399). When Al questioned Bev about her scream, she lied: "There was a spider. A big fat black spider. It . . . it crawled out of the drain" (397). Ironically, instinctively, Beverly knew what It really was, the form beneath the disguises; because Beverly is female, she knows what the boys must risk their lives to uncover and confront. *It* is about sexuality, bloody female sexuality, female sexuality as imagined by a male.

Woman as Object

In *It*, Beverly is Stephen King's ideal woman; as a child her courage facing the monster and surviving her father's abuse suggests that she will mature into a self-reliant, assured woman. Disappointingly, her marriage to Tom Rogan—his battering, her masochism—describe a different Beverly. When Beverly comes home to Derry, she is a woman who needs to be rescued. In Stephen King's nostalgic gender scenario, a strong male must save the beautiful but frightened female from the dangers of the world and threats posed by aggressive, perverted men.[8] Bill, the successful horror novel writer (read as Stephen King), chivalrously emerges from his male quest/adventure plot to rescue the damsel in distress. In King's outrageous erotic fantasy, he modestly describes Beverly's sexual response to Bill: "She became aware that this wasn't going to be just a come; it was going to be a tactical nuke. She became a little afraid" (931).

In an interview with Tony Magistrale, Stephen King describes Beverly as "the symbolic conduit between adulthood and childhood for the boys in the Losers' Club. It's a role that women have played again and again in the lives of boys: the symbolic advent of manhood through the act of sex" (6). In his objectification of woman, female sexuality functions as a male rite of passage.

The subtext of *It* is sexual. The pronoun it—genderless, vague—vacillates as a significator but remains sex-linked throughout the novel. It can be read as sexual intercourse. Stephen King describes it: "[S]*ex must be some unrealized undefined monster; they refer to the act as It. Would you do It, do your sister and her boyfriend do It, do your mom and dad still do IT, and how they never intend to do It*" (1085). It can also be read as repulsive female sexuality, the genesis of all depravity, the wickedness that turns innocent boys into men, forcing them to abandon bicycles named Silver with baseball cards flipping innocently across the spokes, to become bound to mundane, compromising jobs, to grow old and fat and bald and die. Sexual maturity is the evil these misfit boys fear, flee, and surmount for the first time in their secret sexual initiation by Beverly. This initial sexual experience for each of them coincides with end of the groups' first encounter with It and is followed by protracted amnesia.

Monsters and Heroes

It could be sexual intercourse. It could be repulsive female sexuality. But, mostly, It is actually She. It, the monster, is not really androgynous, a point raised at the beginning of the novel when George looked into the sewer and saw Pennywise the Dancing Clown, the principal manifestation of It. George was reminded of "Clarabell, who talked by honking his (or was it her?—George was never really sure of the gender) horn" (13). The question of the clown's gender was restated by Richie when Mike described Its appearance at the parade on Main Street "'But then he turned around and waved to me again and I knew it was him. It was the same man.' 'He's not a man,' Richie said" (712). As a clown using greasepaint to disguise its identity, and in Its other shapes, It exploits a female characteristic, the ability to alter appearance, to change outfits, to use makeup; It has an aptitude for becoming unclear and ambiguous rather than concrete and definable.

Sexual mutilations with a phallic focus are clearly the work of IT/HER. When they found the crew of lumberjacks who were snowed in during the winter of 1979: "All nine hacked to pieces. Heads rolled . . . not to mention arms . . . a foot or two . . . and a man's penis had been nailed to one wall of the cabin" (157). And in 1931, the corpse of the flood victim had a sexual flavor. "The fish had eaten this unfortunate gentleman's eyes, three of his fingers, his penis and most of his left foot" (4).

It. Evil. Unfathomable evil. Mutating, hiding anywhere, everywhere. It could be anyone. It could be your mother. And, the really frightening suggestion in this novel, It is your mother. It, nameless terror. It is bloody, filthy, horrible. It lurks in dark, wet underground caverns. In hidden, secret places. The boy-men heroes have returned to Derry to face IT again, HER, the bitch, the force that is really responsible for their lost youth.

Female sexual imagery intensifies as Its essence is stalked in the sewers under Derry. "The tunnel progressed steadily downward, and that smell—that low, wild stench—grew steadily stronger" (1028). In Stephen King's creation myth, the ultimate evil is repulsive, spiderlike; significantly, It is a pregnant female. "It's *always* been here, since the beginning of time . . . since before there were men *anywhere*" (763). As the origin of evil on earth, the egg-bearing female spider must be conquered, her evil spawn destroyed to prevent unthinkable consequences. To destroy the ultimate female evil, Bill must symbolically rape and dominate her:

It lunged clumsily forward, trying to bite him, and instead of retreating, Bill drove forward, using not just his fists now but his whole body, making himself into a torpedo. He ran into Its gut like a sprinting fullback who lowers his shoulders and simply drives straight ahead.

For a moment he felt Its stinking flesh simply give, as if it would rebound and send him flying. With an inarticulate scream he drove harder, pushing forward and upward with his legs, digging at it with his hands. And he broke through; was inundated with Its hot fluids. They ran across his face, in his ears. he snuffed them up his nose in thin squirming streams.

He was in the black again, up to his shoulders in Its convulsing body. And in his clogged ears he could hear a sound like the steady whack—WHACK—whack—WHACK of a big bass drum, the one that leads the parade when the circus comes to town with its compliment of freaks and strutting capering clowns . . .

He plunged his hands into It, ripping tearing, parting, seeking the source of the sound; rupturing organs, his slimed fingers opening and closing . . .

Whack—WHACK—*whack*—WHACK—. . .

Yes! Try this you bitch! TRY THIS ONE OUT! DO YOU LIKE IT? DO YOU LOVE IT? DO YOU? . . .

Bill felt Its body clench around him suddenly, like a fist in a slick glove. Then everything loosened . . . At the same time he began pulling back, his consciousness leaving him. (1093–94)

It, the noble quest to rid the world of evil, is the playing out of oedipal male fantasies, sexual intercourse with the monster/mother. Significantly, the final battle with It/Her, is clearly a sexual attack. In "The Laugh of the Medusa," Hélène Cixous locates patriarchal definitions of sexuality: "Men still have everything to say about their sexuality, and everything to write. For what they have said so far stems, for the most part, from the opposition activity/passivity, from the power relation between a fantasized obligatory virility meant to invade, to colonize, and the consequential phantasm of woman as a 'dark continent' to penetrate and to 'pacify'" (1091). In the final battle with It/Her, she is indeed a "dark continent" to be "penetrated" and "pacified." For Stephen King, female sexuality remains terrifying, an evil to be subdued, kept in its rightful place. Burns and Kanner locate female sexuality in the King canon: "Menstruation, mothering, and female sexual desire function as bad omens, prescient clues that something will soon be badly awry" (160).

The Denouement—Back to the Past

Bill survived the odyssey into the depths of sinister, powerful female sexuality and emerged victorious, reborn. Unfortunately, Audra, his wife, is now catatonic. Bill, of course, rescues her too. He knows exactly what to do. Bill pulls a relic of his youth out of a convenient garage, his old bike, and proves that pure male courage can fix anything, even "a corpse-like wife." She recovers fully due entirely to Bill's courageous, dangerous bike ride; she is happily terrified. All is well. We know this because of Bill's "huge and cheerful erection" (1137).

    It is a feast of unfettered male fantasy. The hero subdues the greatest evil in the universe, which is, of course, a potent, fecund, sexual female. Cixous identifies repressive trends in this nostalgic form of male writing as precluding the possibility of change:

I mean it when I speak of male writing. I maintain unequivocally that there is such a thing as *marked* writing; that, until now, far more extensively and repressively than is ever suspected or admitted, writing that has been run by a libidinal and cultural—hence political, typically masculine—economy; that this is a locus where the repression of women has been perpetuated, over and over, more or less consciously, and in a manner that's frightening since its often hidden or adorned with the mystifying charms of fiction; that this locus has grossly exaggerated all the signs of sexual opposition (and not sexual difference), where woman has never *her* turn to speak—this being all the more serious and unpardonable in that writing is precisely *the very possibility of change*, the space that can serve as a springboard for subversive thought, the precursory movement of a transformation of social and cultural structures. (1092–93)

The world order at the culmination of King's epic gender myth is nostalgic. The patriarchal hierarchy is restored; pliant, submissive females dedicate themselves to their men, who alone possess the secrets of the universe.

NOTES

    1. Describing Adrian Mellon's sobbing boyfriend, Gardener could not feel empathy, a strategy that distances, centers, and privileges "normal" male sexuality in comparison to marginalized "queer" sexuality. "Harold Gardener recognized the reality of Don Hagarty's grief and pain, and at the same time found it impossible to take seriously" (17).

    2. Thomaston, angry over the murder, hopes for the conviction of Garton, Dubay, and Unwin. "I'm going to put them in the slam my friend, and if I hear they got their puckery little assholes cored down there at Thomaston, I'm gonna send them cards saying I hope whoever did it had AIDS" (38). Later, Richie Tozier, in an irreverent spoof, tells a joke as the character Kinky Briefcase, Sexual Accountant: "I had a fellow come in the other day who wanted to know what the worst thing was about getting AIDS . . . I told him right away—trying to explain to your mother how you picked it up from a Haitian girl" (61). King, again careful to distance himself from a judgmental position, uses references to AIDS and homosexuality as a physical marker of difference. In the implied opposition of heterosexual/homosexual, homosexual is clearly the degraded term. The

The Denouement—Back to the Past

Bill survived the odyssey into the depths of sinister, powerful female sexuality and emerged victorious, reborn. Unfortunately, Audra, his wife, is now catatonic. Bill, of course, rescues her too. He knows exactly what to do. Bill pulls a relic of his youth out of a convenient garage, his old bike, and proves that pure male courage can fix anything, even "a corpse-like wife." She recovers fully due entirely to Bill's courageous, dangerous bike ride; she is happily terrified. All is well. We know this because of Bill's "huge and cheerful erection" (1137).

    It is a feast of unfettered male fantasy. The hero subdues the greatest evil in the universe, which is, of course, a potent, fecund, sexual female. Cixous identifies repressive trends in this nostalgic form of male writing as precluding the possibility of change:

I mean it when I speak of male writing. I maintain unequivocally that there is such a thing as *marked* writing; that, until now, far more extensively and repressively than is ever suspected or admitted, writing that has been run by a libidinal and cultural—hence political, typically masculine—economy; that this is a locus where the repression of women has been perpetuated, over and over, more or less consciously, and in a manner that's frightening since its often hidden or adorned with the mystifying charms of fiction; that this locus has grossly exaggerated all the signs of sexual opposition (and not sexual difference), where woman has never *her* turn to speak—this being all the more serious and unpardonable in that writing is precisely *the very possibility of change*, the space that can serve as a springboard for subversive thought, the precursory movement of a transformation of social and cultural structures. (1092–93)

The world order at the culmination of King's epic gender myth is nostalgic. The patriarchal hierarchy is restored; pliant, submissive females dedicate themselves to their men, who alone possess the secrets of the universe.

NOTES

    1. Describing Adrian Mellon's sobbing boyfriend, Gardener could not feel empathy, a strategy that distances, centers, and privileges "normal" male sexuality in comparison to marginalized "queer" sexuality. "Harold Gardener recognized the reality of Don Hagarty's grief and pain, and at the same time found it impossible to take seriously" (17).

    2. Thomaston, angry over the murder, hopes for the conviction of Garton, Dubay, and Unwin. "I'm going to put them in the slam my friend, and if I hear they got their puckery little assholes cored down there at Thomaston, I'm gonna send them cards saying I hope whoever did it had AIDS" (38). Later, Richie Tozier, in an irreverent spoof, tells a joke as the character Kinky Briefcase, Sexual Accountant: "I had a fellow come in the other day who wanted to know what the worst thing was about getting AIDS . . . I told him right away—trying to explain to your mother how you picked it up from a Haitian girl" (61). King, again careful to distance himself from a judgmental position, uses references to AIDS and homosexuality as a physical marker of difference. In the implied opposition of heterosexual/homosexual, homosexual is clearly the degraded term. The

first victim of the 1985 spree is a marker for social deterioration that has occurred since 1958.

3. Boutillier, police officer investigating the murder accuses Chris Unwin: "You threw the little queer into the Canal" (18). Webby Garton describes Adrian Mellon as a "fucking faggot" when interrogated by the police. (21). Officer Machen tells the bullies "about the bumpunchers I'm neutral" (23). Boutillier arguing for suppression of evidence about the clown figure, offers his inferred opinion of gay men: "The guy was a fruit, but he wasn't hurting anyone" (38).

4. According to Doane and Hodges: "Oppositions tend to operate on a hierarchical rather than an equal basis: one term is degraded, the other exalted. Opposition is a power game. The opposition male/female, to give another example crucial to our analysis, is also typically hierarchical. The disparaged term 'female' helps preserve the value and integrity of the privileged term, 'male'" (9).

5. As noted in Ellen Friedman's article.

6. *Für Elise* is specifically mentioned four times, George's mother's piano playing, three more—a total of seven references in thirteen pages.

7. "(sometimes amplified to 'big for his age')" (185).

8. These men include Al Marsh, the battering father whose violence masks incestuous desire and Tom Rogan whose sadistic control ranges from emotional manipulation to premeditated violence that ends in hot sex.

WORKS CITED

Burns, Gail E., and Melinda Kanner. "Women, Danger and Death: The Perversion of The Female Principle in Stephen King's Fiction." *Sexual Politics and Popular Culture*. Edited by Diane Raymond. Bowling Green: Bowling Green State University Popular Press, 1990, 158–171.

Cixous, Hélène. "The Laugh of the Medusa." *The Critical Tradition. Classic Texts and Contemporary Trends*. Edited by David H. Richter. New York: St. Martin's, 1989, 1090–1102.

Doane, Janice, and Devon Hodges. *Nostalgia and Sexual Difference: The Resistance to Contemporary Feminism*. New York: Methuen, 1987.

Freud, Sigmund. "Creative Writers and Daydreaming." *The Critical Tradition. Classic Texts and Contemporary Trends*. Edited by David H. Richter. New York: St. Martin's, 1989, 651–55.

Friedman, Ellen G. "Where Are the Missing Contents? (Post)Modernism, Gender, and the Canon." *PMLA* 108 (1993): 240–52.

King, Stephen. *It*. New York: Viking, 1986.

Magistrale, Tony. *Stephen King The Second Decade, "Danse Macabre" to "The Dark Half."* New York: Twayne, 1992.

Winter, Douglas E. *Stephen King: The Art of Darkness*. New York: Signet, 1986.

V

Masculine Power and the "Problem" of the Female Body

The Traffic in Women

Stephen King's 1983 horror novel *Christine* (as well as John Carpenter's movie of the same name) is a curious amalgamation of so many stories we've heard before: the 1950s teen romance, the male coming-of-age narrative, the myth of the evil machine.[4] It's *Pygmalion* and *Carrie* and *Frankenstein* and *American Graffiti* all rolled into one narrative *vehicle*. Further, it's a novel of nostalgia for a powerful American past and a novel marking the death of the American romance with the automobile, itself emblematic of American power and progress in 1950s postwar culture. The novel, in fact, seems a perverse echo of the nostalgic television series *Happy Days*. The names of the show's lead character and of the soda shop proprietor, Richie Cunningham and Arnold respectively, are combined in the name of the novel's main character, Arnold Richard Cunningham. The stories of romance, horror, and nostalgia contaminate one another in King's text, and the nostalgia for past narratives foregrounds the violence and power inequities of both gender and sexuality inscribed therein.

In the novel, Arnie Cunningham, a stereotypical nerd, must buy a car and obtain a girlfriend in order to construct himself as an autonomous male, wielding financial/sexual power and divorcing himself from overprotective parents and a protective best friend, Dennis Guilder, the high school jock who narrates most of the novel. But this narrative of a young man coming to power is complicated by his relations with other men, and also by the car, Christine, and the girlfriend, Leigh Cabot. Across the bodies of Christine and Leigh, the desires, anxieties, jealousies of other men are cathected or exchanged. Both car and woman become vehicles of homosocial exchange within the social spaces inscribed in the novel, primarily those of the father-son relationship, adolescent male friendship, and romantic triangle(s).

Dennis Guilder, the narrator, begins the novel: "This is the story of a lover's triangle, I suppose you'd say—Arnie Cunningham, Leigh Cabot, and, of course, Christine" (1). But that "of course" is a bit disingenuous, for the Arnie/Leigh/Christine triangle is only one triangle among many in the novel. In fact, the primary triangle might arguably be that of Arnie, Leigh, and Dennis, the most traditional triangle and the one Dennis admits late in the novel—the triangle in which "the Best Friend steps in" (224). The relationship between Arnie and Dennis is repeatedly triangulated—not only by Leigh (the girlfriend) and by Christine (the car), but also by Arnie's overprotective parents, Michael and Regina Cunningham, professors who teach at Horlicks University (King's less-than-subtle and sexist dig at academics); by the former owner of Christine, Roland LeBay, whose ghost comes back to haunt both the car and Arnie; and by Will Darnell, the owner of a garage who rents space to Arnie and who later involves him in illegal, interstate commerce. Dennis says of the time that Arnie spends working on Christine in Darnell's garage, "And goddammit, was I *jealous*? Was that what it was?" (68).

Sedgwick ties the romantic triangle to the homosocial transactions of patriarchal culture, in which heterosexuality is bound to traffic in women: "the use of women as exchangeable, perhaps symbolic, property for cementing the bonds of men with men" (25–26). Dennis and Arnie's relationship is part of a complex web of relationships, of male social space and homosocial commerce—of men circulating cars and women among themselves. LeBay sells Christine to Arnie, who rents space from Darnell in which to work on "her." Dennis "steals" Arnie's girlfriend. Arnie admits that the primary reason he asks Leigh out is his jealousy in imagining her with other men (163). In other words, he asks her out not for herself, not because he desires her, but because she is desired by other men. Ironically, he later says that Christine had been "waiting for the right buyer": the one "who would love her for herself alone" (319).

Although Arnie rejects his stereotypically wimpy father and castrating mother,[5] he adopts two alternative fathers (or fathers-in-law): Darnell, the garage owner, and LeBay, who sells Christine to Arnie, an exchange of feminized property. Stephen Bayley calls the transaction, which occurs in a chapter entitled "Arnie Gets Married," "a complex litter of meanings, combining sex and money and ownership in a trilogy of intense eroticism" (29). When Arnie and Dennis stop to look at the car, Dennis thinks of LeBay as "a very old pimp huckstering a very young boy" (34). As Arnie later imagines the transaction, it is a marriage in a used car lot, Darnell the best man, Christine the bride, and LeBay rising to give away the bride (317–18). Dennis remembers Arnie's first view of the car as "love at first sight" (63), and he later portrays the relationship as a sexual addiction or obsession—"you're hooked right through the fucking bag, aren't you?" he asks Arnie. Arnie thinks of Christine in sexual/romantic terms as a "perfect" spouse, "waiting faithfully" on him: "She would never argue or complain, Arnie thought. She would never demand. You could enter her anytime and . . . rest in her warmth. She would never deny. . . . *She loved him*" (319). Even Dennis's even-tempered and rational father speaks of the purchase "as if . . . Arnie had gotten married" (63). The purchase of a car is figured in the images of the traffic in women—both prostitution and marriage (in which a man "gives" his daughter to another man). LeBay further equates cars and women when he compares "the smell of a brand-new car," which is "about the finest smell in the world," with that of female genitalia (10), a remark that Arnie later echoes by equating driving and sex (413). LeBay himself had been in love with the car: An acquaintance says of him that he "treated it like it was a woman. . . . He loved that fucking car. . . . He didn't give a shit for his wife" (396–97). Leigh calls Arnie's relation with Christine "a disturbing parody of the act of love" (196).

That cars are women is no new metaphor, though it becomes a bit tiresome in the novel. But the novel does foreground it as a learned, male metaphorization. Dennis—who has nightmares about Christine "bearing down on him in the high womanscream of burning rubber" (226)[6]—says, "it's from your father that you get the magic, the talismans, the words of power. If the car won't start, curse it . . . and be sure you curse it female" (36). It is a repeated motif that by the middle of the novel has a horrific effect, combining discourses of eroticism, homosociality, manipulation, and violence, so that men working together on a car becomes a symbolic gang-rape:

Inside, the world was full of the echoey, evocative bang of tools and the sound of men working on cars and hollering profanity at the rolling iron they were working on. Always the profanity, and always female in gender: come offa there, you bitch, come loose, you cunt, come on over here, Rick, and help me get this twat off. (120)

Like LeBay, these men not only compare cars to women, but specifically to female genitalia, and the pun in the last phrase portrays men working on a car together as men having sex with a woman.[7]

In this textual world of banging tools and sexualized cars, only Leigh questions the association of gender and cars, even as she reinforces it. Dennis briefly resists calling the car "Christine"—"I didn't like it," he says, though he immediately compares Arnie's purchase to a man "who meets a showgirl, indulges in a whirlwind courtship, and ends up with a hangover and a new wife on Monday morning" (63). It is Leigh who tells Arnie that cars are girls. When Leigh asks Arnie "which you love more," he says, "I thought girls were supposed to be jealous of other girls. Not cars." She answers, "Cars *are* girls. Didn't you know that?" (194). King adds:

Cars are girls, she had said. She hadn't been thinking of what she was saying; it had just popped out of her mouth. And it certainly wasn't always true; she didn't think of their family sedan as having any particular gender; it was just a Ford. (195)

But Christine is a girl (even if King does, for the moment, undercut Leigh's moment of insight). Leigh tells Arnie that she cannot make out with him in the car, because—as she later tells herself—"it was like making love inside the body of her rival," it was a "perversion." To ride in Christine, adds Leigh, is to be "swallowed" in her (196). Christine—mouth or womb—is female, and to Leigh, making love to Arnie in the car would be to make love inside the body of another woman.

Christine and Leigh are in many ways interchangeable goods in the novel's systems of exchange. Leigh does not ask Arnie whom he loves more, but *which* he loves more, grammatically portraying both as things. Not only does Leigh recognize that cars are girls and that their rivalry is a sexual rivalry, but Christine may emblematize for Leigh her own disenfranchisement, especially because her dreams about gender and power inevitably turn to cars and driving, to being forced as a child to ask for dolls for Christmas rather than the red racing car she really wanted because it was a "boy toy" (204–5). Worse, the metaphor of cars as women is reversible in the novel, for in this text, women are cars. Dennis, madly in love with Leigh, compares her to a new car: "Like that long-ago Plymouth that had rolled out of Detroit on a carrier in 1957, she was, in a sense, still under warranty" (427). He notes elsewhere that "Leigh Cabot didn't have any rust on her rocker panels" (141).

Cars and women—as goods, bodies, and commodified sexuality—are items of exchange; they mark off the proper versions and property of male society. However, this metaphor not only underlines the novel's homosociality, it also indicts and contaminates its users as well. If women are cars, then all bodies are machines, indicating an anxiety about bodies and bodily identity. Drugs, alcohol, and sex are, for Dennis, compulsive "engines" (62), people are "in gear" (221), minds in "overdrive" (337), and most dramatically, the car's body and men's bodies replicate one another. LeBay dies when Christine is vandalized (182)—an equation Dennis makes specific when he imagines their having similar injuries (to eyes and headlights). And Arnie's complexion gets better in tandem with Christine's repairs (120). Finally, when Christine hunts one victim while panting like an animal (289), the text immediately reverses the metaphorization, and the last breath of Buddy Repperton, the victim, slips out "like auto exhaust" (293).

The Gold Key to the Crapper

The anxiety about the body finds further expression in an anxiety about anality—the body's wastes, the body's orifices, its penetrable boundaries. Within the various frames of male social relations in the novel, male power and the gift of (female) goods are inextricably linked to violence and defilement. Every frame of exchange becomes in some way marked by refuse, by the remainders and reminders of parodic, illegitimate, or "unnatural" exchanges. The continued return to scatological language and the continued motif of shit, both literal and symbolic, mark an anxiety about the aggressive homoerotics of social space in the novel.

If it is Dennis and LeBay who mark—with Arnie—the homosocial systems of the novel (the erotic triangle, the marriage exchange), it is Darnell who more clearly marks the defilement integral to these systems of exchange. His is the realm of illicit commerce. Not only does he traffic in alcohol, tobacco, and cocaine illegally (242, 412), but it is Darnell who emphatically collapses money, power, and privilege into the language of shit. As he had previously hired LeBay, Darnell hires Arnie as a runner, and he gives Arnie a garage door opener, to give him easy access to garage space and illegal goods. King adds, "It [the door opener] was, perhaps, Darnell's version of a gold key to the crapper" (242)—the true sign of privilege, the locked executive restroom.

The movie version of the novel repeats and amplifies the image of the gold key. When Arnie first arrives at the garage in the movie, Darnell warns him that he has no privileges yet: "Don't think you've got the gold key to the crapper." And he continues this language of scatology and anality, talking about "shitpiles" of money and "money falling out of my asshole." In Darnell's world, privilege and socioeconomic power become access—secret, powerful, privileged access—to shit. When Arnie works the circuits of illegal interstate commerce, he transports the contraband in the secret compartment of a car's trunk, goods cleverly inaccessible in the rear of Darnell's 1966 Chrysler Imperial. Similarly, in the short story "Rita Hayworth and the Shawshank Redemption," from King's 1982 collection *Different Seasons*, Andy, who is raped by "killer queens" in prison (21) and examined anally by the guards, gets back at them by using money he has secreted in his anal cavity, and his friend (the narrator) smuggles his story out of prison the same way Andy smuggled money in.[8]

Throughout *Christine*, anal language functions as a discourse of both power and aggression, further collapsing structures of violence and privilege. Arnie, becoming or echoing LeBay, keeps inveighing against the "shitters" of the world—it is LeBay's signature word that Arnie adopts. But shit as both a marker of aggression and an item of exchange is literalized when the town hoodlums destroy Christine and, in a final and crucial act of defilement, defecate on her dashboard (213). This act is the pivot of the novel: After this moment, every relationship in the novel is markedly changed, and the killings begin. After Christine smashes the first of the boys, Moochie Welch, the invective is returned, and Moochie is metaphorized as shit to be scraped up with a shovel. (Implied, perhaps, is that Moochie is the one who actually defecated on Christine.) Arnie actually calls Moochie shit only in the movie version. In the book, it is the police investigator, Rudy Junkins, who says of Moochie, "Isn't that what you're supposed to do with shit? Scrape it up with a shovel?" (257) But he is mocking Arnie's unbelievably flippant dismissal of the dashboard defecation. Arnie pretends to be unaffected by the vandalistic destruction of his car, and he keeps repeating, about the excrement, "Shit wipes off" (256). In between these utterances, a mechanic in the garage curses his car, female of course, chanting, "Oh shit on you, you whore"—a textual echo of Christine's desecration (257).

It is surely no accident that at the novel's end, Dennis crushes Christine inside of Darnell's garage, the space of shit, with a sewage truck named Petunia. Calling the truck a "kaka sucker" (263), he tells its owner, "I want to get rid of some shit" (265). And he proceeds to use it to restore order, to kill Christine, to clean up that defiled social space and homosocial order. But the social space is still tainted. The smell of shit remains and reminds. Petunia still smells of sewage and Christine of dead bodies, the excess and the (living) dead she leaves in her wake. It is surely no accident either that when Darnell is arrested for his illegal business, the police again use anal language for the restoration of social order: "Get this bag of shit out of here" (336).

In her analysis of the movie *To Live and Die in L. A.*, Sharon Willis ties anal language not only to illicit commerce (counterfeit money) and male aggression, but to the homoerotics of commerce and the corollary homophobia of the narrative as well—male aggression is figured repeatedly in images of male rape (16–19). Sedgwick writes of Dickens's *Our Mutual Friend*, "[It] is the only English novel that everyone says is about excrement in order that they may forget that it is about anality" (*Between Men*, 164), and she connects the traditional and Freudian criticism of acquisition, of "filth and lucre," to anal eroticism. Similarly, economic and social power and issues of control are tied to the bodily images of anality in King's *Christine*. Moochie Welch, the novel's "sack of 'shit'" is also literally a sack of money—he had been begging for spare change outside a concert, and as he ran away from Christine, the pockets of his pants and parka jingled with over thirty dollars' worth of nickels and dimes. But in the emphatically homosocial textual realm of Christine, both homophobia and aggression play an inevitable part in the textual trajectory of the anal theme. As Willis explains, "male homosocial bonding . . . depends on keeping its distance, through repression and violence, from homosexuality; hence it depends, in its historical construction, upon homophobia" (18).

When the ghost of LeBay actually takes over Arnie, Arnie/LeBay finds himself saying,

and those shitters with their fancy goddam cars and the trunks full of golf-clubs those goddam officers I'd like to bend them over this here lathe I'd play some golf with them I could find the right hole to put those little white balls in you bet your ass. (317)

Later, while drinking beer with Dennis, Arnie/LeBay throws his empty cans into a wastebasket, saying, "Watch me put it up the little tramp's ass, Dennis" (408). Both the wastebasket and "the right hole to put those little white balls in" are aggressive images of anal rape. The "little tramp" is an image of waste (a wastebasket) and of power; the name refers not to a woman, but to Charlie Chaplin and indirectly to Hitler—one of LeBay's obsessions (429). The other image suggests the multiple rape of powerful men (military officers); anal rape becomes an expression of power over them. The double-bind of the image of anal rape is its aggressive masculinity and its possible homoeroticism. In a textual world of relentless heterosexuality, such an image may symbolize the presumed "unnaturalness" of other exchanges in the novel (such as the illegal commodities hidden in the trunk), but it also continues the dynamics of homophobia and misogyny because the powerless—male or female—are always the "fucked."

Like a Couple of Queers

Late in the novel, Dennis wonders if this has only been the story of two childhood friends growing apart and of his own consequent "fixation on Christine, the wedge that had come between [them]" (439). One might thus read the novel as a narrative of the movement from adolescent same-sex relationships to adult heterosexual relations.[9] Even such a traditional psychological narrative may be marked by anxieties about homosexual desire and female sexuality, and to simply dismiss the narrative in such a way—as only a narrative of boyhood friends sexually and socially growing apart—is to dismiss the overwhelming homosociality the novel inscribes, indicts, and evades. As Dennis himself says of such an interpretation, "It ignored the hard facts, but it was comfortable"

(439). For Dennis, such an interpretation ignores the unbelievable "hard facts" of a sentient car and a ghost; it allows Dennis and Leigh to live "ordinary lives." For the contemporary reader, such a reading ignores the overwhelmingly gendered and sexualized social systems of the novel; it ignores the commodification of women that the sexualized car suggests, and it ignores the homosociality that the ghost represents—a father proffering a woman's body to his son, a father taking over the son's body.[10]

Such a reading is perhaps also comfortable, because it allows Dennis (and the reader) to ignore the sexual anxieties at work in the relationship between Dennis and Arnie. When Dennis asks himself, after Christine begins to take up Arnie's time, "was I jealous?" (68), the answer is an emphatic, albeit evasive, yes. When Dennis's new, buxom girlfriend wants him to take her to a local make-out spot, he admits, "I should maybe have been thinking about the promise of her breast, but instead I found myself thinking about Arnie" (83). In the narrative of the romantic triangle, the real bond being delineated is that between the male rivals, "the bond between rivals in an erotic triangle . . . being even stronger, more heavily determinant of actions and choices, than anything in the bond between either of the lovers and the beloved" (Sedgwick, *Between Men,* 21). The real bond developed by the novel is that between Dennis and Arnie. Dennis notes, as he attempts to comfort Leigh, "I saw all too clearly what comforting her could lead to. Arnie was between us—and part of myself was, too. I had known him for a long time. A long good time" (381). It is as if the relationship with Arnie takes emotional and temporal precedence over that with Leigh. Leigh drops out of the romantic plot at the end, marrying an IBM customer service representative rather than Arnie or Dennis. Arnie dies—appropriately enough, in a car accident with his mother—and Dennis concludes the tale of Arnie, "Rest in peace, Arnie. I love you, man" (497).

In the novel, the heterosexual love triangle is bound to a homosexual panic, the fear and loathing provoked when the affection between men begins to become eroticized.[11] When the female body—car or woman—is erased from the exchange, or when the male body itself becomes feminized, the erotic potential of homosociality seems to necessitate homophobia and a panic about homosexuality. Arnie is repeatedly feminized in the novel, his body and his psyche marked as feminine and permeable. Not only do the school bullies call Arnie "Cuntface" (145), but Dennis himself feminizes Arnie in his narration. He calls Arnie's laughter "hysterical" and feminine (49), he protects him at school, and he notes that Arnie's first job, flagging for a road crew, is a "girl's job"—in fact, Arnie fills in for the girl who quit because she became pregnant (12).

At one point, when Arnie, who seems "hysterical" and "haglike," starts crying, Dennis hugs him:

I knew what to do. Reluctantly, not wanting to, I slid across the seat and put my arms around him and held him. I could feel his face, hot and fevered, mashed against my chest. We sat that way for maybe five minutes, and then I drove him to his house and dropped him off. After that I went home myself. Neither of us talked about it later, me holding him like that. No one came along the sidewalk and saw us parked at the curb. I suppose if someone had, we would have looked *like a couple of queers.* I sat there and held him and loved him the best I could and wondered how come it had to be that I was Arnie Cunningham's only friend, because right then, believe me, I didn't want to be his friend. (56, emphasis added)

This scene between Dennis and Arnie is not marked by the aggressive anality of LeBay, though Arnie does late in the novel include Dennis among the "shitters" of the world—"You stole my girl . . . you're just a *shitter*, like all the rest of them" (454). But the scene is marked by King's obsession with the anal because Dennis says he would rather be "standing in front of a pay toilet stall with diarrhea and no dime" than holding his hysterical friend, thus equating homosexual panic with an excremental anxiety (indeed, the problem of control of the sphincter). This scene also prefigures Leigh's refusal to embrace Arnie in Christine; these two embraces (or lack thereof) frame the sexual politics of Arnie's purchase of and obsession with Christine, and both encounters (the actual and the feared) take place in a car, stereotypical realm of teenage sexuality.

More importantly, for Dennis, this is a scene of both tenderness and disgust; a poignant aporia, it is unspeakable ("Neither of us talked about it later"). Douglas Keesey, in his analysis of homophobia in King's fiction, footnotes this scene—among several—as indicative of "the fear that male bonding will be seen as gay attraction," which is, "pervasive in King's fiction," and which he ties to Sedgwick's descriptions of homosexual panic (Keesey, 199, n. 4).[12] This is not to say that Dennis is homosexual, but to note the homoerotic and homophobic tension of the text. Male tenderness must be held at a homophobic arm's length. To "[love] him the best I could" is to hate and disavow that love: to not talk about it, to wish to be somewhere else, someone else. He doesn't want to be Arnie's friend because of the fear that to others— and perhaps to Arnie or himself—it will seem that he really wants to be Arnie's lover. Late twentieth-century American culture, as the text indicates, fosters an anxiety about and a disjuncture in the relations of men with men, rigorously policing the proper exchanges of homosocial bonds: cars and women, not embraces. In such a culture, as a character says in another King story, there is "no room for the hommasexshul" (*Night Shift*, 263).

Hard Bodies, Soft Bodies

For Arnie, at one point in the novel, homosexual panic is all too real. Christine has been his symbolic phallus, his source of potency (200). But when he is arrested with Darnell's goods in his trunk (hidden in the special compartment in the rear of Darnell's Imperial), he sees his phallic power taken away, his body commodified, and his anal privileges redefined in a realm of violent, erotic, and oppressive homosocial power: "His panic-stricken mind spun up a kaleidoscope of jumbled images. . . . Prison bars, blued steel. A judge bending down from a high bench. . . . Big bull queers in a prison yard looking for fresh meat. Christine riding the conveyor into the carcrusher in the junkyard" (338). The police penetrate his car's trunk, three men gathered around the rear of the car, one policeman accusing Arnie of being "an asshole," another policeman's body phallically "almost entirely in the trunk; only his blue-gray-clad legs stuck out" (339). Arnie begins to think of Christine to reassure himself, as, throughout the novel, he has touched or caressed her hard body to gather confidence—"He groped back behind him, touched Christine—her hard, cool, reassuring surface—and things dropped back into place again" (329). (Arnie constantly caresses the car, "seeming to draw strength from it" [180]. Her "solidity" seems "to comfort him" [255].) Christine's "hard" body, phallic and impermeable (and "behind" him), is Arnie's support, a comfort to his fears of psychic and bodily permeability, which are figured in the image of "big bull queers" who surely echo the rapists of "Shawshank Redemption."[13]

Although Arnie's terror at arrest is of his body's penetrability—vividly imagined in the image of anal rape—a more frightening terror might be his loss of both identity and body to a usurping male, not in sex, violence, or confinement, but in possession. Arnie's other father figure, Roland LeBay, who sells him Christine, returns as a ghost to inhabit both the car and Arnie's body. The ghost in the car becomes the ghost in the machine, and Arnie's body gives birth to his own violent father, the ghost of LeBay "coalescing" inside him (351). At one point an "apparition" appears in the car beside Arnie. At first he sees that it is the ghost of LeBay, then it seems to be an aged version of himself. Arnie thinks to himself, "This version of himself and Roland D. LeBay could have been son and father: the resemblance was that great" (322). The ghost embodies the perverse patriarchal lineage of the father usurping the body of the son.

But that apparition—like many of the apparitional bodies in Christine—dissolves, both literally and figuratively. The body shrivels and decays in front of Arnie, "rotting before his very eyes" (322). The bodies associated with Christine are never solid.[14] Dennis repeatedly characterizes his perception of LeBay within Arnie in images of a drowned man (337). Arnie's identity seems liquid, LeBay's face ever protruding, taking over, or pushing through Arnie's body. When LeBay begins to take over, Arnie's face "roils" (456), his body shudders and convulses "as if a basket of snakes had been dumped inside his clothes" (457). His language and his body, even a characteristic back injury, gradually replicate LeBay. The signature of Arnie also becomes that of Roland LeBay—which Dennis and Leigh find out with a bit of detective work (386–90)—not only representing the fact that LeBay's ghost is taking over Arnie's body (as it had the car), but also indicating the importance of the patronymic, the father's name. If Christine is Arnie's symbolic phallus, his sense of power, it is only because it is bestowed by LeBay, who represents the perverse law of the patriarchy that structures the narrative.

This return of the ghost is an intrusion of the past, a return of history and his story. Arnie talks, says his father, "as if this were the fifties instead of the seventies" (468). Christine, narrative and car, facilitates a nostalgia for past narratives. (The movie visually quotes James Dean's *Rebel Without A Cause*.) The car's odometer runs only backwards, and the radio plays only oldies. Set in 1978 and published in 1983, this novel is an elegy to the American romance with the automobile. King notes the degeneration of neighborhoods, the transformation of "desirable neighborhoods" into "exurban sprawl" (44). He notes in particular the renaming of a street: Barnswallow Drive, the center of a residential neighborhood, becomes JFK Drive, a strip of gas stations and fast-food restaurants on the way to the Pennsylvania Turnpike. The loss of a mythic American past is doubly marked in the street name (after the assassination of John F. Kennedy) and the transformation of neighborhoods into aesthetically displeasing roadside culture.

But the novel is perhaps also an indictment of our romantic desires for past narratives and our blindness to the repression that haunts them. In this novel, the return to nostalgic history involves the return of a repressed history, a kind of return of the living dead figured in the misogyny and homophobia that linger with us. The nostalgia for past narratives releases the violence inscribed therein and foregrounds a history marked by male power and male privilege: a horrific story, in which women and/as cars delineate a homosocial culture, and in which ghosts and shit mark the violence, repression, and the homosexual panic integral to that culture. If the automobile may be said to both *shape* and *haunt* American imagination (Dettelbach, 120), King's *Christine* foregrounds both the gender dynamics that shape American (car) culture and the sexual anxieties that haunt it. Dennis asks himself midway through the novel:

Buy an old car and it will what? Change your head, your way of thinking . . . ? If we follow this line of reasoning to the bitter end, ladies and gentlemen, where does it take us?
Where indeed? (138)

Where indeed. To a social and textual realm in which women and cars are interchangeable goods, and where homosexuality is a frightening category of experience. To a world in which "cars are girls," one in which a man may claim to have "built the Ferrari" of his daughter's body and now "want the keys back," rather than let her assert her own subjectivity. To a culture in which misogyny and homophobia are intimately connected. In fact, to a culture not so very different from our own.

NOTES

1. See Stephen Bayley's *Sex, Drink, and Fast Cars* for an extended analysis of the female symbolism of automobiles. See also *Driving Passion: The Psychology of the Car*, by Peter Marsh and Peter Collett, which refers briefly to King's *Christine* in relation to

the themes of the car as a weapon and as a love object (170, 198). On the broader significance of the automobile in American culture, see *The Automobile Age* and *The Car Culture*, by James Flink; *The Automobile in American Culture*, edited by David L. Lewis and Laurence Goldstein; *Roadside America: The Automobile in Design and Culture*, edited by Jan Jennings; and *In the Driver's Seat: The Automobile in American Literature and Popular Culture*, by Cynthia Golomb Dettelbach. Dettelbach's book appeared before the publication of King's *Christine*, but her chapter on "Dreams of Possession, Nightmares of Being Possessed" (90–120) provides a useful analysis of many of the themes that surface in *Christine*. Finally as a contrast to King's *Christine*, see J. G. Ballard's 1973 novel *Crash*, a disturbingly erotic novel that finds in the imagery of automobile accidents an equation of sex, technology, and violence. Unlike the determinedly heterosexual and homophobic narrative of Stephen King's *Christine*, *Crash* is bisexual, even polymorphously perverse.

2. On the exchange of women as property, see, for example, Lévi-Strauss's 1949 *The Elementary Structures of Kinship*; Irigaray's *This Sex Which Is Not One*; Rubin's "The Traffic in Women: Notes on the 'Political Economy' of Sex"; and Sedgwick's *Between Men*, especially the chapter on "Gender Asymmetry and Erotic Triangles." (See also Emma Goldman's "The Traffic in Women," an earlier economic analysis of prostitution and the "white slave trade.") Both Irigaray and Rubin reread Lévi-Strauss's analysis through the lens of feminist theory. Sedgwick builds upon their analyses, but where Irigaray fails to distinguish between the social construction of male-male bonds and the actual demonization of male-male sex (see, for example, Irigaray 192), Sedgwick points out the simultaneous homosocial and homosexual dynamics at work in the traffic in women and the disavowal of the homosexual at work in the hegemony of the homosocial. I am especially indebted to Sedgwick's work. On the necessity of the homophobic impulse in Western homosocial cultures see Sedgwick's *Between Men* (3, 18–20, 25–27).

3. Verena Lovett, who examines in detail the menstrual imagery of King's 1974 novel *Carrie*, dismisses *Christine* as simply comparable to "misogynistic pulp fiction," a novel about "the tensions of masculinity" rather than the "female energy" she finds significant in other King texts (174). She fails to take into account the fact that, although women in the novel are minor characters, the car Christine, emphatically a female entity, is a primary character. There is female energy in this text, but, as I demonstrate, it is tied to misogynistic fear and homophobia, both of which structure the novel's "tensions of masculinity."

4. The myth of the evil or sentient machine is a common theme in King's fiction. See "Uncle Otto's Truck" in *Skeleton Crew* and "Trucks" in *Night Shift*.

5. King depicts both parents as "caricatures" (to use King's own word for Arnie's father). Both are academics. Michael, Arnie's father, is a mournful, vegetarian history professor who mopes around in cutoffs playing a recorder. Regina, his mother, is a cold, domineering English professor who wants to crush any sense of teenage rebellion. (See 17–18, 23.)

6. This screaming is a characteristic feature of Christine. For example, "the car was still shrieking like an insanely angry, murderous woman" (240), and "he heard the car's engine scream. The sound was like the shriek of a woman who scents treachery" (368).

7. It is perhaps worth noting here that one character in the novel (who is sitting in a gas station, masturbating) reads a pornographic novel entitled "Swap-Around Pammie," which features a woman who "had gotten it from just about everyone" (360–61). In the

novel's male and automotive (sexist and misogynistic) world, women are repeatedly shared by men.

8. The implication, then, for the reader is that text he or she is holding is the transcript of that secreted (or excreted) text. The movie version also seems to foreground the anality of the story. Andy escapes from prison through the sewage system, and he slides out of a sewage pipe in a scene that can only be described as excremental.

9. Earlier in the novel, Dennis says he feels like someone whose best friend has married a "high-riding dyed-in-the-wool bitch," "You don't like the bitch," he says, and she doesn't like you, so "you just close the door on that room of your friendship," or, more likely, "you find your friend letting go of you, usually with the bitch's enthusiastic approval" (70). Such imagery furthers the interpretation of the narrative as a movement from adolescent male bonding to adult heterosexuality.

10. Both LeBay and Christine are the catalysts of the perverse proliferations of triangulating desire. When LeBay takes over the body of Arnie, Dennis says Arnie and Leigh's relationship becomes "a perversion on perversion—LeBay, Leigh, and Christine in some hideous *ménage à trois*" (446). And Dennis says of his budding relationship with Leigh, "Arnie was between them, and almost surely always would be. Arnie and his lady" (224), referring, of course, to Christine.

11. In *Between Men*, Sedgwick uses the term "homosexual panic" to denote the perceived social threat of "blackmailability," "the interiorized and psychologized homophobia inherent in Western homosocial bonding, which enforces the disjuncture between homosexual desire and homosocial relations" (89–90). Later, in the *Epistemology of the Closet*, Sedgwick enlarges the definition to take into account the legal use of the term, "homosexual panic" being a defense used in court to prevent or lighten the sentencing of those who commit antigay bias crimes (gay-bashing, assault, murder), a defense based on the "assumption that hatred of homosexuals is so private and so atypical a phenomenon in this culture as to be classifiable as an accountability-reducing illness." Sedgwick notes that the defense is so widely accepted that it in fact proves just the opposite, that hatred of homosexuals is "even more public, more typical, hence harder to find any leverage against than hatred of other disadvantaged groups" (*Epistemology of the Closet*, 19–21). This defense, in fact, was used as recently as 1993 in the state of Texas, in relation to the murder of Tommy Music in Midland in April 1993. His murderers got a lighter sentence because they claimed they became "momentarily irrational with fear" when Music allegedly made sexual advances. (For a discussion of this case and its implications, see Garry Boulard's article, "The Anti-Twinkie Defense" in *The Advocate*, June 14, 1994.)

12. Much of Keesey's analysis is an attempt to recuperate King's fiction from the charge of homophobia. His reading of *It* is a sophisticated and perhaps convincing attempt to prove that, at least in that novel, "Only by facing up to one's fear of effeminacy, only by acknowledging the monstrousness of homophobia, can one learn to live with others and with the Otherness in oneself" (198). However, despite Keesey's compelling reading of *It*, I find *Christine* to be much less nuanced: It is a text in which the repeated denigration or objectification of the female and the aggressive anality between men reinforces misogyny and homophobia in ways that are both unsubtle and unredeemable through any kind of creative reading.

13. Frank Darabont, the director and screenwriter of the 1994 movie version, distanced himself from the homophobia possibly represented in the "bull queers," insisting that they are not gay but rapists who substitute men when women are not

available. (See "The Buzz" in *The Advocate*, 4 April 1995.) The rapists, however, are still labeled "queens" or queers; they are still marked as homosexual.

14. Christine carries the ghosts of her victims. A car full of rotting corpses appears at a gas station for one of the final murders (362–63), and the rotting dead—in various states of dismemberment or decay—appear as wedding guests in Arnie's dream of marriage to Christine (318).

WORKS CITED

Ballard, J. G. *Crash*. New York: Farrar, 1973.

Bayley, Stephen. *Sex, Drink, and Fast Cars*. New York: Pantheon, 1986.

Boulard, Garry. "The Anti-Twinkie Defense." *The Advocate*, 14 June 1994, 33–38.

"The Buzz" Rev. of *The Shawshank Redemption*. *The Advocate*, 4 April 1995, 70–71.

Carpenter, John. Dir. *Christine*. Columbia Pictures, 1983.

Darabont, Frank. Dir. *The Shawshank Redemption*. Columbia Pictures, 1994.

Dettelbach, Cynthia Golomb. *In the Driver's Seat: The Automobile in American Literature and Popular Culture*. Westport: Greenwood, 1976.

Flink, James J. *The Automobile Age*. Cambridge: MIT Press, 1988.

——. *The Car Culture*. Cambridge: MIT Press, 1975.

Goldman, Emma. "The Traffic in Women." *Anarchism and Other Essays*. 1917. New York: Dover, 1969, 177–94.

Irigaray, Luce. *This Sex Which Is Not One*. Translated by Catherine Porter. Ithaca: Cornell University Press, 1985.

Jennings, Jan, ed. *Roadside America: The Automobile in Design and Culture*. Ames: Iowa State University Press, 1990.

Keesey, Douglas. "'The Face of Mr. Flip': Homophobia in the Horror of Stephen King." *The Dark Descent: Essays Defining Stephen King's Horrorscape*. Edited by Tony Magistrale. Westport, CT: Greenwood, 1992, 187–201.

King, Stephen. *Christine*. New York: Viking, 1983.

——. *Different Seasons*. New York: Viking, 1982.

——. *Night Shift*. Garden City, NY: Doubleday, 1978.

——. *Skeleton Crew*. New York: Putnam's, 1985.

Lévi-Strauss, Claude. *The Elementary Structures of Kinship*. 1949, 1967. Translated by James Harle Bell, John Richard von Sturmer, and Rodney Needham. Edited by Rodney Needham. Boston: Beacon, 1969.

Lewis, David L., and Laurence Goldstein, eds. *The Automobile and American Culture*. Ann Arbor: University of Michigan Press, 1980, 1983.

Lovett, Verena. "Bodily Symbolism and the Fiction of Stephen King." *Gender, Genre, and Narrative Pleasure*. Edited by Derek Longhurst. London: Unwin Hyman, 1989, 157–76.

Marsh, Peter, and Peter Collett. *Driving Passion: The Psychology of the Car*. Boston: Faber and Faber, 1986.

"Perspectives." *Newsweek*, 27 June 1994, 13.

Rubin, Gayle. "The Traffic in Women: Notes on the 'Political Economy' of Sex." *Toward an Anthropology of Women*. Edited by Rayna R. Reiter. New York and London: Monthly Review, 1975, 157–210.

Sedgwick, Eve Kosofsky. *Between Men: English Literature and Male Homosocial Desire*. New York: Columbia University Press, 1985.

——. *Epistemology of the Closet*. Berkeley: University of California Press, 1990.
Simmons. Lydia. "Not from the Back Seat." *The Automobile and American Culture*. Edited by David L. Lewis and Laurence Goldstein. Ann Arbor: University of Michigan Press, 1980, 1983, 153–58.
Willis, Sharon. "Disputed Territories: Masculinity and Social Space." *Camera Obscura: A Journal of Feminism and Film Theory* 19 (January 1989): 4–23.

The Rape of Constant Reader: Stephen King's Construction of the Female Reader and Violation of the Female Body in *Misery*

Kathleen Margaret Lant

> Is the pen a metaphorical penis?
>> Sandra Gilbert and Susan Gubar
>> *The Madwoman in the Attic* (3)

"Here's your book, Annie," he panted, and his hand closed on more paper. This bunch was out, dripping wet, smelling sourly of spilt wine. She bucked and writhed under him. The salt-dome of his left knee whammed the floor and there was excruciating pain, but he stayed on top of her. *I'm gonna rape you, all right Annie. I'm gonna rape you because all I can do is the worst I can do. So suck my book. Suck my book. Suck on it until you fucking CHOKE.* He crumpled the wet paper with a convulsive closing jerk of his fist and slammed it into her mouth, driving the half charred first bunch farther down.

>> Stephen King
>> *Misery* (292)

> Is the pen a metaphorical pistol? Are words weapons with which the sexes have fought over territory and authority?
>> Sandra Gilbert and Susan Gubar
>> *No Man's Land* (3)

> Writing a book is a little like firing an ICBM . . . only it travels over time instead of space.
>> Stephen King
>> *Misery* (257)

In the past few years, Stephen King's relationship with his audience has taken several horrifying turns. King is arguably the best selling,[1] certainly the most lavishly rewarded,[2] author in American history, and his rise to this position may have had some rough moments at the beginning, when—as he puts it—"I began to have long talks with myself at night about whether or not I was chasing a fool's dream" ("On Becoming a Brand Name," 19). But oddly enough, King seems to be facing the most taxing and draining moments of his career at the zenith of his success. As King himself asserts, "I started out as a storyteller; along the way I became an economic force" (Beahm, 17), and the popularity of the stories that have made him such an economic force has cost him dearly. George Beahm, compiler of the exhaustive *Stephen King Companion*, asserts that "King is a publishing phenomenon and . . . a celebrity in his own right" (16) but adds that this very success has not been good for King:

He is a victim of his own celebrity status. King is a household name, a contemporary figure of popular culture. His face is recognizable, in part because of the many book-jacket photos and the media interviews, but mostly because of the campy American Express ad in which he played himself. When you're famous, popular, and rich, he has found out, everyone wants a piece of you. Understandably, that is what King detests the most; he called it in his *Time* profile "the cult of the celebrity." (Beahm, 17)

King can no longer attend conventions or book fairs; he is so heavily in demand that he finds himself threatened physically by the affection of his fans. He cannot comply with his publishers' desires to participate in book signings because, as Beahm explains, "experience has shown him that the lines may be longer than he can accommodate in a single session" (17). Richard Panek reports that fans often camp outside his Bangor, Maine, home (32), and King's safety and the safety of his family are now less than secure, a situation that seems to trouble King greatly. In fact, in 1985 he said of his career, "Sometimes I feel like Mickey Mouse in *Fantasia*. I knew enough to get the brooms started, but once they start to march, things are never the same" (Panek, 29).

In fact, King and his family have been forced to learn the dangers of King's popularity. In April of 1991, King's wife, Tabitha, was surprised in their home by an intruder carrying a fake bomb. Apparently the would-be terrorist, Eric Keene, a native of San Antonio, Texas, was convinced that King had stolen the plot of his novel *Misery* from a woman Keene claimed to be his aunt, Anne Hiltner. To make matters more complex, it seems that Hiltner herself has written to King for about ten years, accusing him of burglarizing her Princeton, New Jersey, home 150 times ("Man Threatens to Blow Up Stephen King's Home").

Another obsessive fan, Steven Lightfoot, a twenty-eight-year-old native of San Francisco, has recently made himself conspicuous in Bangor, Maine, King's hometown, sporting a bumpersticker on his van that reads, "Photos prove it's Stephen King, not Mark David Chapman, getting John Lennon's autograph. No joke, folks" ("Personals"). Lightfoot's point is, of course, that it was King and not Chapman who murdered Beatle John Lennon. And—the odd connections seem to multiply—King himself relates an incident in which the deeply disturbed Chapman approached King—before Chapman murdered Lennon—asking King for an autograph and a picture; King obliged him, later realizing that the person who "described himself as *my number-one fan* was in fact the man who killed John Lennon" (Beahm, 248). And King's secretary, Shirley Sonderegger, reports that King's fans "look to Steve for everything," including advice and money (Spignesi, 28–29). Some of their intrusions are, as she puts it, "just crazy stuff"; in fact, she says that King once received a box with "the bones and hair of several dead kittens" (29).

King's fans have made a heavy impact upon King's work as well as upon his life. In fact, he feels his own creativity threatened at times by their demands and their devotion. King has complained bitterly for years about the strange requests fans impose upon him—requests for information, for resurrection of favorite characters, for books on cherished subjects, for King's fulfillment of the fantasies he has stimulated in his fans. According to Richard Panek, it became clear early in King's career that he would not be able to keep up with his audience's insatiable and vociferous lust for his works: "Always a workaholic who churned out five to 10 pages every day except Christmas, the Fourth of July and his birthday, King now couldn't produce fast enough to meet popular demand. By 1982 he'd published 10 books in eight years not including the [pseudonymous] Bachmans" (30), and by 1990, he had written thirty book-length works (Spignesi, 150). The pressure to produce is accompanied by the pressure to create repeatedly on command the works that most please the clamorous throngs who buy those novels. King relates his vulnerability as a writer to the kinds of work he produces:

There is no particular danger in writing what I will call, for want of a better term, "serious fiction." In writing popular, commercial fiction, there is nothing but danger. The commercial writer is easy to bribe, easy to subvert, and he knows it. I have felt this much more strongly in the last two or three years than ever before. ("On Becoming a Brand Name," 16)

King seems to have made every effort both to protect himself physically from his eager audience and to preserve his creative autonomy. In addition to increasing security in his home in Bangor ("Break-In Rattles Writer Stephen King"), King has made a serious effort to extend his creative experiments into areas other than those approved by his fans. In 1982 he offered his readers *Different Seasons*, which he concluded with a somewhat defensive "Afterword": "I got typed [as a horror writer] and I don't much mind—after all, I write true to type . . . at least, *most* of the time. But is horror *all* I write? If you've read the foregoing stories, you *know* it's not" (501). And, although she focuses upon King as a horror writer, Elizabeth Young points to the fact that *Misery* and *The Dark Half* "have been highly self-referential, dealing with the collapse of the boundaries between life and fiction faced by professional authors" (34). Early in King's career (1978), John D. MacDonald emphasized King's creative autonomy when he asserted, "He does not write to please you. He writes to please himself" (ix). And during that same period, King himself insisted, in the foreword to his collection *Night Shift*, that he wrote for himself:

I didn't write any of the stories which follow for money, although some of them were sold to magazines before they appeared here and I never once returned a check uncashed. . . . I didn't write them for money; I wrote them because it occurred to me to write them. I have a marketable obsession. (xiii)

Despite King's efforts to shield himself personally and artistically, his fans have cost him dearly and frightened him badly. *Playboy* interviewer Eric Norden asked King, "Are you ever worried about a mentally unstable reader's emulating your fictional violence in real life?" and King replied, "Sure I am; it bothers me a lot" (quoted in Beahm, 42). And concerning his status as a celebrity, he remarked, "The occupational hazard of the successful writer in America is that once you begin to be successful, then you have to avoid being gobbled up. America has developed this sort of cannibalistic cult of celebrity, where first you set the guy up, and then you eat him" (quoted in Beahm, 247). In a telling harmony of metaphors, Kim Newman echoes King's fears of his audience and his concerns for his own creative autonomy in her review of his novel *Misery* (1987); Newman writes, "There are obvious parallels [in the novel] with King's own well-publicised feelings that his chosen genre has been eating him alive" (30).

Ever Et Raw Meat?

Although Stephen King has made clear his fears, frustrations, and angers over his audience for a very long time and although he has touched in many of his works—both fiction and non-fiction—on the issue of creativity, *Misery* (1987) is probably King's most thorough and complex exploration of the powers of his own mind, of the powers of the artist, of the pressures of the audience, and of the workings of creativity. King had clearly reached a crisis in his relationship with his audience during the period when he published this novel, and the fact that he published a vituperative and belittling piece on his devoted audience—"'Ever Et Raw Meat?' and Other Weird Questions"—during the same year that *Misery* appeared makes clear his concern with this constellation of issues.[3] In this novel, King expresses his intense feelings of anger at the demands his readers make by creating Annie Wilkes, a demented fan who, after a series of fortuitous events, manages to make romance writer Paul Sheldon her captive and torture and terrorize him into writing the novel she wants him to write. She is the embodiment of King's worst fantasies about fans out of control or readers run amok. She is the fan, his "number one fan," who will corrupt his work, pervert his style, and even endanger his life. As Newman puts it, *Misery* is a "writer's nightmare" (30), the nightmare of loss of creative power.

What is most horrifying about King's fantasy on the theme of creativity, however, is not his depiction of Annie Wilkes's insane victimization of Paul Sheldon, not his graphic descriptions of how Annie torments Paul mentally, humiliates him, and finally cuts him—quite literally—to pieces. The horror in the novel resides in King's own view of the creative process and, primarily, in the sexual roles he imposes upon that process. In *Misery*, creativity is solely a masculine prerogative, for the artist is male, and both the reader and the character/antagonist—made one in Paul Sheldon's vicious and dangerous fan Annie Wilkes—are female. The artist's power, moreover, is conveyed in terms of his sexuality; as a sexually potent male, Paul Sheldon is creative. When Annie Wilkes—as the subject of Stephen King's art and as the consumer of Paul Sheldon's art—inhibits or usurps the creative process, she threatens the artist's autonomy and his masculinity. She immobilizes him, she even begins to cut off parts of his body, hinting that ultimately she will excise that most essentially masculine part—she will castrate him. With her power as audience, she threatens to render Paul Sheldon—physically, emotionally, and artistically— impotent. She effects a metaphorical and a real cannibalization, to use King's frightened term, of Paul Sheldon, the stand-in for Stephen King.

The reception *Misery* garnered from reviewers when it was released in 1987 offers another testament to the absolute devotion of the very fans King insults and ridicules in this novel. Despite the hostile attitude he harbors toward his audience, many reviews were quite ecstatic over the work, completely unaware—apparently—of the implications of King's novel. Carolyn Banks, for instance, calls *Misery* King's "most heavily autobiographical and funniest work" (1), and John Katzenbach praises King's work, saying *Misery* "creates strengths out of its realities" (20). Another *New York Times* reviewer, Christopher Lehmann-Haupt—apparently striving to give King all the credit he can—asserts that the novel concerns "the torture of being a writer" (C17). Both Katzenbach and Lehmann-Haupt apparently neglect to acknowledge the very position they occupy as readers while they praise King's vituperative and violent assessment of readers and reviewers.

Oddly, the original jacket of the hardcover edition of *Misery* announced that *Misery* is "a love letter to King's fans" (Hoppenstand and Browne, 14), but several readers have termed the novel "hate mail" (Hoppenstand and Browne, 14; and Beahm, 249). Other reviewers, too, have been severely critical—not so much of the novel as a novel but rather of the angry and twisted attitudes that shape it. Darlene James calls *Misery* "both a profound comment on the potential price of commercial success and a hefty chunk of self-pitying narcissism from a successful writer groaning all the way to the bank" (51). And David Brooks charges that "Mr. King is taking a not-too-subtle slam at his audience, which only wants lightweight output," going on to assert that because *Misery* "is selling like mad . . . It just goes to show you that some people don't know when they've been insulted" (28). King was perhaps more sensitive to the anger in his work than his readers were because he originally intended to publish *Misery* under his Richard Bachman pseudonym. According to Kim Newman, the only reason he allowed the novel to appear under his name was that his Bachman identity had recently been revealed (30). And very shortly after the novel's appearance, Tabitha King, who as King's wife might share some insight into his view of his fans, went quickly to King's defense, asserting—despite the evidence in the novel to the contrary—that "Paul Sheldon is *not* Stephen King, just as Annie Wilkes is not the personification of the average Stephen King fan" (Spignesi, 114). The speediness and the vehemence of Tabitha King's retort cause one to wonder if she perceives the depth of King's insult to his audience even as she denies it.

"Binge-Eating, Depressive Woman" as Reader

If—in *Misery*—Stephen King maliciously turns the creative effort into a vicious battle between artist and audience and if he uses this novel as an opportunity to effect some revenge upon that audience he has come to hate so vehemently, we might expect to find hints in his other works of the shape his fury is beginning to take. We might examine his comments on creativity to see how and why his metaphors become so stridently aggressive by the time he writes *Misery*. If, as Karen Stabiner, observes, King presents in this novel "Everyreader" as a "binge-eating, depressive woman" (8), if the novel is, as an anonymous reviewer in *Booklist* asserts, a "misogynist fantasy" ("Upfront: Advance Review," 1153), and if the novel offers the darkest implications of our culture's view of creativity, surely evidence exists elsewhere in King's monumental and effusive output that reveals this tendency developing.

Probably the first issue of note with respect to King's view of the creative process and his part in it is that he feels somewhat insecure about his own efforts. His protagonist Paul Sheldon is, like King himself, a popular writer; whereas King is known for his horror fiction, Paul is famous for his genre romance tales about a figure (Misery Chastain) whom even he finds objectionable and insufferable; in fact, when Sheldon finally kills off Misery and moves on to more serious writing, he says "Free at last! Free at Last! Great God Almighty, I'm free at last! The silly bitch finally bought the farm!" (13). As a popular novelist, King, like Paul Sheldon, writes what he calls "plain fiction for plain folks, the literary equivalent of a Big Mac and a large fries from McDonald's" (*Different Seasons*, 504), and it is clear that he is what Richard Panek quite accurately terms "the Joe Sixpack of literature" (30). In fact, King even defines himself as a "brand name author . . . one who is known for a certain genre of the popular novel" ("On Becoming a Brand Name," 15). But King's secure position in popular fiction has not kept him from larger dreams; he admits,

I'd like to win the National Book Award, the Pulitzer Prize, the Nobel Prize. I'd like to have someone write a *New York Times Book Review* piece that says "Hey, wait a minute guys, we made a mistake—this guy is one of the great writers of the 20th century." But it's not going to happen. (quoted in Goldstein, 8)

And even as he is hurt by and yet hardened to the critical establishment's unwillingness to take him seriously, he is also victimized by his own susceptibility to criticism of his work in his chosen genre: "I obsess over the possibility of bad reviews and brood over them when they come" (*Four Past Midnight*, xiii).

King's double insecurity about his work—is he good enough to be taken seriously and is he even good enough to write that which is not taken seriously—is reflected in Paul Sheldon's goals in *Misery*. First, Paul decides to stop writing genre fiction and to move to a more critically acceptable effort; he gives up the saccharine and predictable stories about Misery for a novel called *Fast Cars* (a novel about a young street-wise male as opposed to the Misery series that concerns a glamorized, long-suffering female), which convinces him—as he completes it—that he is finally a writer of merit: "*You may have just won next year's American Book Award, my friend*," he tells himself (14). Second, however, it becomes clear that Paul is not easily going to escape the demands of his fans. He is the prisoner of Annie Wilkes (he has been injured in an automobile accident from which Annie has rescued him, and she has imprisoned him and nursed him in her deserted Colorado mountain farm), and he comes to realize that Annie is a "dangerously crazy" (8) woman who wants him to bring back the character Misery he created in his successful romance novels. In order to stay alive and to placate the controlling and demanding reader which Annie has proven herself to be, Paul must renounce his more ambitious efforts by burning his only copy of *Fast Cars*, and he must again prove himself as a genre writer; he must resurrect Misery, continue the *Misery* series, and do so in such a way as to appease this voracious audience. He must succeed in writing romance novels that Annie will love, he must continue to satisfy his popular audience. Moreover, he must write in such a way that he never stoops to cheap tricks or flashy effects to achieve Misery's resurrection, for his reader Annie is exacting and rigorous. When Sheldon offers Annie his first compulsory effort at a new Misery novel, Annie rejects it, saying "It's not right. . . . I said it wasn't *right*. It's a cheat. You'll have to change it" (97–98). Annie's attitude prompts Sheldon to consider his own feelings about Annie as audience and fan: "Had he once thought of her as the perfect audience? Oh Boy. *Have to give you credit, Paul—when you make a mistake, you go whole hog.* Constant Reader had just become Merciless Editor" (98).

Obviously, the significant question King raises about creativity here is this: Who guides the creative effort? In whose control is this creative process? As Darlene James puts it, "The plot [of *Misery*] provokes questions about the relationship between a book's producer and its consumer, a fiction writer and a fictional character. Who, ultimately, is in control? *Misery* implies that its millionaire author feels terrorized by his massive audience" (51). King himself has noted his ambivalence in dealing with his audience: "I am concerned with my readership. But it's kind of a combination love letter/poison-pen relationship, a sweet-and-sour thing. . . . I feel I ought to write something because people want to read something. But I think, 'Don't give them what they want, give them what you want'" (quoted in Goldstein, 6).

In understanding the dynamic of this power struggle between creator and those who consume or enjoy the fruits of that creativity (and who in turn reward and further inspire the creator), it is necessary to uncover the gender marking King imposes upon his metaphors for that process. What is perhaps most appalling about King's view of the creative enterprise is that the powerful agent in that act is male and that the passive recipient of the act is female. Paul Sheldon is the artist who is put upon by his "number one fan" Annie Wilkes, a woman who perverts and destroys his creative efforts. And it is clear that King's criticism of Annie Wilkes for overstepping the bounds of appropriate female behavior reflects a more extensive hostility toward women. King seems to harbor a certain anger toward those females who thwart him intellectually; he describes how, earlier in his life, he discovered the writer Loren Singer: "I happened to borrow a novel titled *The Parallax View* from the Bangor Public Library. I didn't take it out because it looked particularly good; I took it out because the old ladies with the blue rinses had, as usual, gotten to the library earlier in the day and taken everything that was good" (quoted in Underwood and Miller, *Fear Itself*, 17). And even King's enthusiastic readers seem to concur with him that the market for popular fiction is controlled by women, and they conclude that King has achieved his great success in part by learning successfully to respond to the needs of this powerful force. Gary Hoppenstand and Ray Browne assert that

King's spectacular entry into the mass market arena [with *Carrie* in 1974] was even more spectacular when considering the paperback audience of the time: well-educated middle-class women, and the predominant taste of that audience: sex/money/power thrillers and romances. (1)

Hoppenstand and Browne go on to observe that King has finely cultivated an understanding of his audience's needs and that, even chafing at the restraints of that audience, King continues to please:

he possesses an intimate understanding of what his audience desires of his work. He plays *The Author* myth for his cult following for even though he protests at times about this type of devoted reader, he does nothing to change the *status quo* . . . It's as if he fears severing the line of communication with *The Following* since *The Following* tells him what they want from him, what it takes to produce a bestseller. (5)

In meeting what Hoppenstand and Browne call the "emotional needs of his audience," King has, they point out, directed his work "at the foundation of the paperback mass market: women and adolescents" (5). And though *Misery* offers a very negative view of the connection King has forged with his audience, he clearly has exploited his audience's input; in fact, elsewhere he is often appreciative of his audience. In his introduction to *Four Past Midnight*, King applauds his readers for liking *Different Seasons*, which was not his usual effort: "God bless and keep Constant Reader; the mouth can speak, but there is no tale unless there is a sympathetic ear to listen" (xiv). In his introduction to his collection of short stories *Skeleton Crew*, King is again quite friendly toward the audience that supports him: "I hope you'll like this book, Constant Reader" (16). Oddly enough, he uses this very phrase, "Constant Reader," to refer to Annie Wilkes in *Misery*.

Despite the fact that King acknowledges his debt to "Constant Reader," he seems to rage when this figure exceeds its authority. And in coming to terms with the power of his reader, King conceives of his audience—in its most negative sense—as female, as demandingly and voraciously and belittlingly female. And because for King his own creativity seems connected ineluctably to his masculinity, King describes the connection between writer and reader in sexual terms. Again, he is the seducer, the aggressor, the masculine force, and his audience is the female—that being who must be taken. King asserts, in *Skeleton Crew*, that "reading a good long novel is in many ways like having a long and satisfying affair," and—of course—he as the writer and we as the readers are the somewhat reluctant and demuring participants in that affair. He goes on to say that a short story somewhat attenuates the intensity of this affair: "A short story is a different thing altogether—a short story is like a quick kiss in the dark from a stranger. That is not, of course, the same thing as an affair or a marriage, but kisses can be sweet, and their very brevity forms their own attraction" (17).

King carries this sexual metaphor into his remarks to his audience in several of his works. He frequently presents himself as a seducer and renders his audience as the reluctant yet interested object in need only of a bit of encouragement to succumb with a sigh of pleasure. He admits that he likes to coax his audience into a position of vulnerability: "I'm not really interested in killing somebody in the first paragraph of a novel. I want to be your friend. I want to come up to you and put my arm around you and say, 'Hey, you want to see something? It's *great*! Wait till you *see* it! You'll *really* like this thing'" (Underwood and Miller, *Bare Bones*, 4). In discussing himself as a reader, King's word choice reveals the same sexual positioning; he admits that he read Tolkien with enthusiasm because "Tolkien and his hobbits simply ravished me"—not "pleased," or "entranced," or "fascinated," but "ravished" ("What Stephen King Does for Love," 240).

And King begins his introductory note to *Four Past Midnight* with a rather innocent invitation: "Well, look at this—we're all here. We made it back again. I hope you're half as happy to be here as I am. Just saying that reminds me of a story, and since telling stories is what I do for a living (and to keep myself sane), I'll pass this one along" (xii). He sets up the same sort of intimacy in his foreword to *Night Shift*, when he says "Let's talk, you and I. Let's talk about fear. . . . Where I am, it's still dark and raining. We've got a fine night for it. There's something I want to show you, something I want you to touch. It's in a room not far from here—in fact, it's almost as close as the next page" (xi, xxii). In his introduction to *Skeleton Crew*, the sexual implications of King's invitations become more overt: "*Wait—just a few minutes. I want to talk to you*

. . . and then I am going to kiss you. Wait" (13), and he ends his introduction with the promise of more intimacies: "Okay—commercial's over. Grab onto my arm now. Hold tight. We are going into a number of dark places, but I think I know the way. Just don't let go of my arm. And if I should kiss you in the dark, it's no big deal; it's only because you are my love" (17–18).

The preceding passage reveals most clearly King's construction of the perfect relationship between reader and writer. The writer is in charge, he is masculinely assertive, and he will impose himself upon his reader as he desires. The appropriate reader goes quietly along for the ride and accedes to the writer's demands for obedience and intimacy. In his nonfiction work on horror in movies and novels, *Danse Macabre*, King makes more clear his view of writing as a blatantly sexual seduction with appropriate roles for writer and reader; if we view dancing as a figure for romantic or sexual intimacy, King's use of that metaphor is especially telling: "[T]he work of horror really is a dance—a moving, rhythmic search. And what it's looking for is the place where you, the viewer or the reader, live at your most primitive level" (17–18).

What is most perplexing about King's use of this metaphor is the danger and violence with which he infuses it; it is as though his dance, his shared intimacy between reader and writer, is an exercise of power and imposition very much like a rape: "The good horror tale will dance its way to the center of your life and find the secret door to the room you believed no one but you knew of" (18). For King, then, horror is "combat waged in the secret recesses of the heart" (25), warfare in the realms of trust and intimacy, but warfare for which the victim/reader is partly responsible, for the horror writer finds our secret joy, our hidden guilty passions. The writer is, however, in control, and even as he frightens us, we defer to his power. As King invites us to enter this engagement with him, he insists upon making us aware of the threat involved. Our fears notwithstanding, though, we will enter this relationship, for he is the leader in this *pas de deux*. He writes, "It's a dance. And sometimes they turn off the lights in this ballroom. But we'll dance anyway, you and I. Even in the dark. Especially in the dark. May I have the pleasure?" (28). By the end of *Danse Macabre*, King makes more overt the sexual content of his relationship with his reader, but he renders it innocent and playful: "My, look at this . . . I do believe the sun is coming up. We have danced the night away, like lovers in some old MGM musical. . . . I cannot tell you how much I've enjoyed the evening" (375).

When viewed in terms of this sexual metaphor for the relationship between writer and reader, King's increasing hostility toward his demanding audience makes perfect sense. In King's paradigm, the ideal audience is constructed as the ideal woman, following compliantly in the *danse macabre*—uncomplaining, undemanding, receptive, appreciative, and grateful. But like those voracious "blue headed ladies" of the Bangor library, King's audience insists on causing trouble. His readers make demands, lodge complaints, ask pointed and stupid questions, grumble bitterly, and—like recalcitrant and intractable women—these readers must be brought into line with a show of force. Of course the most potent show of force available to men in dealing with defiant and assertive women is rape. As Susan Brownmiller put it in her groundbreaking study *Against Our Will,*

Rape [is] . . . not only a male prerogative, but man's basic weapon of force against woman, the principal agent of his will and her fear. His forcible entry into her body, despite her physical protestations and struggle, [is] . . . the vehicle of his victorious conquest over her being, the ultimate test of his superior strength, the triumph of his manhood. (14)

And Carol Vance, observing that "the threat of sexual attack [serves] as a powerful reminder of male privilege, constraining women's movement and behavior" (3), may be said to take Brownmiller's observations one step further in asserting that rape and physical violence directed against women serve to punish women who prove troublesome or rebellious: "[G]ross and public departures from 'good' woman status . . . still invite—and are thought to justify—violation" (4). As we shall see, this is just King's strategy in dealing with the allegorical conflict between writer Paul Sheldon and reader Annie Wilkes. Annie's body becomes the receptacle for Paul's words and his work, but when she begins to take control of Paul's efforts, when she directs and leads instead of appreciating and following, she must be reminded of her place—she is woman/ reader. Upon her body, Paul Sheldon will reassert and reaffirm his creative potential.

His Number-One Fan

That *Misery* offers King's most definitive work on creativity and the problems of the writer as brand name is clear from the first few chapters of the book. In fact, King sets up the conflicts Paul Sheldon will face and establishes the means by which he will work out the problem of being a famous and very popular writer early in the novel. Stephen King, working through his alternate, Paul Sheldon, begins his novel with the quintessential creative act of Western culture, bringing order out of chaos; not only are King's initial images effective in conveying the power that creativity holds for King, but they are almost arrogant in their positioning of the creative artist. Chapter 1 offers the reader meaningless letters on the page as an introduction into the world of Paul Sheldon:

umber whunnn

yerrnnn umber whunnnn

fayunnnn

These sounds: even in the haze. (3)

As the narrative begins, Paul Sheldon brings order by making sense of these words ("your number one fan"), and King appropriates biblical language for Paul's painful awakening: "Let there be light (even of the hazy variety), and the light was good, and so on and so on" (3). But our "god" in this novel finds himself helpless; he lies in bed after an automobile accident, he is in pain, he drifts in and out of consciousness, and he seems to be held captive by the woman who claims to be an admiring fan. Paul's identity is clearly bound up with his writing, for as the haze clears sufficiently for him to remember who he is, he identifies himself first and most aggressively as a writer. In his delirium, his childhood name flickers in and out of his mind—*"that's my name Paulie I'm Paulie"* (4). His captor refers to him as "Paul," and he recognizes his name is Paul Sheldon (6), but it is not until he reaches full consciousness that he claims his complete name along with his most essential orientation: "He was Paul Sheldon, who wrote novels of two kinds, good ones and best-sellers" (6).

The conflict between Paul Sheldon and Annie Wilkes, author and reader, begins with the ambiguity of Annie's position as Paul's nurse; she saves him after his accident, but the fact that she saves him makes him completely dependent upon her, for not only are his legs shattered, *"pulverized"* as King puts it (36), but he has also become dependent upon the drug Novril, which Paul discovers is a "pain-killer with a heavy codeine base" (8). From the outset, Annie Wilkes invades Paul Sheldon's consciousness; she is as powerful and as mysterious as the African goddess of the H. Rider Haggard stories with whom Paul associates her (7), and she forces herself upon him. The first words he hears and the first lines we read in the novel are her claim that she is his "number one fan." And in more and more pernicious ways she begins to invade Paul. In an apparently innocent act, designed only to save Paul's life, she has fed him intravenously. But Paul comes to perceive that she has invaded his body in order to make him well, for ultimately she uses this invasion of his body to claim him as her own: "'I fed you intravenously,' she said. 'Through tubes. That's what those marks on your arms are.' She looked at him with eyes that were suddenly flat and considering. 'You owe me your life, Paul. I hope you'll remember that. I hope you'll keep that in mind'" (16).

Paul's victimization at Annie's hands, the victimization he must ultimately punish her for, evolves at two levels. In the first place, he is completely dependent upon her for the painkillers he craves and the care he needs, and in the second place she begins to struggle with him over whether he will even live. Only a few pages into the novel, Paul refers to Annie's treatment of him as rape: Not only has she invaded his body with drugs and tubes, but she has, he asserts, caused him to be "raped back into life" (6). As Paul has lain sleeping, he apparently stopped breathing, and Annie performed mouth-to-mouth resuscitation upon him. Paul, even this close to death, is appalled at the stench of Annie's breath because it represents almost a sexual violation of him: "[S]he had forced [her breath] into him the way a man might force a part of himself into an unwilling woman" (4), and that part of Annie, a "mixed stench of vanilla cookies and chocolate ice cream and chicken gravy and peanut-butter fudge," revolts him so deeply that it makes him live:

> *"Breathe, goddam you!"* the unseen voice shrieked, and he thought *I will, anything, please just don't do that anymore, don't infect me anymore,* and he *tried,* but before he could really get started her lips were clamped over his again, lips as dry and dead as strips of salted leather, and she raped him full of her air again. (5)

Paul breathes in order to "flush the smell and taste of her out of him" (5). In viewing Annie as Paul's number one fan here, we must note as well that what she has done literally—and the story plays cruelly with the literal levels of language—is to *inspire* Paul, to fill him with air and spirit, the will to live and then the will to create. She has done what a good fan should do; she has given her author a reason to live and write, but there is something fundamentally unwholesome about this relationship.

Paul is not, however, violated simply by Annie's presence and her power; he is also violated by her forcing him to accept her version of reality. She chooses that he will live, and he lives; she chooses that he will eat, and he eats; she chooses that he will write, and he writes. As he does so, the role reversal that forms the basis for the conflict between Paul and Annie intensifies. Not only has Annie usurped a male prerogative, to use Brownmiller's term, in "raping" Paul, but now she begins to impose *her* story on *his* experience. He is, after all—both as a character and as a stand-in for King himself—the writer, the creator; she is—at least at the level at which King operates—only a character and—at the level at which Paul operates—only a fan. Sheldon's greatest distress seems to arise as Annie demotes him from creator to created.

Curiously, it is not Annie's emotional or aesthetic power that allows her to assume the position Paul has occupied; rather it is the power of the material, the real, that affords her the ability to command Paul Sheldon's attention and obedience. She holds Paul Sheldon's bread and butter, quite literally, in her hands—as his captor/nurse and as his number one fan who buys his books. Paul lives or dies—as a man and as a writer—if Annie his reader desires it. Now Annie has the power of the storyteller; now she dictates how the narrative will unfold:

> It was while he ate the soup that she told him what had happened, and he remembered it all as she told him, and he supposed it was good to know how you happened to end up with your legs shattered, but the manner by which he was coming to this knowledge was disquieting—it was as if he was a character in a story or a play, a character whose history is not recounted like history but created like fiction. (10)

And in a complex and interesting contrapuntal dialogue—his portion expressed only within his own mind—Annie continues to create Paul's history while he seeks to assert himself by remembering his most recent literary effort. The dialogue continues for over a page, Paul silently—and sadly, because he is the wordsmith here—asserting himself against Annie:

The new novel was called *Fast Cars*, and he hadn't laughed when it was done. He just sat there in front of the typewriter for a moment, thinking *You may have just won next year's American Book Award, my friend.* And then he had picked up—

"a little bruise on your right temple, but that didn't look like anything. It was your legs . . . I could see right away, even with the light starting to fade, that your legs weren't—"

the telephone and called room service for a bottle of Dom Perignon. (13–14)

Obviously, despite her consistent show of force against Paul, Annie Wilkes does not consciously imagine herself to be a match for Paul Sheldon; she is quite content to be his fan and to allow him to be the creative force behind the novels she loves; she tells him "that she had read each of his eight novels at least once, and had read her *very* favorites, the *Misery* novels, four, five, maybe six times. She only wished he would write them faster" (9). What then has gone wrong with this relationship between creator and consumer? What threat does Annie Wilkes pose to Paul Sheldon; why—when power falls so completely into the audience's hands—does the audience become so dangerous to the writer?

The Spirit of Fan-Love

King's marking of his typical audience as female reveals a good deal about what he values in an audience and how he perceives that the relationship between reader and writer should function. To understand King's metaphorical use of Annie as a stand-in for his audience, we must take into consideration the symbolic function of the female body in western culture. As Susan Rubin Suleiman puts it, "The cultural significance of the female body is not only . . . that of a flesh and blood entity, but that of a *symbolic construct*" (2). And in her brilliant discussion of the role of the female in film, Laura Mulvey characterizes woman's relationship to "patriarchal society" in this way: "Woman then stands in patriarchal culture as signifier for the male other, bound by a symbolic order in which man can live out his phantasies and obsessions through linguistic command by imposing them on the silent image of woman still tied to her place as bearer of meaning, not maker of meaning" (7). In this role, the female body cannot function as a representative for the assertive female self; the female body is, rather, read or experienced as an emblem of another's, a male's, pleasure, not as a proclamation of self-identity; the woman's function is to provide a counterbalance to the roles assigned to the more powerful male: "In a world ordered by sexual imbalance, pleasure in looking has been split between active/male and passive/female. The determining male gaze projects its phantasy onto the female figure which is styled accordingly" (11).

In this way, King relegates Annie to two important functions in *Misery*. In the first place, she is the symbolic construct, as Suleiman calls it, by means of which King himself projects his fantasies concerning audience and audience demands upon the body of Annie Wilkes: In terms of the view of creativity that King constructs in *Misery*, Paul Sheldon's audience is female and ignorantly so:

[W]hile she might be crazy, was she so different in her evaluation of his work from the hundreds of thousands of other people across the country—ninety percent of them women—who could barely wait for each new five-hundred page episode in the turbulent life of the foundling who had risen to marry a peer of the realm? (25)

Oddly, it is Annie's very ignorance and her transient passivity that make her a good audience for Paul's romance novels: "Annie Wilkes was the perfect audience, a woman who loved stories without having the slightest interest in the mechanics of making them. She was the embodiment of that Victorian archetype, Constant Reader" (57).

And secondly, Annie is for Paul the incarnation of all those fans who threaten him and thwart his creative potential. In both cases, the best Annie is the most passive Annie, the quietest Annie, the least demanding Annie; she most fully embodies *"that spirit of . . . of fan-love"* (28, King's ellipses) as King terms it. Like a good character and like a good reader, Annie exists to be contemplated or manipulated by the active artist/writer—Paul or King. For King—who is the "maker of meaning"—she is the symbol that realizes his fears about audience; she is "the bearer of meaning." As a character, she is for Paul—like King, the "maker of meaning" within the novel—that force through which his work is most fully realized. She is—or should be—the appreciative, accepting audience. In neither case is Annie the "maker of meaning" herself. And this is, of course, the very problem with *Misery*. Annie has transcended her function as "bearer of meaning" and thereby has imperiled the creative dynamic by which both Stephen King and Paul Sheldon operate.

King's conflation of creativity and sexuality, his unrelenting use of sexuality as a metaphor for creativity, becomes clear when we contemplate Annie's madness, and Paul Sheldon declares several times that she is, indeed, mad: *"I am in trouble here. This woman is not right"* (13). In the first place, Annie is not acceptably feminine: She is, in fact, repulsively unattractive. She is fat, she is slovenly, she smells, and she is insane. In short, she is not a desirable partner for this reader-writer *pas de deux*. Paul's descriptions of Annie are curious, though, for they reveal that it is more than her unattractiveness that bothers him; what he seems to hate most about her is her impregnability. Annie cannot—it seems—be entered:

[S]he gave him a disturbing sense of *solidity*, as if she might not have any blood vessels or even internal organs; as if she might be only solid Annie Wilkes from side to side and top to bottom. . . . It seemed to him that if he made the first two fingers of his hand into a V and attempted to poke them up her nostrils, they might go less than an eighth of an inch before encountering a solid (if slightly yielding) obstruction; that even her gray cardigan and frumpy house skirts and faded outside-work jeans were part of that solid fibrous unchannelled body. (7)

And here we find a clue to the dangers of the audience. As Paul has revealed, 90 percent of his readers are female, but Annie renounces her essential femaleness, at least as it is constructed in Western culture. She spurns receptivity and passivity, the pregnability that Paul has told us she lacks, and arrogates powers to herself that are rightfully the powers of the artist. She begins to tell Paul what to write. She makes demands. She—with his injury—finds herself in the position of being able to "rape" Paul with pills and with humiliation. When she discovers that he has killed off the deplorable character—at least from his perspective—Misery, Annie demands that he write a novel in which he resurrects this character. She will remain resistant to Paul; she will demand her own way. And, of course, Annie's way is not the way of the real artist who knows his good work. To Paul and to King himself, Annie is ignorant and presumptuous, like a woman who doesn't know what is good for her. And as a reader she lacks refinement and intelligence. She prefers the romantic Misery series to a tough new work about a car thief: *"She doesn't like the new book because she's too stupid to understand what it's up to. . . . Too stupid? No. Too set. Not just unwilling to change, but antagonistic to the very idea of change"* (25).

At Paul's initial refusal to comply with Annie's requests for more fiction about Misery, Annie begins a series of violations that uncover the absolute terror that lies behind King's anger at his fans' demands. First, Annie forces Paul to burn his prized *Fast Cars* manuscript, then she cuts off his foot because she knows he is trying to escape her, and finally she cuts off his thumb. Each stage in her humiliating and vengeful assault upon Paul seems to make real King's feeling that his fans are slowly but surely consuming him—bit by bit, inch by inch. And each assault is underscored by Paul's real fear that Annie will castrate him and King's real fear that his audience is depriving him of his creativity—very closely associated for him with his masculine sexuality, with his power to assert, enter, dominate, and control. As Annie begins to assert herself against Paul, as she begins to make insistent demands concerning his work, Paul feels the assaults in his groin: "The pain throbbed in his legs and made a deep steel circlet around his crotch. He had touched himself down there, and he thought his pelvis was intact, but it felt twisted and weird" (17), and "[h]is thighs, crotch, even his penis, were all still mottled with fading bruises" (35–36). Not only did the crash that brought him under Annie's power break his "writing bone" (104) as Paul puts it, but he realizes as Annie continues to threaten him, as she literally "hobbles" him (205), that he has lost his manhood. His writing, his power, his masculinity are conflated, and Annie has control of all in this novel of horror. When Annie gives Paul a defective typewriter, he bewails his lost manhood at the same time that he mourns his lost power to create. He is too afraid to ask even for a decent typewriter: "Once there had been a man who would at least have *asked*. . . . *He* had been that man, and he supposed he ought to be ashamed, but *that* man had had two big advantages over this one: *that* man had had two feet . . . and two thumbs" (211–12).

The problem for Paul is that he needs Annie, and he knows it—despite his fears that she will, as he puts it "castrate him" (202) literally and creatively and despite her threats to do so: "You're lucky I didn't cut off your man-gland. I thought of it, you know" (251). Paul asserts, "A person might as well not write a book at all, if there's no one around to read it" (161). And Annie, as the powerful audience, knows this too; she tells Paul somewhat threateningly, "You owe me your life, Paul. I hope you'll remember that" (16). But the irony of Paul's relationship with his audience is that his creative power is firmly identified with his power as a male, and yet the demands of his audience, Annie's demands, threaten to unman him. As Paul Sheldon describes the hold a writer has on his audience, he talks about the "gotta," as in "I think I'll stay up another fifteen-twenty minutes, honey, I gotta see how this chapter comes out" (224), the force that makes a reader need the writer, crave the writer's words, cling to the writer as a dependent slave. In *Misery*, King characterized this force in crudely sexual terms:

The gotta. Nasty as a hand job in a sleazy bar, fine as a fuck from the world's most talented call-girl. Oh boy it was bad and oh boy it was good and oh boy in the end it didn't matter how rude it was or how crude it was because in the end it was just like the Jacksons said on the record—don't stop til you get enough. (224–25)

Thinking about his creative process and his audience's role in that process, Paul foregrounds the sexuality of it:

But hadn't there also been some sort of fuck, even if of the driest variety? Because once he started again . . . well, she wouldn't interrupt him while he was working, but she would take each day's output as soon as he was done . . . he knew this by now, just as sexually acute men know which dates will put out at the end of the evening and which ones will not—to get her fix. To get her *gotta*. (226)

She's Gotta Have It

The relationship between audience and writer is, thus, sexual, aggressively and specifically heterosexual, in that the writer "fucks" the audience—as King puts it; he provides the audience with pleasures, the "gotta," that the audience, lacking a penis, cannot provide itself. The ideal audience is passive and accepting, totally within the thrall of the writer's sexual/creative power just as the ideal woman is submissive and silent in the traditional paradigm for heterosexuality. In their discussion of the manner in which heterosexuality has been constructed in America, Barbara Ehrenreich, Elizabeth Hess, and Gloria Jacobs foreground these qualities of heterosexuality by observing that the traditional sexual arrangement in Western culture may be seen as "a condensed drama of female passivity and surrender" (5). They go on to assert that even in the twentieth century, "Heterosexual sex has had many uses, but it has had, over and over, one social meaning, and that is male domination over women" (203). But Annie Wilkes—because she is an overbearing and demanding fan/woman—has perverted and reconstructed the essentially heterosexual relationship between writer and reader. Not only does she refuse her role as passive object, but she also continues to usurp Paul's power to create.

With respect to Annie's creativity, King sets up an odd—but probably inadvertent—parallel with Sandra Gilbert and Susan Gubar's conceptualization of the angry, creative female spirit, "the madwoman in the attic." For Annie is a crazed artist in her own right, but her "art" has consisted of a series of grisly murders and the book she creates from these murders. Thus, Annie further rejects her role as "bearer of meaning" rather than "maker of meaning" by her hidden and bizarre creative efforts. Annie has sequestered herself on her mountain farm because she has been accused of—and actually committed—a series of murders, and her narrative of the murders has proven powerful because she has managed to convince the authorities and the courts that she is innocent. Like Gilbert and Gubar's madwoman, she has been selfish and fiendishly forceful: "[C]ommitted only to their own private ends, these women are accidents of nature, deformities meant to repel, but in their very freakishness they possess unhealthy energies, powerful and dangerous arts" (Gilbert and Gubar, *Madwoman*, 29). What Paul Sheldon discovers in finding the record of Annie's crimes is that Annie has actually written her own book. She is not simply a fan of his; she is a creator as well, for she has kept detailed scrapbooks chronicling all her killings. Annie is a serial killer who has put some pride and much energy into her work; as he examines the record Annie has kept of her victims, Paul says, "This book, dear God, this book was so *big*" (176). It comes as no surprise, given Paul Sheldon's equation of sexuality with creativity, his projection of his creative powers onto his penis, that the first thing he notices about Annie Wilkes's book is its size.

And oddly, Annie proves a worthy competitor in this creative competition, as effective at the craft of writing as Paul Sheldon, for she has laid hold of him with the "gotta." Despite his horror at what Annie has done, Paul continues to read her book: "[H]e bent over the book again. In a weird way it was just too good to put down. It was like a novel so disgusting you just have to finish it" (179). Ultimately the struggle between Paul and Annie comes down to a struggle of texts; will Paul's story be told or will Annie's? Who will have the power to create? For as he reads further in her scrapbook, Paul discovers that he will be the next to die: "He turned the page and looked at the last clipping—at least so far—and suddenly his breath was gone. It was as if, after wading grimly through the almost unbearable necrology in the foregoing pages, he had come face to face with his *own* obituary" (185). Either Paul will author this story, and Annie will die, or Annie will strip Paul of his creative power, his masculinity, his right to "fuck her," and he will die.

In fact, Annie has so completely disempowered Paul as a writer and as a man that Paul must construct a new metaphor for creativity, one that expresses his dependence upon Annie Wilkes and her mastery over him—he has become Scheherazade to her Shahriar. Just as Scheherazade had to provide the powerful emperor with tales to prolong her life, Paul must entertain Annie in the way she demands. As long as Paul can keep Annie interested in the story he weaves, the Misery novel she forces him to write, she will—she must—let him live. He says to himself, "*you owe her* [his character Misery] *your life, such as that may be . . . because you turned out to be Scheherazade after all, didn't you?*" (220–21).

To be sure, Paul's willing acceptance of this transformed state fills him with self-loathing, and—as his metaphors reveal—makes clear how he feels about the abject obedience, both creative and sexual, to which Annie has reduced him. When Annie requests that Paul reveal the end of the Misery story before he writes it, he understands that his hold on his audience is still a sexual hold—although by now he has been reduced, in his terms, to the female position: "'I can't do that,' he said . . . *Because you wouldn't respect me in the morning*" (228). And he asserts that it was his earlier novel, his novel about men and crime and the real world—*Fast Cars*—that could have saved him from the prostitution to which the popular Misery novels consigned him:

I'm no whore. Fast Cars was about not being a whore. That's what killing that goddamned bitch Misery was about, now that I think about it. I was driving to the West Coast to celebrate my liberation from a state of whoredom. What you did was to pull me out of the wreck when I crashed my car and stick me back in the crib again. Two dollar straight up, four dollar I take you aroun the worl. (66)

The question for Paul Sheldon as for Stephen King is how to right this creative relationship gone awry. How is Paul to reclaim his masculinity and his creativity? The answer is obvious—he must assert himself sexually against the woman who has refused to afford him access to her body, who—in Paul's words—feels like "clots and roadblocks rather than welcoming orifices" (7); he must reestablish his sexual and creative dominance, repositioning Annie in her appropriate role as bearer of meaning rather than maker of meaning. In a study of rape and representation, Lynn Higgins and Brenda Silver assert that "rape and rapability are central to the very construction of gender identity," that "the social positioning of women and men" is set and perpetuated by the literary and artistic representations which demonstrate acceptable power relationships between men and women" (3). In order to reassert the gender identity necessary for creativity in Stephen King's metaphorical universe, Annie must be raped, for as Ehrenreich, Hess, and Jacobs point out, "sex is the ratification of male power" (203). Thus Annie's orifices must be filled—especially her demanding mouth— her power overthrown, and her sexual and creative passivity re-imposed. In a scene more horrible than any King has written, Paul Sheldon rapes Annie Wilkes with his book. He takes his power—pen, penis, book, now a single emblematic unity—into his hands and violates Annie with this power. He forces that book down her throat, screaming, "*I'm gonna rape you, all right Annie. I'm gonna rape you because all I can do is the worst I can do. So suck my book. Suck my book. Suck on it until you fucking CHOKE*" (292). To secure his retaken position, Paul must kill Annie, and after a prolonged and horrifying struggle he does, but she lives in his head; the memory, the force of the demented fan haunts him: "I think she's dead. But be careful. If she's still alive . . . dangerous . . . like a rattlesnake" (300).

Ironically, for all of Paul's hatred of Annie as audience, she guarantees his publishing success, for after he heals from the nightmare of his captivity, he releases the book that she forced him to write—*Misery's Return*. As Paul's agent, Charlie, tells him, "This book is going to outsell everything in the world" (304). King is not quite finished playing with us by this point; in fact, almost obsessively he seems forced to call to our attention the fact that there is some connection between our demands for his work and Annie's demands for Paul Sheldon's novels. As Paul discusses his new novel with Charlie, his agent tells him: "We all ought to be down on our knees thanking God that the story *in* the book is almost as good as the story *behind* the book." What his agent refers to, of course, is the torment to which Annie has subjected Paul. By implication the novel we hold in our hands—*Misery*—has grown out of the torment to which we—the demanding and voracious, the unappealingly female audience—have subjected King himself. With this in mind, we remember the dedication of the book—"This is for Stephanie and Jim Leonard, who know why. Boy, *do* they"—and the fact that Mrs. Leonard was King's secretary for many years (Spignesi, 100), the woman who protected King from his fans—number one and otherwise.

By the end of *Misery*, Stephen King answers very clearly the questions posed by Sandra Gilbert and Susan Gubar in their works *The Madwoman in the Attic* and *No Man's Land*. In considering the metaphors for women's creativity in nineteenth-century literature, they wondered whether the pen was not a metaphorical penis; in examining the place of the woman writer in the twentieth century, they asked whether the pen had become a metaphorical pistol. To both of these questions Stephen King seems to answer resoundingly, "Yes!" For his penis is linked very strongly to his creativity, and his creativity is most clearly a weapon by means of which, when as an audience we behave properly, he pleases, but by means of which, when we transcend the bounds of appropriate behavior, he punishes. His greatest moments of creative joy seem to come when he can reduce us to the submissive position of female audience to his masculine creator. As he puts it in a discussion of "Apt Pupil," "I thought to myself, 'Gee, I've done it again. I've written something that has really gotten under someone's skin.' And I do like that. I like the feeling that I reached between somebody's legs like that" (quoted in Beahm, 250).

NOTES

1. If comparisons to other popular figures are significant, an anonymous commentator in the *Economist* deems King as much a star as Eddie Murphy or Michael Jackson, likening him as well to Stephen Spielberg ("Author as Star," 97); in a review of *Misery* in *New Statesman*, Kim Newman concurs that King is as impressive in his popularity and impact as Spielberg, as does Karen Stabiner, in a review of *Misery*, which appeared in the *L.A. Times*. In *Variety*, Charles Kipps termed King "a 1-man entertainment complex," going on to report that "Twenty-one of his books and short stories have been made into movies, and another five are in development. King has

written several screenplays, produced some of the films and even directed one of them" (3).

George Beahm opines that

As a writer, King has arrived in grand style, like few other writers in our time. He was on the cover of *Time* magazine. He has had almost as many books written *about* him as those written by him. He has won numerous awards in the fantasy and science-fiction fields. A university is collecting his work seriously—the Special Collections at the University of Maine at Orono. He commands the enviable position of usually being able to pick and choose his projects. Publishers love him because he's their money machine and keep him happy at all costs. He is, in short, a power unto himself in the comparatively small world of book publishing. (17)

In fact, an entire newsletter, *Castle Rock*, provided fans with information on King and his projects from 1985 until 1989 (Spignesi, 102–26).

And although King has been, as one reader puts it, "scorned by the cognoscenti" ("Author As Star," 97) and given "critical short shrift" according to Michelle Slung, he seems to motivate enthusiasts and scholars alike to write about him. According to George Beahm, as of 1990 a total of twenty-nine books had been written on King or were in the works with publishers eagerly awaiting their completion (326–30); Stephen Spignesi sets the number at a more modest twenty-seven (673). Even those who approach him with a critical or scholarly spirit find themselves gushing with the enthusiasm of a devoted fan. Douglas E. Winter dedicates his *Stephen King: The Art of Darkness* "to Steve and Tabby, for caring" (xiv), and Peter Straub admits that he "became evangelical about Stephen King" (9).

2. Elizabeth J. Young declares that King is "the world's best-selling author" (34), and Darrell Schweitzer calls King "arguably the most successful fiction writer of any kind active today in the English language" (5). Richard Panek reports that King's "cottage industry has grown at a rate that scares even King himself. In the last two years [since 1989] he made a reported $22 million, and he's currently in the middle of a four-book contract worth a record $32 million to $40 million" (29). Panek goes on to assert that King's price is "the highest in the history of publishing" (30). In 1989, *Forbes* compiled a list of the forty highest-paid entertainers, and King ranked twenty-third, earning $25 million in two years, making him the highest-earning novelist on the list ("Author as Star," 97). According to Charles Kipps, the "King empire" brings in over $100 million a year from "various entertainment ventures" (3).

3. "'Ever Et Raw Meat?' and Other Weird Questions" offers King's most uncharitable view of his audience. He ridicules questions such as "How do you start a novel" and "Who is your favorite writer" as well as belittling readers for even expressing interest in his work and his work habits. Curiously, he concludes his tirade with the assurance that "no one—at least no one with a modicum of simple human kindness—resents questions from people who honestly want answers" (7), yet his whole piece, as its title reveals, springs from the premise that readers are somehow presumptuous and ridiculous for their interest in the writers they most revere.

WORKS CITED

"Author As Star." *Economist*, 18 March 1989, 97.

Banks, Carolyn. Review of *Misery*, by Stephen King. *Book World* [*Washington Post*], 14 June 1987, 1 and 14.

Beahm, George. *The Stephen King Companion.* Kansas City: Andrews and McMeel, 1989.

"Break-In Rattles Writer Stephen King—Will Lock Gate." *San Francisco Chronicle,* 29 April 1991, three star edition, D2.

Brooks, David. "Bookshorts: Numbing, Chilling, Thrilling." Review of *Misery,* by Stephen King, *Wall Street Journal,* 23 June 1987, 28.

Brownmiller, Susan. *Against Our Will: Men, Women, and Rape.* New York: Simon and Schuster, 1975.

Ehrenreich, Barbara, Elizabeth Hess, and Gloria Jacobs. *Re-Making Love: The Feminization of Sex.* Garden City: Anchor/Doubleday, 1986.

Gilbert, Sandra, and Susan Gubar. *The Madwoman in the Attic: The Woman Writer and the Nineteenth-Century Literary Imagination.* New Haven and London: Yale University Press, 1979.

———. *No Man's Land: The Place of the Woman Writer in the Twentieth Century.* Vol 1: "The War of the Words." New Haven and London: Yale University Press, 1988.

Goldstein, Bill. "King of Horror." *Publishers Weekly* 24 January 1991, 6–9.

Higgins, Lynn A., and Brenda R. Silver, eds. "Introduction: Rereading Rape." *Rape and Representation.* New York: Columbia University Press, 1991, 1–11.

Hoppenstand, Gary, and Ray B. Browne, eds. *The Gothic World of Stephen King: Landscape of Nightmares.* Bowling Green: Bowling Green State University Popular Press, 1987.

James, Darlene. Review of *Misery,* by Stephen King. *Maclean's,* 20 July 1987, 51.

Katzenbach, John. "Sheldon Gets the Ax." Review of *Misery,* by Stephen King. *New York Times Book Review,* 31 May 1987, 20.

King, Stephen. *Danse Macabre.* New York: Everest, 1981.

———. *Different Seasons.* New York: New American Library, 1982.

———. "'Ever Et Raw Meat?' and Other Weird Questions." *New York Times Book Review,* 6 December 1987, 7.

———. *Four Past Midnight.* New York: Signet, 1990.

———. *Misery.* New York: Viking, 1987.

———. *Night Shift.* New York: Signet, 1978.

———. "On Becoming a Brand Name." Foreword to *Fear Itself: The Horror Fiction of Stephen King.* Edited by Tim Underwood and Chuck Miller. San Francisco: Underwood-Miller, 1982, 15–42.

———. *Skeleton Crew.* New York: Putnam's, 1985.

Kipps, Charles. "King's Tale of Mystery & Intrigue—And That's Just His Contract." *Variety,* 29 November 1989, 3.

Lehmann-Haupt, Christopher. "Books of the Times." Review of *Misery,* by Stephen King. *New York Times,* 8 June 1987, C17.

MacDonald, John D. "Introduction." *Night Shift: Excursions into Horror.* By Stephen King. New York: Signet, 1978, vi–x.

"Man Threatens to Blow Up Stephen King's Home." *San Francisco Chronicle,* 23 April 1991, three star edition, A3.

Mulvey, Laura. "Visual Pleasure and Narrative Cinema." *Screen* 16 (1975): 6–18.

Newman, Kim. "Horror: Body Snatcher." Review of *Misery,* by Stephen King. *New Statesman,* 18 September 1987, 30–31.

Panek, Richard. "King's Ransom." *M. Inc* 8, 5 (1991): 29–32.

"Personals." *San Francisco Chronicle*, 29 June 1992, three star edition, D3.

Schweitzer, Darrel, ed. *Discovering Stephen King*. Mercer Island: Starmont, 1985.

Slung, Michelle. "In the Matter of Stephen King." *Armchair Detective* 14 (1981): 147–49.

Spignesi, Stephen. *The Complete Stephen King Encyclopedia: The Definitive Guide to the Works of America's Master of Horror*. Chicago: Contemporary, 1991.

Stabiner, Karen. "The Misery of Stephen King." Review of *Misery*, by Stephen King. *Los Angeles Times Book Review*, 10 May 1987: 8.

Straub, Peter. "Meeting Stevie." Introduction to *Fear Itself*. Edited by Tim Underwood and Chuck Miller. San Francisco: Underwood-Miller, 1982, 7–13.

Suleiman, Susan Rubin. Introduction. *The Female Body in Western Culture: Contemporary Perspectives*. Edited by Susan Rubin Suleiman. Cambridge: Harvard University Press, 1986, 1–4.

Underwood, Tim, and Chuck Miller, eds. *Bare Bones: Conversations on Terror with Stephen King*. New York: McGraw-Hill, 1988.

——. *Fear Itself: The Horror Fiction of Stephen King*. San Francisco: Underwood-Miller, 1982.

"Upfront: Advance Review." Review of *Misery*, by Stephen King. *Booklist*, 1 April 1987, 1153.

Vance, Carol S. "Pleasure and Danger: Toward a Politics of Sexuality." *Pleasure and Danger: Exploring Female Sexuality*. Edited by Carol S. Vance. Boston: Routledge & Kegan Paul, 1984, 1–27.

"What Stephen King Does for Love." *Seventeen*, April 1990, 240–41

Winter, Douglas E. *Stephen King: The Art of Darkness*. New York: NAL, 1984.

Young, Elizabeth J. "Best of Horror: Printers' Devils." *New Statesman and Society* 3, 130 (1990): 34–35.

Selected Bibliography

Works by Stephen King

"The Boogeyman." *Night Shift*. Garden City, NY: Doubleday, 1978, 98–107.

Carrie. New York: Signet, 1974.

Christine. New York: Viking, 1983.

Cujo. New York: The Mysterious Press, 1981.

Danse Macabre. New York: Everest, 1981.

The Dead Zone. New York: Viking, 1979.

Different Seasons. New York: Signet, 1982.

Dolores Claiborne. New York: Viking, 1993.

"'Ever Et Raw Meat?' and Other Weird Questions." *New York Times Book Review*, 6 December 1987, 7.

Four Past Midnight. New York: Signet, 1990.

Gerald's Game. New York: Viking, 1992.

It. New York: Viking, 1986.

Misery. New York: Viking, 1987.

Night Shift. New York: Signet, 1978.

"On Becoming a Brand Name." Foreword to *Fear Itself: The Horror Fiction of Stephen King*. Edited by Tim Underwood and Chuck Miller. San Francisco: Underwood-Miller, 1982, 15–42.

Pet Sematary. Garden City, NY: Doubleday, 1983.

"The Raft." *Skeleton Crew*. New York: Putnam's, 1985, 245–70.

Rage (as Richard Bachman). New York: New American Library, 1977.

"The Reach." *The Dark Descent*. Edited by David G. Hartwell. New York: Doherty, 1987, 15–30.

The Running Man (as Richard Bachman). New York: New American Library, 1982.

The Shining. New York: Doubleday, 1977.

Skeleton Crew. New York: Putnam's, 1985.

The Stand. Garden City, NY: Doubleday, 1978.

Other Works

Abraham, Karl. *Selected Papers of Karl Abraham*. Translated by Douglas Bryan and Alix Strachey. Brunner/Mazel Classics in Psychoanalysis, 3. 1927. New York: Brunner/Mazel, 1979, 326–32.

"Author As Star." *Economist*, 18 March 1989, 97.

Ballard, J. G. *Crash*. New York: Farrar, 1973.

Banks, Carolyn. Review of *Misery*, by Stephen King. *Book World* [*Washington Post*], 14 June 1987, 1 and 14.

Barnes, Clive. "Musical 'Carrie' Soars on Blood, Guts and Gore." *New York Post*, 13 May 1988.

Bayley, Stephen. *Sex, Drink, and Fast Cars*. New York: Pantheon, 1986.

Beahm, George, ed. *The Stephen King Companion*. Kansas City: Andrews and McMeel, 1989.

——. *The Stephen King Story*. Kansas City: Andrews and McMeel, 1992.

Benjamin, Jessica. *The Bonds of Love: Psychoanalysis, Feminism, and the Problem of Domination*. New York: Pantheon, 1988.

Bercovitch, Sacvan. *The Puritan Origins of the American Self*. New Haven: Yale University Press, 1975.

Bettelheim, Bruno. *The Uses of Enchantment: The Meaning and Importance of Fairy Tales*. New York: Vintage, 1989.

Bleiler, E. F. "Stephen King." *Supernatural Fiction Writers: British Writers of the Interbellum Period*, Vol. VIII. Edited by E. F. Bleiler, Vol. 2: A. E. Coppard to Roger Zelazny. New York: Scribner's, 1985.

Bosky, Bernadette Lynn. "Playing the Heavy: Weight, Appetite, and Embodiment in Three Novels by Stephen King." *The Dark Descent: Essays Defining Stephen King's Horrorscape*. Edited by Tony Magistrale. Westpart, CT: Greenwood, 1992, 137–56.

Boulard, Garry. "The Anti-Twinkie Defense." *The Advocate*, 14 June 1994, 33–38.

"Break-In Rattles Writer Stephen King—Will Lock Gate." *San Francisco Chronicle*, 29 April 1991, three star edition, D2.

"Broadway Goes for Blood." *Newsday* (New York), 8 May 1988.

Brooks, David. "Bookshorts: Numbing, Chilling, Thrilling." Review of *Misery*, by Stephen King. *Wall Street Journal*, 23 June 1987, 28.

Brownmiller, Susan. *Against Our Will: Men, Women, and Rape*. New York: Simon and Schuster, 1975.

Burns, Gail E., and Melinda Kanner. "Women, Danger, and Death: The Perversion of The Female Principle in Stephen King's Fiction." *Sexual Politics and Popular Culture*. Edited by Diane Raymond. Bowling Green, OH: Bowling Green State University Popular Press, 1990, 158–72.

Bushman, Richard. "Jonathan Edwards as Great Man: Identity, Conversion, and Leadership in the Great Awakening." *Soundings* 52 (1969): 15–46.

"The Buzz" Rev. of *The Shawshank Redemption*. *The Advocate*, 4 April 1995, 70–71.

Carpenter, John. Dir. *Christine*. Columbia Pictures, 1983.

Chodorow, Nancy. *The Reproduction of Mothering: Psychoanalysis and the Sociology of Gender*. Berkeley: University of California Press, 1978.

Cixous, Hélène. "The Laugh of the Medusa." Translated by Keith Cohen and Paula Cohen. *Signs: Journal of Women in Culture and Society* 1 (1976): 875–93.

Clark, Michael. "Witches and Wall Street: Possession Is Nine-Tenths of the Law." *Herman Melville's Billy Budd, Benito Cereno, Bartleby the Scrivener, and Other Tales*. Edited by Harold Bloom. New York: Chelsea, 1987, 127–47.

Clover, Carol J. *Men, Women, and Chain Saws: Gender and the Modern Horror Film*. Princeton: Princeton University Press, 1992.

Cohn, Norman. "Le Diable au Coeur." Review of *The Origin of Satan*, by Elaine Pagels. *The New York Review of Books*, 21 September 1995, 18–20.

Collings, Michael R. *The Many Facets of Stephen King*. Starmont Studies in Literary Criticism, 11. Mercer Island, WA: Starmont, 1985.

———. *Stephen King as Richard Bachman*. Starmont Studies in Literary Criticism, 10. Mercer Island, WA: Starmont, 1985.

———. *The Stephen King Phenomenon*. Starmont Studies in Literary Criticism, 14. Mercer Island, WA: Starmont, 1987.

Collings, Michael R., and David Engebretson. *The Shorter Works of Stephen King*. Starmont Studies in Literary Criticism, 9. Mercer Island, WA: Starmont, 1985.

Collins, James. "What Could We Have Been Thinking?" *Spy*, April 1991, 48.

Connor, Jeff. *Stephen King Goes to Hollywood*. New York: New American, 1987.

Creed, Barbara. *The Monstrous-Feminine: Film, Feminism, Psychoanalysis*. London: Routledge, 1993.

Darabont, Frank. Dir. *The Shawshank Redemption*. Columbia Pictures, 1994.

Davis, Jonathan P. *Stephen King's America*. Bowling Green, OH: Bowling Green State University Popular Press, 1994.

Deleuze, Gilles. *Masochism:* Coldness and Cruelty *by Gilles Deleuze and* Venus in Furs *by Leopold von Sacher-Masoch*. New York: Zone Books, 1991.

Demos, John. *Entertaining Satan: Witchcraft and the Culture of Early New England*. Oxford: Oxford University Press, 1982.

Dettelbach, Cynthia Golomb. *In the Driver's Seat: The Automobile in American Literature and Popular Culture*. Westport, CT: Greenwood, 1976.

Detweiler, Robert. *Breaking the Fall: Religious Readings of Contemporary Fiction*. San Francisco: Harper and Row, 1987.

Dika, Vera. *Games of Terror. "Halloween," "Friday the 13th," and the Films of the Stalker Cycle*. Rutherford, NJ: Fairleigh Dickinson University Press; London and Toronto: Associated University Presses, 1990.

Doane, Janice, and Devon Hodges. *Nostalgia and Sexual Difference: The Resistance to Contemporary Feminism*. New York: Methuen, 1987.

Douglas, Mary. *Implicit Meanings: Essays in Anthropology*. Boston: Routledge & Paul, 1975.

———. *Natural Symbols: Explorations in Cosmology*. New York: Random, 1970.

Ehrenreich, Barbara, Elizabeth Hess, and Gloria Jacobs. *Re-Making Love: The Feminization of Sex*. Garden City, NY: Anchor/Doubleday, 1986.

Elliott, Emory, ed. *Puritan Influences in American Literature*. Urbana: University of Illinois Press, 1979.

Erickson, Kai T. *Wayward Puritans: A Study in the Sociology of Deviance*. New York: Wiley, 1966.

Evans, Sara M. *Born for Liberty: A History of Women in America*. New York: Macmillan, 1989.

Faludi, Susan. *Backlash: The Undeclared War Against American Women*. New York: Crown, 1991.

Fiedler, Leslie. "Fantasy as Commodity and Myth." *Kingdom of Fear: The World of Stephen King*. Edited by Tim Underwood and Chuck Miller. New York: Signet, 1986, 47–52.

Flink, James J. *The Automobile Age*. Cambridge: MIT Press, 1988.

——. *The Car Culture*. Cambridge: MIT Press, 1975.

Foucault, Michel. *The History of Sexuality*. Translated by Robert Hurley. New York: Pantheon, 1978.

Freud, Sigmund. "Creative Writers and Daydreaming." *The Critical Tradition. Classic Texts and Contemporary Trends*. Edited by David H. Richter. New York: St. Martin's, 1989, 651–55.

——. "Femininity." *The Women and Language Debate*. Edited by Camille Roman, Suzanne Juhasz, and Christanne Miller. Rutgers: Rutgers University Press, 1994.

——. "The Uncanny." Translated by James Strachey. Vol. 17 of *The Standard Edition of the Complete Psychological Works of Sigmund Freud*. 24 Vols. London: Hogarth, 1986, 219–52.

Friedan, Betty. *The Feminine Mystique*. New York: Norton, 1963.

Friedman, Ellen G. "Where Are the Missing Contents? (Post)Modernism, Gender, and the Canon." *PMLA* 108 (1993): 240–52.

Gilbert, Sandra, and Susan Gubar. *The Madwoman in the Attic: The Woman Writer and the Nineteenth-Century Literary Imagination*. New Haven: Yale University Press, 1979.

——. *No Man's Land: The Place of the Woman Writer in the Twentieth Century*. Vol 1: "The War of the Words." New Haven: Yale University Press, 1988.

Goldman, Emma. "The Traffic in Women." *Anarchism and Other Essays*. 1917. New York: Dover, 1969, 177–94.

Goldstein, Bill. "King of Horror." *Publishers Weekly*, 24 January 1991, 6–9.

Gulzow, Monte, and Carol Mitchell. "'Vagina Dentata' and 'Incurable Venereal Disease' Legends from the Viet Nam War." *Western Folklore,* 39 (1980): 306–16.

Hall, David D. *Witch-Hunting in Seventeenth Century New England: A Documentary History, 1638–1692*. Boston: Northeastern University Press, 1991.

——. *Worlds of Wonder, Days of Judgment: Popular Religious Belief in Early New England*. New York: Knopf, 1989.

——, ed. *The Antinomian Controversy, 1636–1638: A Documentary History*. Boston: Northeastern University Press, 1991.

Hall, David, John M. Murrin, and Thad W. White, eds. *Saints and Revolutionaries: Essays on Early American History*. New York: Norton, 1984.

Hanson, Clare. "Stephen King: Powers of Horror." *American Horror Fiction: From Brockden Brown to Stephen King*. Edited by Brian Docherty. New York: St. Martin's, 1990, 135–54.

Hartwell, David G., ed. *The Dark Descent*. New York: Doherty, 1987.

Hatlen, Burton. Interview. *Stephen King's America*. Edited by Jonathan P. Davis. Bowling Green, OH: Bowling Green State University Popular Press, 1994, 141–60.

Heldreth. Leonard G. "Viewing 'The Body': King's Portrait of the Artist as Survivor." *The Gothic World of Stephen King: Landscape of Nightmares*. Edited by Gary Hoppenstand and Ray B. Browne. Bowling Green, OH: Bowling Green State University Popular Press, 1987, 64–74.

Heller, Terry. *The Delights of Horror: An Aesthetics of the Tale of Terror.* Urbana: University of Illinois Press, 1987.

Henry, William A. "The Biggest All-Time Flop Ever." *Time,* 30 May 1988, 65.

——. "Getting All Fired Up over Nothing." *Time,* 23 May 1988, 80.

Herron, Don. "The Summation." *Reign of Fear: The Fiction and the Films of Stephen King.* Edited by Don Herron. Novato, CA: Underwood-Miller, 1992, 209–47.

Higgins, Lynn A., and Brenda R. Silver, eds. "Introduction: Rereading Rape." *Rape and Representation.* New York: Columbia University Press, 1991, 1–11.

Hoppenstand, Gary, and Ray B. Browne, eds. *The Gothic World of Stephen King: Landscape of Nightmares.* Bowling Green, OH: Bowling Green State University Popular Press, 1987.

Horney, Karen. "The Dread of Women." *The International Journal of Psycho-analysis* 13 (1932): 348–60.

Irigaray, Luce. "Body Against Body: In Relation to the Mother." *Sexes and Genealogies.* Translated by Gillian C. Gill. New York: Columbia University Press, 1993.

——. *This Sex Which Is Not One.* Translated by Catherine Porter. Ithaca: Cornell University Press, 1985.

Jackson, Rosemary. *Fantasy: The Literature of Subversion.* New York: Methuen, 1981.

James, Darlene. Review of *Misery,* by Stephen King. *Maclean's,* 20 July 1987, 51.

Jancovich, Mark. *Horror.* London: Batsford, 1992.

Jennings, Jan, ed. *Roadside America: The Automobile in Design and Culture.* Ames, IA: Iowa State University Press, 1990.

Jones, Ann Rosalind. "Writing the Body: Toward an Understanding of *l'Écriture feminine.*" *The New Feminist Criticism: Essays on Women, Literature, and Theory.* Edited by Elaine Showalter. New York: Pantheon, 1985, 361–77.

Kael, Pauline. *When the Lights Go Down.* New York: Holt, Rinehart and Winston, 1980.

Karlsen, Carol F. *The Devil in the Shape of a Woman: Witchcraft in Colonial New England.* New York: Random House, 1987.

Katzenbach, John. "Sheldon Gets the Ax." Review of *Misery,* by Stephen King. *New York Times Book Review,* 31 May 1987, 20.

Keesey, Douglas. "'The Face of Mr. Flip': Homophobia in the Horror of Stephen King." *The Dark Descent: Essays Defining Stephen King's Horrorscape.* Edited by Tony Magistrale. Westport, CT: Greenwood, 1992, 187–201.

Kipps, Charles. "King's Tale of Mystery & Intrigue—And That's Just His Contract." *Variety,* 29 November 1989, 3.

Kissel, Howard. "Don't 'Carrie' Me Back to Ol' Virginny." *Daily News,* 13 May 1988.

Kramer, Mimi. "Bloody Awful." *New Yorker,* May 1988, 85.

Kristeva, Julia. *Powers of Horror: An Essay on Abjection.* Translated by Leon S. Roudiez. New York: Columbia University Press, 1982.

——. *Strangers to Ourselves.* Translated by Leon S. Roudiez. New York: Columbia University Press, 1991.

Kroll, Jack. "Shakespeare to Stephen King." *Newsweek,* 23 May 1988, 73.

Lawrence, D. H. *Studies in Classic American Literature.* New York: Viking, 1964.

Lederer, Wolfgang. *The Fear of Women.* New York: Grune, 1968.

Legman, G. *No Laughing Matter. An Analysis of Sexual Humor.* Bloomington: Indiana University Press. Vol. 1, 1968; Vol. 2, 1975.

Lehmann-Haupt. Christopher. "Books of the Times." Review of *Misery,* by Stephen King. *New York Times,* 8 June 1987, C17.

Lerner, Gerda. *The Creation of Patriarchy*. New York: Oxford University Press, 1986.

Levin, Harry. *The Power of Blackness: Hawthorne, Poe, Melville*. New York: Knopf, 1964.

Lévi-Strauss, Claude. *The Elementary Structures of Kinship*. 1949, 1967. Translated by James Harle Bell, John Richard von Sturmer, and Rodney Needham. Edited by Rodney Needham. Boston: Beacon, 1969.

Lewis, David L., and Laurence Goldstein, eds. *The Automobile and American Culture*. Ann Arbor: University of Michigan Press, 1980, 1983.

Lovett, Verena. "Bodily Symbolism and the Fiction of Stephen King." *Gender, Genre, and Narrative Pleasure*. Edited by Derek Longhurst. London: Unwin Hyman, 1989, 157–76.

MacDonald, John D. "Introduction." *Night Shift: Excursions into Horror*. By Stephen King. New York: Signet, 1978, vi–x.

Magistrale, Tony. *Landscape of Fear: Stephen King's American Gothic*. Bowling Green, OH: Bowling Green University Popular Press, 1988.

——. *The Moral Voyages of Stephen King*. Starmont Studies in Literary Criticism, 25. Mercer Island, WA: Starmont, 1989.

——. *Stephen King The Second Decade, "Danse Macabre" to "The Dark Half."* New York: Twayne, 1992.

——, ed. *The Dark Descent: Essays Defining Stephen King's Horrorscape*. Westport, CT: Greenwood, 1992.

"Man Threatens to Blow Up Stephen King's Home." *San Francisco Chronicle*, 23 April 1991, three star edition, A3.

Marsh, Peter, and Peter Collett. *Driving Passion: The Psychology of the Car*. Boston: Faber and Faber, 1986.

Martin, Wallace. *Recent Theories of Narrative*. New York: Cornell, 1986.

Mather, Cotton. *Wonders of the Invisible World*. Boston, 1693; reprint, John Russell Smith, 1862.

Moers, Ellen. *Literary Women*. New York: Doubleday, 1976.

Moore, R. I. *The Formation of a Persecuting Society: Power and Deviance in Western Europe, 950–1250*. New York: Basil Blackwell, 1987.

Mulvey, Laura. "Visual Pleasure and Narrative Cinema," *Screen* 16 (1975): 6–18.

Neumann, Erich. *The Great Mother: An Analysis of the Archetype*. Translated by Ralph Manheim. Princeton: Princeton University Press, 1963.

Newhouse, Tom. "A Blind Date with Disaster: Adolescent Revolt in the Fiction of Stephen King." *The Gothic World of Stephen King: Landscape of Nightmares*. Edited by Gary Hoppenstand and Ray B. Browne. Bowling Green, OH: Bowling Green State University Popular Press, 1987, 49–55.

Newman, Kim. "Horror: Body Snatcher." Review of *Misery*, by Stephen King. *New Statesman*, 18 September 1987, 30–31.

Panek, Richard. "King's Ransom." *M. Inc* 8, 5 (1991): 29–32.

"Personals." *San Francisco Chronicle*, 29 June 1992, three star edition, D3.

"Perspectives." *Newsweek*, 27 June 1994, 13.

Pharr, Mary Ferguson. "A Dream of New Life: Stephen King's *Pet Sematary* as a Variant of *Frankenstein*." *The Gothic World of Stephen King: Landscape of Nightmares*. Edited by Gary Hoppenstand and Ray B. Browne. Bowling Green, OH: Bowling Green State University Popular Press, 1987, 115–25.

———. "Partners in the *Danse*: Women in Stephen King's Fiction." *The Dark Descent: Essays Defining Stephen King's Horrorscape*. Edited by Tony Magistrale. Westport, CT: Greenwood, 1992, 19–32.

Pribek, Thomas. "Witchcraft in 'Lady Eleanor's Mantle.'" *Studies in American Fiction* 15 (1987): 95–100.

"Rape in America, A Report to the Nation." National Victim Center and Crime Victims Research and Treatment Center, 1992.

Rich, Frank. "'I Just Want to Set the World on Fire.'" *New York Times*, 13 May 1988, C3, p. 1.

Rubin, Gayle. "The Traffic in Women: Notes on the 'Political Economy' of Sex." *Toward an Anthropology of Women*. Edited by Rayna R. Reiter. New York and London: Monthly Review, 1975, 157–210.

Schweitzer, Darrel, ed. *Discovering Stephen King*. Mercer Island, WA: Starmont, 1985.

Sedgwick, Eve Kosofsky. *Between Men: English Literature and Male Homosocial Desire*. New York: Columbia University Press, 1985.

———. *Epistemology of the Closet*. Berkeley: University of California Press, 1990.

Selden, Raman. *A Reader's Guide to Contemporary Literary Theory*. Lexington: University of Kentucky Press, 1989.

Senf, Carol. "Donna Trenton, Stephen King's Modern American Heroine." *Heroines of Popular Culture*. Edited by Pat Browne. Bowling Green, OH: Bowling Green State University Popular Press, 1987, 91–100.

Shelley, Mary. *Frankenstein or The Modern Prometheus*. 1818. Edited by James Rieger. Indianapolis: Bobbs-Merrill, 1974.

Showalter, Elaine. *A Literature of Their Own: British Women Novelists From Brontë to Lessing*. Princeton: Princeton University Press, 1977.

Siegel, Carol. *Male Masochism: Modern Revisions of the Story of Love*. Bloomington: Indiana University Press, 1995.

Simmons. Lydia. "Not from the Back Seat." *The Automobile and American Culture*. Edited by David L. Lewis and Laurence Goldstein. Ann Arbor: University of Michigan Press, 1980, 1983, 153–58.

Simon, John. "Blood and No Guts." *New York*, 23 May 1988, 60.

———. *Reverse Angle: A Decade of American Films*. New York: Clarkson N. Potter, 1982.

Slater, Philip. *The Glory of Hera: Greek Mythology and the Greek Family*. 1968. Boston: Beacon, 1971.

Slung, Michelle. "In the Matter of Stephen King." *Armchair Detective* 14 (1981): 147–49.

Spignesi, Stephen. *The Complete Stephen King Encyclopedia: The Definitive Guide to the Works of America's Master of Horror*. Chicago: Contemporary Books, 1991.

Stabiner, Karen. "The Misery of Stephen King." Review of *Misery*, by Stephen King. *Los Angeles Times Book Review*, 10 May 1987: 8.

Stallybrass, Peter, and Allon White. *The Politics and Poetics of Transgression*. London: Methuen, 1986.

Starkey, Marion. *The Devil in Massachusetts: A Modern Enquiry into the Salem Witch Trials*. New York: Knopf, 1949.

Stout, Harry S. *The New England Soul: Preaching and Religious Culture in Colonial New England*. New York: Oxford University Press, 1986.

Straub, Peter. "Meeting Stevie." Introduction to *Fear Itself*. Edited by Tim Underwood and Chuck Miller. San Francisco: Underwood-Miller, 1982, 7–13.

Suleiman, Susan Rubin. Introduction. *The Female Body in Western Culture: Contemporary Perspectives*. Edited by Susan Rubin Suleiman. Cambridge: Harvard University Press, 1986, 1–4.

Thomas, Keith. *Religion and the Decline of Magic*. New York: Scribner's, 1976.

Thompson, Bill. "A Girl Named Carrie." *Kingdom of Fear: The World of Stephen King*. Edited by Tim Underwood and Chuck Miller. New York: Signet, 1986, 29–34.

Trevor-Roper, Hugh. *The European Witch-Craze of the Sixteenth and Seventeenth Centuries and Other Essays*. New York: Harper, 1969.

Underwood, Tim, and Chuck Miller, eds. *Bare Bones: Conversations on Terror with Stephen King*. New York: McGraw-Hill, 1988.

———. *Fear Itself: The Horror Fiction of Stephen King*. San Francisco: Underwood-Miller, 1982.

"Upfront: Advance Review." Review of *Misery*, by Stephen King. *Booklist*, 1 April 1987, 1153.

Vance, Carol S. "Pleasure and Danger: Toward a Politics of Sexuality." *Pleasure and Danger: Exploring Female Sexuality*. Edited by Carol S. Vance. Boston: Routledge & Kegan Paul, 1984, 1–27.

Weisman, Richard. *Witchcraft, Magic, and Religion in Seventeenth-Century Massachusetts*. Amherst: University of Massachusetts Press, 1984.

"What Stephen King Does for Love." *Seventeen*, April 1990, 240–41

Willis, Sharon. "Disputed Territories: Masculinity and Social Space." *Camera Obscura: A Journal of Feminism and Film Theory* 19 (January 1989): 4–23.

Wills, Garry. *Under God: Religion and American Politics*. New York: Simon and Schuster, 1990.

Winer, Linda. "'Carrie': Staging a Horror on Broadway." *Newsday*, 13 May 1988.

Winter, Douglas E. *Stephen King: The Art of Darkness*. 1984. New York: New American, 1986.

Women's Action Coalition Stats: The Facts About Women. New York: The New Press, 1993.

Wood, Gary. "King's Boxoffice Bite." *Cinefantastique* 21, 4 (February 1991): 38.

Wood, Robin. "Cat and Dog: Lewis Teague's Stephen King Movies." *Gender, Language, and Myth: Essays on Popular Narrative*. Edited by Glenwood Irons. Toronto: University of Toronto Press, 1992, 303–18.

Wornom, Howard. "Terror in Toontown." *The Stephen King Companion*. Edited by George Beahm. Kansas City: Andrews and McMeel, 1989, 155–60.

Yarbro, Chelsea Quinn. "Cinderella's Revenge—Twists on Fairy Tale and Mythic Themes in the Work of Stephen King." *Fear Itself: The Horror Fiction of Stephen King*. Edited by Tim Underwood and Chuck Miller. New York: Signet, 1982, 67–71.

Young, Elizabeth J. "Best of Horror: Printers' Devils." *New Statesman and Society* 3, 130 (1990): 34–35.

Ziff, Larzer. *Puritanism in America: New Culture in a New World*. New York: Viking, 1973.

Zonana, Joyce. "'They Will Prove the Truth of My Tale': Safie's Letters as the Feminist Core of Mary Shelley's *Frankenstein*." *The Journal of Narrative Technique* 21 (1991): 170–84.

Index

About the Editors and Contributors

LINDA ANDERSON
Linda Anderson is an associate professor of English at Virginia Polytechnic Institute and State University (Virginia Tech), where she teaches literature and writing. Her principal areas of specialization are Shakespeare and other Renaissance literature. She is the author of *A Kind of Wild Justice: Revenge in Shakespeare's Comedies* (1987) and of articles in such journals as *Studies in English Literature 1500–1900* and *The Upstart Crow.*

LEONARD CASSUTO
Leonard Cassuto is associate professor of English at Fordham University. He is the author of *The Inhuman Race: The Racial Grotesque in American Literature and Culture* (1997).

ANDRÉ L. DECUIR
André L. DeCuir is an Assistant Professor of English at Muskingum College in New Concord, Ohio. While he has published and presented papers on the works of Mary Shelley, George Eliot, and Thomas Hardy, he is also interested in the aesthetics of horror fiction, Victorian and modern.

EDWARD J. INGEBRETSEN
Edward J. Ingebretsen, S.J. is an Associate Professor of English at Georgetown University. He has published widely in American poetics and in American cultural studies. Publications include *Robert Frost: A Star in a Stone-Boat* (1995) and *Maps of Heaven, Maps of Hell: Religious Terror as Memory from the Puritans through Stephen King* (1996). He is currently working on a book-length reading of the gothics of American politics, "Making Monsters: The Politics of Persuasion."

DOUGLAS KEESEY

Douglas Keesey is an Associate Professor of English at California Polytechnic State University, San Luis Obispo, where he teaches twentieth-century fiction and film. He has edited books on Stephen King's *Pet Sematary* and *It*, and published essays on Stephen King's treatment of politics (*A Casebook on the Stand*) and homophobia (*The Dark Descent: Essays Defining Stephen King's Horrorscape*). He also has a book on Don DeLillo in Twayne's United States Authors Series.

KATHLEEN MARGARET LANT

Peggy Lant is a Professor of English and Coordinator of Instructional Technology in the College of Liberal Arts at California Polytechnic State University, San Luis Obispo. On leave from Cal Poly, she is currently serving as Special Assistant for Online Programs in Extended Education at California State University, Hayward. She teaches American literature, women writers, and electronic communication and authoring. She has published work on distance learning and on Kate Chopin, Harriet Beecher Stowe, Louisa May Alcott, Charlotte Perkins Gilman, Sylvia Plath, Tennessee Williams, Stephen King, and others.

EDWARD MADDEN

Ed Madden, an assistant professor of English at the University of South Carolina, teaches and writes on modernism, 20th-century poetry, and queer theory. Recent publications include essays on Victorian poetry, psychoanalysis, Radclyffe Hall, and poetry about AIDS. He is currently completing a book on the image of Tiresias in modernist literature.

CAROL A. SENF

An associate professor in The School of Literature, Communication, and Culture at the Georgia Institute of Technology, Carol Senf is especially interested in the relationship between high culture and popular culture. In addition to this essay on King, she has written several others, including "Donna Trenton, Stephen King's Modern American Heroine" and "Stephen King's Modern Interpretation of the Frankenstein Myth," as well as prepared the entry on King for *The Dictionary of Literary Biography: American Novelists Since World War II*. She has also written essays on the Brontës, George Eliot, Charles Dickens, Sarah Grand, and Bram Stoker. Her most recent publications include *The Critical Response to Bram Stoker* (Greenwood, 1994) and *Dracula* (1998). A Midwesterner by birth, she and her husband, Jay, have lived in Atlanta since 1980. They have two sons, Jeremy and Andy, who are native Atlantans.

KAREN THOENS

Karen Thoens is a graduate student in the Ph.D. program in English at the Graduate School of the City University of New York. Her academic interests include cultural studies and modern women writers. Her essay, *"Alien 3, Frankenstein's Daughter: Warnings to Women About Technology and Childbirth,"* was published in *Echoes and Mirrors: Comparative Studies in Film.* She teaches English and Women's Studies at Pemberton Township High School.

THERESA THOMPSON
Theresa Thompson is an assistant professor at Valdosta State University in Georgia, where she teaches twentieth-century British and Post-Colonial literature. She has published articles on Virginia Woolf, D.H. Lawrence, and Edward Said. She received her Ph.D. from Washington State University in 1994.